LEADERSHIP FOR LITERACY

Forrest P. Chisman
and Associates

LEADERSHIP FOR LITERACY
The Agenda for the 1990s

Jossey-Bass Publishers
San Francisco • Oxford • 1990

LEADERSHIP FOR LITERACY
The Agenda for the 1990s
by Forrest P. Chisman and Associates

Copyright © 1990 by: Jossey-Bass Inc., Publishers
350 Sansome Street
San Francisco, California 94104
&
Jossey-Bass Limited
Headington Hill Hall
Oxford OX3 0BW

Library of Congress Cataloging-in-Publication Data

Chisman, Forrest P., date.
    Leadership for literacy: the agenda for the 1990s/Forrest P.
Chisman and associates.
        p.   cm. — (The Jossey-Bass higher education series)
    Includes bibliographical references.
    ISBN 1-55542-247-0
    1. Literacy — United States.   2. Reading (Adult education) — United
States.   3. Literacy programs — United States.   4. Literacy —
Government policy — United States.   I. Title.   II. Series.
LC151.C45   1990
374'.012 — dc20   90-4254
                                                             CIP

Manufactured in the United States of America

JACKET DESIGN BY WILLI BAUM

FIRST EDITION

Code 9056

The Jossey-Bass
Higher Education Series

Consulting Editor
Adult and Continuing Education

Alan B. Knox
University of Wisconsin, Madison

For Harold W. McGraw, Jr.,
Dan Lacy,
and Gail Spangenberg,
who started us down this road

Contents

▟▙ Preface

The adult literacy problem in the United States has become an issue of monumental importance. It is an issue that has indisputable bearing on the maintenance of social stability, the values of our democracy, and the lives of adults whose basic skills are deficient. By the start of the twenty-first century, this issue also will have a decisive bearing on our economy: Although the number of adults now receiving some form of literacy instruction is large, not enough such adults are achieving the skills that will be required to keep the United States competitive in world markets in the year 2000.

Purpose and Organization of the Book

Leadership for Literacy was written not to delve into why adults did not learn when they were children but to investigate why they are not learning now and what we as a nation can do to develop a more literate citizenry and workforce. Of course, significant progress has already been made by dedicated individuals in the literacy field, and we have learned valuable lessons from literacy initiatives undertaken over the last decade or so. The challenge now is to use what we have learned to solve the problem of adult literacy. To do so, we must recognize and overcome the weak points in our present system of literacy service: The public policies designed to instigate and fund a response to the problem are fragmented; many of the institutions and programs that must implement the response are inadequate; and the intellectual bases for program development, design, implementation, and evaluation have many short-comings.

The authors of *Leadership for Literacy* share the purpose of many in the field: to develop a national agenda for leadership and action on all fronts—political, institutional, and intellectual. Their goal is to build on the existing foundations and create a strengthened and integrated system of adult literacy service. In keeping with this goal, each chapter first specifies the short-comings of an important component of the literacy system, such as federal policy, the literacy profession, or research and development. Beginning with this practical discussion of barriers to success and opportunities for improvement, the authors then propose what needs to be done in each case. They present goals that must be pursued vigorously over the next decade and beyond by an array of literacy leaders, including researchers; staff members of educational institutions; program administrators; literacy instructors; employers; and government policymakers and administrators at the federal, state, and local levels. Each chapter concludes with a set of immediate priorities that should be key elements in a national agenda over the next three to five years. These concluding sections should be especially useful to policymakers and to program planners and designers.

Because this book has been designed as a leadership agenda and a call to action for all in the adult literacy field, the authors illustrate their claims and proposed solutions with specific examples but not with the exhaustive documentation of a scholarly text. Moreover, they have made every effort to set forth specific proposals—recommendations for actions that are based on what we know about the existing literacy system, that are doable and economically feasible, and that *by themselves* will make a difference both immediately and in the long term. The strategies proposed are therefore evolutionary in nature, building on the strengths and opportunities inherent in the existing system through planned, coordinated change.

Overview of the Contents

The first four chapters map the current state of the literacy field, its programs, and its practitioners. In Chapter 1, Forrest P. Chisman begins by defining the literacy problem: 20 to 30 million Americans who are seriously handicapped in their work and in their everyday lives by deficient basic skills. These basic skills include not only reading, writing, and verbal communication in English, but also math and problem-solving abilities. Chisman then shows the social and economic stakes that all Americans have in solving the problem of adult literacy. He outlines the current response to the problem by government as well as by community organizations and indicates where and how the current response falls short.

Chapter 2, by Hanna A. Fingeret, surveys the state of the art in literacy instruction. Fingeret presents an overview of four "domains of change" in adult literacy instruction: theories of learning, goals of learning, the expanding role of students, and control of the instructional system. Fingeret provides a well-focused snapshot of a fast-moving picture, in which forces for change are competing with strong tendencies toward the status quo.

In Karl O. Haigler's view, linkages — that is, effective cooperative relationships — among literacy programs and other interested agencies are an important and necessary part of the near-term agenda for solving the adult literacy problem. In Chapter 3, Haigler points out that literacy programs today generally exist on the margin, among the last to be funded and the first to be cut. He believes that strong linkages can help relieve this situation, and he identifies nine barriers that often prevent such connections from being formed or being effective. He cautions, however, that building linkages must be viewed as one strategy in the development of a national literacy system and not as a goal in itself.

Chapter 4 focuses on the instructors, administrators, and institutions making up the literacy profession today. Susan E. Foster identifies the shortcomings in training, standards of practice, and the institutional infrastructure that stand in the way of advancement of the literacy profession. She clarifies the steps needed to build an adult literacy profession capable of helping adults attain significant improvements in literacy skills — a task that will require commitment and cooperation from state governments, public officials, private employers, volunteers, literacy providers, and students themselves.

The research and technology that are needed to improve literacy instruction are the subject of the next two chapters. In Chapter 5, Judith A. Alamprese reviews current research and development in the adult literacy field and makes specific recommendations for putting research results to use in the field. She suggests that expanding our knowledge of how adults' skills and abilities can be improved is a critical step in solving the adult literacy problem. Alamprese points to the factors that have contributed to our present limited investment in building an intellectual base in adult literacy. In her view, adequate funding of research and widespread dissemination of findings can do much to upgrade the practice of basic skills instruction, but a solution to the problem will mean forming new alliances among researchers, practitioners, and learners and creating new roles for institutions.

In Chapter 6, Arnold H. Packer and Wendy L. Campbell suggest several ways the literacy field can benefit from computer technology. They identify factors that have hindered the use of computers in literacy instruction, including incomplete development and evaluation of products and institutional barriers to investing in technology. Estimating the true potential of computer-based instruction involves three sets of cost-benefit calculations: those of learners, providers, and funders.

Workforce literacy is the focus of Chapter 7, in which Forrest P. Chisman and Wendy L. Campbell discuss how we as a nation can most effectively narrow the job-skills gap. First, we must acknowledge the true dimensions, causes, and implications of the problem; then we must overcome ingrained institutional inertia to establish effective, relevant, and accountable programs to raise basic skills to the level required by a competitive, high-productivity economy.

The large and rapidly growing demand for instruction in English as a Second Language (ESL) is the subject of Chapter 8. William B. Bliss vividly illustrates the gravity of the problem, which is exacerbated by increasing demand, inadequate supply, and diverse needs. The answer, he argues, lies in linking federal funds to the demand; bringing the nation's immigration policy into line with demographic and economic imperatives; removing logistical and other barriers to increasing participation in ESL programs; creating a full-time, professional teaching force; investing in research and development; and, finally, promoting better attitudes toward immigrants.

The final three chapters of this book examine the role of government in solving the adult literacy problem. In Chapter 9, Jack A. Brizius discusses the role of states, pointing out that states now spend more than the federal government on basic skills instruction. He surveys existing literacy programs and policies in several states and then outlines the steps that states must take to build an improved system of literacy service. Key issues concern strategic planning, motivation of adult students, program effectiveness, program expansion, professionalism of literacy staff, adoption of instructional technology, evaluation of programs, and allocation of new resources.

Forrest P. Chisman discusses the federal role in adult literacy in Chapter 10. While other entities, including states, cities, employers, unions, and voluntary groups, will retain most of the responsibility for delivering literacy service, Chisman believes the federal government must play a crucial leadership role. The federal role involves creating conditions within which other agencies can find and implement a solution to the adult literacy problem. Chisman begins by examining recent federal legislation that bears on adult literacy and its implications for the literacy field. He shows that federal actions have raised questions for all the players in the literacy field, among them learners, teachers, program administrators, state and federal officials, employers, vendors, individuals in the voluntary sector, and members of the research community. Federal action is needed in four key functions: building greater expertise within the literacy field, upgrading the proficiencies of literacy professionals, improving coordination among programs and agencies, and filling service gaps created by recent legislation.

While previous chapters present specific recommendations for the near term, Forrest P. Chisman argues in Chapter 11 that near-term agendas must be evaluated in the context of a larger vision that encompasses long-term goals, the cost of achieving those goals, the individuals and agencies that should bear the responsibility for achieving them, changes in the paradigm and provision of literacy services, and changes in the literacy system's governance that will be required to fully implement the adult literacy agenda. He concludes with a call to literacy leaders to embrace change in directing the nation toward solving the adult literacy problem.

Acknowledgments

Support for the research and writing contained in this book was drawn from grants to the Southport Institute for Policy Analysis for its Project on Adult Literacy from the following sources:

The Annenberg Fund, Inc.
Carnegie Corporation of New York
Chase Manhattan Bank
The Chicago Tribune Foundation
Exxon Corporation
The Gannett Foundation
The William & Flora Hewlett Foundation
IBM Corporation
The William R. Kenan, Jr., Charitable Trust
Harold W. McGraw, Jr.
Morgan Guaranty Trust Company
The Charles Stewart Mott Foundation
The Rockefeller Foundation
Travelers Corporation Foundation
Xerox Corporation

We would like to express our gratitude to all these sources of support. The opinions expressed in this book, however, are ours alone and do not necessarily reflect the views of either the funders of the Adult Literacy Project or the institutions with which we are affiliated.

We would also like to express our deep appreciation to Wendy L. Campbell of Research Findings in Print for her invaluable contribution in managing the editorial process and our gratitude to Lys Ann Shore for her excellent editorial work. We also thank Alan B. Knox, consulting editor in adult and continuing education for Jossey-Bass, for his insightful suggestions and wise judgment, and Lynn D. W. Luckow, executive editor at Jossey-Bass, for his unfailing encouragement, understanding, and support.

Washington, D.C. Forrest P. Chisman
February 1990

📖 The Authors

Judith A. Alamprese is director of the Education & Training Group at COSMOS Corporation in Washington, D.C. She received her B.A. degree (1969) from Emmanuel College and her M.A. degree (1980) from Syracuse University, both in sociology. Her research activities have primarily involved adult learner assessment, program evaluation, organizational change, and policy development. Her work in adult education includes the codevelopment of the New York State External High School Diploma Program, a competency-based, applied performance process for adults. She has served as adviser to the Kettering Foundation's Literacy Issues Forum, the Kenan Family Literacy Project, the National Adult Literacy Project, and state departments of education. Alamprese's most recent publication on the topic of adult literacy is *Charting Progress: Interim Evaluation Report of the Connecticut Adult Performance Program* (1989).

William B. Bliss is president of Language & Communication Associates in Washington, D.C. He received his B.S. degree (1973) from Boston University in communication and his Ed.M. degree (1976) from Harvard University in education. He has served as adviser on language education and literacy to the Business Council for Effective Literacy, the Educational Testing Service, the American Bar Association, the National Adult Literacy Project, and the U.S. Department of Education and has also served as manager of refugee camp training in the Philippines for the U.S. Department of State. Bliss is the author of several English language textbooks, the most recent of which is *Access: Fundamentals of Literacy and Communication* (1990, with S. J. Molinsky).

Jack A. Brizius is a consultant specializing in public management and policy development. He received his B.A. degree (1968) in public affairs, his M.P.A.U.P. degree (1972) in public affairs and urban planning, and his Ph.D. degree (1974) in public affairs — all from Princeton University's Woodrow Wilson School of Public and International Affairs. In recent years, Brizius has assisted the governors of more than a dozen states. He has also served as consultant to the National Governors' Association, the Southern Growth Policies Board, the Appalachian Regional Commission, the Council of Great Lakes Governors, and the Center for the New West. Before becoming a consultant, Brizius served as director of policy research at the National Governors' Association. He has written or edited several books and is coauthor of *Enhancing Adult Literacy: A Policy Guide* (1987, with S. E. Foster) and *State Literacy Strategies: A Policy Primer* (1989, with S. E. Foster).

Wendy L. Campbell, director of Research Findings in Print, consults with policy institutes and universities to broaden the dissemination of their findings. She received her B.A. degree (1974) from the University of Colorado in geography and pursued graduate studies in labor relations and adult education at Cornell University. Formerly managing editor of *Industrial and Labor Relations Review* and coeditor of *Cornell Journal of Social Relations,* Campbell has reported on and edited evaluations of a variety of programs for educationally and economically disadvantaged adults and compiled *Industrial and Labor Relations Review Cumulative Index, Volumes 1–39* (1987, with B. Keeling). She has also taught literacy and ESL courses both in the United States and abroad and designed management and employee training programs for Cornell University and a major computer manufacturer. Campbell now serves on the boards of two community-based organizations in Rochester, New York.

Forrest P. Chisman is director of the Southport Institute for Policy Analysis and author of *Jump Start: The Federal Role in Adult Literacy* (1989), for which the Southport Institute received the American Association for Adult and Continuing Education's President's Award in 1989. He received his B.A. degree (1966) from Harvard University in government and his D.Phil. degree (1973) from Oxford University in political science. From 1983 to 1988, Chisman was director of the Project on the Federal Social Role, and he was previously an official in the U.S. Commerce Department and program officer of the John and Mary R. Markle Foundation. He is coauthor of *Government for the People: The Federal Social Role* (1987, with A. Pifer) and has written numerous articles on public policy and communications.

Hanna A. Fingeret is associate professor at North Carolina State University and director of the North Carolina Center for Literacy Development. She received her B.S. degree (1972) from Massachusetts Institute of Technology in humanities and science, and her M.S. degree (1979) and her Ph.D. degree (1982) from Syracuse University, both in adult education. Fingeret has been working in adult literacy education for the past eighteen years as a literacy tutor, teacher, program director, trainer, researcher, and consultant. Her research includes field studies of nonreading adults, and she has published widely on literacy topics. Fingeret is the author of *Adult Literacy Education: Current and Future Directions* (1984) and coeditor of *Participatory Literacy Education* (1989, with P. Jurmo). She is also a member of the board of Literacy Network, Inc., a national organization supporting collaborative literacy efforts in the United States.

Susan E. Foster is a partner in Brizius & Foster, a public affairs consulting firm. She received her B.S. degree (1969) from Pennsylvania State University in family studies and her M.S.W. degree (1972) from Rutgers, the State University of New Jersey, in social policy. Foster has had extensive experience in management and policy development at all levels of government and in the private sector. Her areas of expertise include general government management and operations and the human services, including adult literacy, education, vocational education, health care, and teenage pregnancy. Foster is coauthor of *Enhancing Adult Literacy* (1987, with J. A. Brizius) and *State Literacy Strategies: A Policy Primer* (1989, with J. A. Brizius). She currently serves as chairperson of the National Scanning Board.

Karl O. Haigler is special adviser for literacy to the governor of Mississippi. He received his B.A. degree (1970) from Wake Forest University in political science and his M.A. degree (1972) from the State University of New York, Buffalo, in political science. Haigler has worked in education for sixteen years, primarily as a secondary school teacher and administrator. From 1985 to 1988 he served as director of the Adult Literacy Initiative at the U.S. Department of Education. He was also director of the Division of Adult Education, the major federal program that funds adult literacy efforts, from 1986 to 1988. Haigler has contributed to many national literacy projects, including ABC/PBS Project Literacy U.S., the Gannett Foundation Literacy Challenge, the Kenan Foundation Family Literacy Project, Literacy for Jobs and Productivity (a state policy academy), and *The Bottom Line: Basic Skills in the Workplace* (a joint publication of the U.S. Department of Education and the U.S. Department of Labor [1988]).

Arnold H. Packer is president of Interactive Training, Inc., a firm that produces interactive videodisc training courses to teach basic workforce skills. He received his B.M.E. degree (1956) from Brooklyn Polytechnic Institute in mechanical engineering, his M.S. degree (1964) from Sacramento State University in business administration, and his Ph.D. degree (1969) from the University of North Carolina, Chapel Hill, in economics. Packer is a senior fellow at the Hudson Institute and deputy director of the Workforce 2000 study. He is currently directing a related project exploring the use of technology in teaching workforce literacy. From 1977 to 1980, he was assistant secretary for policy, evaluation, and research at the U.S. Department of Labor. Earlier, he was chief economist for the Budget Committee in the U.S. Senate. He has also worked as an economist for the U.S. Office of Management and Budget.

LEADERSHIP FOR LITERACY

1

Forrest P. Chisman

Toward a Literate America: The Leadership Challenge

At least 20 to 30 million adult Americans are seriously handicapped in their work and in their everyday lives by deficient basic literacy skills. This problem casts an ominous shadow over our nation's future as we enter the last decade of the twentieth century. At the same time, there is an unprecedented window of opportunity to come to grips with the adult literacy problem in the United States. Whether we seize that opportunity will depend in large part on how well leaders, both in the literacy field and elsewhere, understand the nature of the problem, the national stake in solving it, and the outlines of an adequate national response.

The Problem

Serious thinking about adult literacy stumbles almost at once over the issue of terminology. Although both the popular press and more specialized media have convinced most people that America has a serious literacy problem, strictly speaking, this concern is directed at a misnomer.

Defining the Problem. In a dictionary definition sense, *literacy* is the ability to read and write at all. Just that. But if public attention focused only on literacy in this narrow sense, it is unlikely that the nation's concern would be very great. At

1

most, 1 or 2 million adult Americans are completely illiterate. And while the United States is, and should be, taking steps to help these people, their numbers are not large enough to explain the public outcry that has developed in recent years.

It is adult literacy in an enlarged sense that has caused such great concern. Reading and writing are valued because they are presumed to be among the basic intellectual skills that everyone needs to function effectively in an advanced society — to earn a living wage, exercise the responsibilities of citizenship, and deal with the challenges of everyday life. But in today's society, reading and writing are not the only intellectual basics required. Most students of the subject would add to the list some ability in mathematics, the ability to communicate clearly, and problem-solving ability sufficient to deal with challenges both on and off the job. Moreover, it seems clear that most people cannot function effectively in American society today unless they can read, write, and speak clearly in English.

A five-part definition of adult literacy — reading, writing, and verbal communication in English as well as ability in math and problem-solving skills — is accepted by most of the recent scholarly literature and is increasingly winning acceptance by policymakers and literacy providers as well (Brizius and Foster, 1987; Carnevale, Gainer, and Meltzer, 1989; Hunter and Harman, 1985). This five-part construct is often referred to as the "basic skills" all adults should master. The term *basic skills* is often used interchangeably with the term *literacy* in discussions of the adult education field and will be so used throughout this book.

Obviously, this concept of literacy is ragged at the edges. People can master the intellectual basics with differing degrees of proficiency. Literacy skills fall along a continuum ranging from a complete inability to perform any one of the five basics to the very highest levels of proficiency. And if literacy is valued primarily because it allows people to function effectively in society, then the ability to read, write, communicate, calculate, and solve problems at the most rudimentary levels is not enough. The critical question about literacy in this enlarged sense is not whether people have mastered the basics *at all* but whether they have mastered them *well enough* to satisfy their own needs and the needs of society — whether, for example, they can hold a decent job, balance a checkbook, understand a newspaper, or fill out a tax form.

Illiteracy is far less of a concern today than the lack of what is often called *functional literacy:* mastering basic skills well enough to meet individual goals and societal demands. Accordingly, throughout this book the terms *literacy* and *basic skills* will refer to functional literacy, understood in this sense.

Unfortunately, this definitional tour de force begs an important question. How well, in fact, must people master the intellectual basics to be considered literate in this enlarged, functional sense? There is not and never will be any single, all-purpose answer to that question. If literacy is defined relative to the needs of individuals and society, different people will need different sets of basic skills, and their needs will probably change over time. The only thing we can say for sure is that the further people move along the literacy continuum, the better off they will be. Yet if this is all we can say, then asking how literate people must be is almost as perplexing as asking how high is up. There are no clear-cut boundaries.

In recent years, however, at least a half-dozen national surveys have tried to approximate a reasonable answer to the question (Brizius and Foster, 1987). Some have tested the ability of people to use literacy skills for a laundry list of everyday tasks. Others have analyzed the literacy requirements of various jobs and compared them against literacy profiles of the public. Still others have applied to adults variations of the tests of grade-level proficiencies in reading and mathematics commonly used to measure the achievements of children. Finally, some studies have relied on respondents' self-reports of their literacy problems.

None of these measures is entirely satisfactory, but the various ways of measuring the literacy problem do at least yield estimates that fall within a common range. Given the considerable differences among the measures employed, this is remarkable in itself. As a result, convergent validity can be claimed for what these various studies show.

The Size of the Problem. The studies show that *at least* 20
to 30 million adult Americans have not mastered basic literacy
skills very well at all. For example, at least that many adults
cannot read and understand a newspaper, balance a checkbook,
use a bus schedule, or in some cases speak the English language
at all. Moreover, at least that many people would not meet the
minimum qualifications for most jobs, and the types of jobs for
which they would qualify are unskilled positions that are few
in number and becoming fewer with each passing year.

Most experts believe that it is extremely misleading to
classify adults in terms of the grade-level attainment measures
used for children, because those measures do not adequately
capture either the abilities or the problems of adults. It is safe
to say, however, that the literacy levels of 20 to 30 million adults
are well below those of the average high school graduate. And
if we used the skills of high school graduates as a benchmark,
the number of adults with serious literacy problems would be
closer to 50 or 60 million.

We do not know as much as we should about the characteristics of people with low literacy skills. In fact, one of the
weakest aspects of the literacy field as a whole is a pervasive in-
adequacy of data. Most of what is known, or thought to be
known, about people with low literacy skills is based on inference
from fragmentary information. But the information that is available supports the following conclusions.

Not surprisingly, most of the 20 to 30 million adults with
very low basic skills are poor or living close to the poverty line,
and they are more likely than other Americans to be unemployed
or only marginally employed. In fact, there appears to be a
strong correlation between limited literacy and virtually every
other indicator of economic and social distress (Berlin and Sum,
1988). For example, a very large percentage of long-term welfare
recipients, the homeless, and teenaged parents have limited literacy skills. And the population in need of literacy services contains disproportionate numbers of African Americans and Hispanic Americans.

The literacy problem in America today can be summed
up this way: *By most measures, at least 20 to 30 million adults do
not have the basic skills required to function effectively in our society, and*

*a large portion of them suffer from economic and social distress that
reasonably can be related to their lack of basic skills.*

The Social Stake

Why should we care? Obviously the fact that 20 to 30 million of our fellow citizens lack the skills required to participate fully in the nation's life arouses humanitarian, civic, and economic concerns.

The Humanitarian Stake. It is the humanitarian appeal that has been in the forefront of recent media attention. The pathos of people unable to read stories to their children or covering up their lack of basic skills on the job, the isolation of people with limited literacy skills — these have been vividly depicted. And most Americans doubtless feel the same sense of national shame about the literacy problem as they feel about the problems of poverty and other social ills.

The family is an especially important focus for humanitarian concerns. As with the cycle of poverty, the cycle of illiteracy tends to be reinforced in the family. Family literacy programs have received considerable attention in recent years because they promise to help break this cycle to the benefit of young people as well as adults.

The Civic Stake. The literacy problem is also an affront to our civic values. It is hard to imagine how people with very limited literacy can be well-informed voters or even how they can learn enough about the issues of the day to be motivated to vote at all.

In the most general sense, literacy is a ticket to economic, social, and political freedom. People with limited basic skills are significantly less free in all respects; their opportunities to participate in American life are blocked at almost every turn. Our nation's history should have taught us that blocked opportunities lead to tragic divisiveness, for which we all pay a terrible price. Limited literacy is one of the many barriers that wall off the underclass from mainstream American life. And lack of proficiency in English is fast creating another "nation within a nation," composed of millions of immigrants as well as some native-born Americans. With nativist sentiments rising in many parts of the country, we face the potential for serious social unrest unless and until we address the need to help all Americans overcome their literacy problems.

But although humanitarian and civic concerns should, and probably do, lead us to care about adult literacy, there are grounds for skepticism about whether those concerns, by themselves, are enough to make the United States mount a substantial response to the problem.

There is no magic in placing the "limited basic skills" label on people. Labels such as "welfare mother," "the working poor," "the homeless," and many others exert essentially the same claim on our sympathies. In reality, these are all overlapping groups of the disadvantaged, and the tortured history of national attitudes and actions toward these groups indicates that we are extremely reluctant to provide assistance to able-bodied adults who are suffering from economic and social distress. The ethic of individualism is so deeply ingrained in most Americans that, more often than not, we respond by blaming the victim — by assuming that it is his or her responsibility to overcome barriers to opportunity, whatever they may be. The usual national response to the problems of able-bodied adults has been weak programs of public assistance coupled with volunteer efforts that cannot possibly match the scale of the problem.

The lesson of our national history is that the only way to catalyze a strong national effort to assist able-bodied adults who are not "succeeding," according to the usual social norms, is to find some direct stake that the rest of us have in fostering their success. And so it is with literacy. There can be no coincidence in the fact that concern over the literacy problem began to increase exponentially in the late 1980s when studies began to document the *economic* stake that the nation as a whole has in this problem.

The Economic Stake. Why should we do something about adult literacy? The most persuasive answer appears to be that literacy is a life-and-death economic issue for the United States, both now and in the coming years, because it is closely linked to economic productivity.

Productivity—the amount of goods and services created by each individual worker—is probably the most salient economic problem of our time. In simplest terms, if productivity is high, our standard of living will be high, because there will be a large supply of national wealth for everyone to share. Unfortunately, American productivity has grown very slowly over the last decade, at the rate of about 1 percent a year—a rate substantially lower than the rates most of our competitors have enjoyed. Growth in income (after adjustments for inflation) has been slow, and most households now need two earners if they want to improve their standard of living. In sectors of the economy where foreign goods are cheap or productivity is especially low, the result has been falling wages. In short, because of low productivity we are all suffering the consequences of a weak economy, and we will continue to suffer those consequences until productivity levels rise.

What can we do about this problem? There are three major components of productivity: capital, technology (including every kind of improved knowledge about how to produce goods and services), and labor skills. The United States now has ample supplies of capital (although too much is imported and some may be poorly used). We are still the world's leader in technology. But we are seriously deficient in the third component of productivity: labor skills. All the capital and technology in the world will not increase productivity without a labor force that has the requisite skills to use the advanced machines and other investments effectively.

One result of the recent drive to increase productivity is that jobs are becoming more technical and complex. Today's employers are looking for *trainable workers* to fill these complex jobs. They need people with a high enough level of basic skills to learn an increasingly broad array of job-specific tasks (Carnevale, Gainer, and Meltzer, 1989; U.S. Department of Labor and others, 1988). And because technologies are changing rapidly, workers must be able to learn new jobs several times in their careers. National productivity can grow only if we have a sufficient supply of trainable workers to fill the demand.

It is fairly clear that we do not. The Hudson Institute's *Workforce 2000* report, as well as other recent literature, shows that the skill levels of a large part of the U.S. labor force are substantially below the level required by today's employers (Johnston and Packer, 1987). The same studies show that unless we do something about the job-skills gap, it will almost surely grow much larger in the future, because employers will continue to seek productivity gains by placing greater demands on workers. Already there are reports of labor shortages in many parts of the United States—not shortages of warm bodies willing to work, but shortages of people with the skills required for today's high-productivity jobs (Finney, 1989).

This is where literacy comes in. At least 75 percent of the estimated U.S. labor force in the year 2000 are adults today—and the figure is well over 50 percent for the year 2010 (Brizius and Foster, 1987). These percentages translate into about 100 million workers. Of this figure, over 15 percent by most estimates—or at least 15 million workers—are seriously deficient in basic skills (National Advisory Council on Adult Literacy, 1986).

Whatever the exact number of workers with basic literacy problems may be, they fall along a continuum from the few million who are completely illiterate to the 5 or 6 million who have limited proficiency in English, and the much larger numbers who simply cannot perform basic skills very well. The ability of many millions of present-day workers to read, write, and communicate clearly in English, to calculate, and to solve problems is well below the level of the average high school graduate. In contrast, the basic skills required for the average entry-level job today are above high school level and increasing rapidly (Johnston and Packer, 1987). The United States simply cannot build and sustain a competitive, high-productivity economy when so many of its workers are so deficient in basic skills.

The *Workforce 2000* report indicates that 35 million Americans will have to improve their abilities if we are to meet the labor needs of the year 2000. The 15 to 20 million people, or more, who have severe basic skills problems are those who must improve their abilities the most. Unless we take steps to upgrade their skills in the very near future, all of us will be worse off.

Our rate of economic growth will stagnate, welfare costs will escalate, foreign competition will make more rapid inroads, and our national standard of living will fall (or at least it will not keep pace with increased standards of living elsewhere in the world).

Moreover, we cannot afford to delay solving this problem. The United States is facing a demographic deadline. Around the year 2010, members of the baby boom generation will begin to retire, placing an unprecedented strain on our economy. The baby boomers must be supported in their retirement years by the relatively small baby bust generation that follows them. Unless we create an economy that is both much larger and much higher in productivity between now and about 2010, the baby bust generation will not be able to shoulder this burden without reducing either its standard of living or the incomes of retirees, or both.

In short, our nation's economic future depends to a very significant extent on whether we can improve the basic skills of today's adults and whether we can do so very soon. This is probably the most compelling stake we all have in the literacy problem.

The Current Response

Despite the enormous economic and social stakes that all Americans have in the issue of adult literacy, the United States has not responded in a way that is at all commensurate with the problem. The present national response takes two forms: (1) *prevention*, through our elementary and secondary school system, and (2) *correction*, through our system for providing adult literacy service.

If schools had always succeeded in teaching basic skills to all children, we would not have a literacy problem today. The existence of the problem is attributable partly to failure of the schools and partly to the fact that even the most prescient educators have always found it hard to anticipate the basic skill needs of tomorrow's society and economy. Even twenty years ago many jobs required only a minimal level of basic skills. In particular, the demand for at least a moderate level of skill in mathematics was not as great then as it is today (U.S. Department of Labor and others, 1988). Educators could believe that little immediate harm would come from letting at least some students slide by with a limited education.

Today there is a strong movement to improve American schools, and to the extent that it succeeds, it will doubtless bring great benefits for the future. But by all indications the school reform movement will take many years to bear fruit. In the interim school systems will continue to release hundreds of thousands of young people with deficient skills each year.

Moreover, even if we created a perfect elementary and secondary school system tomorrow, we still would not solve the adult literacy problem in its most acute form. School reform will not help the 20 to 30 million adults with deficient basic skills who will continue to make up a large part of our labor force well into the twenty-first century. They are out of school and unlikely ever to return. If we cannot solve the problems of these adults, today's children — whether literate or not — will be doomed to grow up in a country that is suffering the agonies of economic decline.

The nation's direct response to the problems of adults with limited basic skills is our adult literacy system. In fact, it is hard to consider it a system at all. Adult literacy service in the United States represents precisely the combination of weak public programs and insufficient voluntary efforts with which this nation characteristically responds to the economic and social problems of able-bodied adults.

The history of efforts to increase adult literacy in America is long and tangled. In the form of a general movement to improve education, it reaches back to the earliest days of settlement. As a movement targeted specifically at adults, it reaches back at least as far as the mid-nineteenth-century era of Reconstruction (when a major effort was mounted to educate freed slaves) and the great waves of immigration of the late nineteenth century (Foner, 1988; Cremin, 1988). Throughout our history adult literacy service has been a combination of programs developed by all levels of government and initiatives by voluntary groups of every imaginable kind. Today's adult literacy effort is the legacy of this long development. Its most salient characteristic is that it is pluralistic in the extreme.

The Governmental Response. An estimated 80 percent to 90 percent of the people who sign up for adult literacy instruction in the United States are served by government-supported programs. It is easiest to visualize the dimensions of this public effort by starting at the federal level. Half a dozen major federal programs, and at least as many lesser programs, provide some support for basic skills education to adults. Almost every cabinet department has responsibility for literacy service of some sort.

The centerpiece of federal efforts has long been the Adult Education Act (AEA). In its original form, the act was Title II-B of the Economic Development Act of 1964, and administrative responsibility for it rested with the Office of Economic Opportunity (National Advisory Council on Adult Literacy, 1980). In 1966, Title II-B programs were transferred to the Elementary and Secondary Education Act of 1965, and responsibility for them was placed in the hands of the Office of Education, and subsequently the U.S. Department of Education.

Almost all of the funds authorized under the Adult Education Act are used to provide grants to states for the establishment of adult literacy programs through state education departments. Funding for the state grant program in fiscal year 1990 was $158 million, and total AEA funding was $185 million. AEA programs provide literacy services to adults at all skill levels up to high school equivalency, including English as a Second Language (ESL) instruction for people with limited English proficiency. Programs funded by the act are not means-tested in any way; they are open to anyone who needs help with basic skills. During the late 1980s about 3 million people were enrolled in these programs each year (U.S. Department of Education, 1986).

Provisions in other pieces of federal legislation permit, but do not require, the use of funds to offer adult literacy service. Among these legislative initiatives are the Carl D. Perkins Vocational Education Act, the Job Training Partnership Act, the Family Support Act amendments to the Aid to Families with Dependent Children program (often called "welfare reform"), and the educational provisions of the Immigration Reform and Control Act of 1986. Each of these programs is funded at $1 billion or more, but there is no reliable information about exactly how much of the funding is devoted to adult literacy, although the portion is surely very small. Smaller programs that provide support include the educational provisions of the Food Stamp Act (funded at $75 million per year), educational services in federal prisons, the VISTA program, and various educational programs for Native Americans.

Since most of these federal programs are grants-in-aid to state and local governments, the pattern of federal programs is to some extent duplicated at the state and local levels. In addition, some states and cities have devoted substantial resources of their own to adult literacy, either by supplementing federally funded programs or by establishing programs of their own.

All told, between 3 million and 4 million people are enrolled in adult literacy programs funded by one or another of these public sources each year (U.S. Department of Education, 1986). Total federal spending is more than $700 million per year, and total public spending by all levels of government is probably about twice that amount, per year, or about $350 to $450 per enrollee. But these are only estimates; no one has ever determined the exact numbers.

Whatever the precise numbers may be, it is obvious that the public effort is far too small to deal with the adult literacy problem. A public response that reaches only several million people cannot hope to reduce the waiting list of 20 or 30 million people who need help. It can barely keep up with the growth of the population in need. It is estimated that each year almost 1 million young people leave school with deficient basic skills and a similar number of immigrants with limited English proficiency enter the country (Pierce, 1988).

Moreover, the public response has neglected several high-priority groups. Most conspicuous is the lack of service to people who are employed. By most estimates, about half of all adults with serious basic skills problems are employed, and upgrading their skills would seem to be the shortest route to achieving national economic gains through investment in literacy. Nevertheless, the only public programs that support service to the employed are the Adult Education Act programs and a few small, experimental efforts. And a perusal of the limited data that are available indicates that most of the service provided to employed people by Adult Education Act programs takes place at the more advanced end of the skills continuum — usually in the form of high school equivalency classes. Although such classes serve a real need, many millions of workers with lower levels of basic skills are still neglected.

Taken as a whole, public support for service to people with limited English proficiency reveals a strange combination of generosity and neglect. Large sums have been appropriated for educational services, including ESL, under the amnesty provisions of the Immigration Reform and Control Act. But only about one-quarter of the people who need ESL service fall under the provisions of the amnesty program, and most of the instruction supported by the Immigration Reform and Control Act is targeted at meeting citizenship requirements, rather than at the broader goal of full proficiency in English. The remaining three-quarters of the ESL population must turn to services available primarily from the overburdened Adult Education Act programs. Over 40 percent of the people who sign up for those programs are enrolled in ESL classes — more than 1 million people (U.S. Department of Education, 1988, unpublished). But allowing for dropouts, the Adult Education Act probably serves about as many learners as the estimated number of new entrants into this country each year who need ESL service (see Chapter 8). At best, public programs are keeping up with the increase in demand for ESL instruction, but it appears that they are not reducing the backlog of people in need of help.

The Community Response. In addition to public programs, volunteer groups, community-based organizations (CBOs), and businesses also provide adult literacy service, but the number of people they teach falls far short of filling the gap left by public programs.

Most volunteer efforts are affiliated with the two large, national volunteer groups, Laubach Literacy Action and Literacy Volunteers of America. Together they serve about 200,000 adults per year, mostly through individual tutoring. Volunteer programs focus almost exclusively on reading and ESL skills, and they primarily serve people with the lowest levels of literacy skills.

CBOs are usually small, local community action organizations. Some are independent, while others are affiliated with larger educational, civic, or cultural groups. Although many are extremely innovative and dedicated to their work, they serve at most another 100,000 adults per year.

A growing number of companies offer some form of literacy instruction to their employees. Many also encourage their managers to volunteer as tutors in local programs. But almost all corporate efforts are very small. At most, a few hundred learners are involved in each case. A few large companies, such as Aetna, Motorola, Polaroid, and the Big Three automakers, have launched larger programs to improve the skills of their workers, and literacy training is a part of those undertakings. In most cases, however, the primary focus is on higher level or job-specific skills, and it is difficult to determine how much attention literacy receives in these more ambitious corporate educational programs.

The Quality of the Response. Overall the nation's response to the adult literacy problem is clearly inadequate in terms of the resources that are devoted to it and the numbers of people who are served. But an even more serious problem is the quality of the national response.

If the reason we care about adult literacy is that 20 to 30 million people are severely handicapped in their work and in their everyday lives by limited basic skills, only programs that help learners achieve skill levels that can be assumed to improve their economic and social conditions should be considered a success. The measure of success is in the real world of everyday life, not in nominal learning gains on a test or scale. Unfortunately, very few programs gather any evidence that would allow us to tell whether they are successful in these real-world terms. But the evidence we do have indicates that most literacy programs achieve extremely limited results.

To begin with, we know that a large portion of the people enrolled in literacy programs learn little or nothing at all. Dropout rates commonly range between 30 percent and 50 percent, and most dropouts leave during the first few weeks of a program (Hunter and Harman, 1985; Diekhoff, 1988; Sticht, 1988). Moreover, the available evidence indicates that the learning gains of people who remain in literacy programs are, on average, very small. A survey of learning gains in the public programs that are usually considered most effective estimated that the average improvement is 1.5 grade levels per year — the equivalent of moving someone from, say, a fifth-grade reading level to a mid-sixth-grade level (Sticht, 1988). And only a small percentage of people remain enrolled in programs for more than one year.

We also know that most of the national literacy effort is targeted at the learners who are easiest to serve. Most programs devote the majority of their resources to high school equivalency courses, to ESL instruction, and to the lowest level readers (U.S. Department of Education, 1986). In contrast, most national surveys indicate that the largest portion of the 20 to 30 million people with seriously deficient basic skills falls somewhere in the middle of the literacy continuum — between the lowest-level readers and the high school equivalency candidates (National Advisory Council on Adult Literacy, 1986; Kirsch and Jungeblut, 1986). In short, the present national effort neglects the largest part of the population in need, and it achieves only minimal gains, on average, with the population it does serve.

Barriers to Quality. This poor track record is all the more disturbing because it appears to be needless. There are programs that have helped people at every level of skills to achieve substantial learning gains (Berlin and Sum, 1988; Lerche, 1985). Why does the overall effort lag behind? The primary reason is that the literacy field is institutionally, intellectually, and politically weak and fragmented. And these structural flaws make it extremely difficult to improve the level of service.

Because the meager funding for adult literacy flows through a multiplicity of different channels, most literacy programs are small. They lack the resources to attract, train, or adequately compensate full-time, professional staff or to provide the materials and other support required for effective teaching. One indication of meager funding is the finding that the amount spent per student hour by public school adult education is only one-sixth the amount spent in employer-sponsored education and training (Anderson and Kasl, 1982). Most literacy instructors are part-time employees — often elementary and secondary school teachers working after hours. Most have received only minimal training in the specialized techniques required for teaching adults. Programs usually lack the resources for adequate preservice or in-service training or for investments in state-of-the-art teaching technology.

Computer-assisted learning systems have demonstrated considerable promise for improving both the quality and quantity of literacy instruction. A number of companies are now marketing such systems, but most literacy program administrators believe they cannot afford to buy the hardware and software involved. And few have the in-house expertise either to make this sort of investment decision or to use the new learning systems to maximum effect.

Of course, literacy programs could overcome some of these problems by pooling their resources to employ, train, and support full-time teachers and to purchase learning technology for joint use. But one of the consequences of the extreme fragmentation in the literacy field is that program boundaries create barriers to cooperative efforts that have proved difficult to overcome.

Another consequence of fragmentation has been that literacy instruction in the United States rests on extremely weak intellectual foundations. The proliferation of small, largely isolated programs in the public and private sectors has resulted in a great diversity in methods of instruction. This is not troublesome in itself; there is probably no single best way to teach basic skills. But there are also no very effective mechanisms to help instructors make informed choices among instructional approaches. The existing mechanisms for sharing information — such as meetings, training institutes, and publications — are few and far between, and their quality often is not very high. As a result, instructors often function well below the present state of the art at its best, and there is a great deal of re-inventing of the wheel in the literacy field.

Moreover, there is a paucity of basic or applied research devoted to upgrading the state of the art based on any instructional approach or to developing wholly new systems for adult learning. At most, a dozen first-rate researchers focus their energies on this field. Recent contributions from related scholarly fields are scattered. Without a doubt, the legacy of decades of research is far from trivial and certainly has contributed to improving the field. Nevertheless, many aspects of literacy instruction are still poorly understood, many essential tools of the trade (such as testing instruments) are inadequate, our base of knowledge about the literacy problem is small, and practitioners are too often unaware of what *is* known by people at the center of research activity (see Chapter 5).

One consequence of these intellectual shortcomings is that literacy instruction rarely extends beyond instruction in reading and writing, and sometimes mathematics. Although communication and problem-solving skills are widely acknowledged to be key factors in enabling adults to cope with social and economic problems, little is known about how to impart these skills to adults.

There is also far too little solid research on individualized instruction or learning in context, although many people in the literacy field believe these are the most effective approaches to teaching basic skills (Brizius and Foster, 1987; Mikulecky and Diehl, 1980; Sticht, 1987). These approaches are based on the idea that instruction is most effective and beneficial to learners if it is tied to solving the types of problems that each learner faces and to mastering other skills — such as how to succeed in a certain line of employment — that may be immediately relevant to their everyday lives. Nevertheless, there is very little systematic understanding of how to tailor instruction to individual needs in these ways. "One size fits all" literacy instruction is still the norm.

Another result of the intellectual shortcomings of the literacy field is a lack of standards and a resulting lack of accountability. A wide array of tests to diagnose basic skills difficulties has been developed, and some are widely used. But researchers and practitioners generally agree that none of these assessment tools is adequate to capture the complete range of learners' needs, to plan teaching strategies, or to measure gains in ways that will ensure that the instruction received actually contributes to the learners' ability to function more effectively at work, at home, or in society.

Nor are there commonly accepted criteria for how teachers should be trained or how curricula should be structured. As a result, it is virtually impossible to hold programs or individual instructors accountable for their performance. And very little effort has been made to do so. Neither public policy nor administrative practices generally contain significant incentives for effective instruction, disincentives for failure, or even any requirement that the outcomes of literacy programs must be measured. Usually, programs are evaluated only by head counts—the number of people enrolled—and not by how much participants learn or what difference the instruction they receive makes in their lives.

There is also very little understanding of how to structure and manage programs for some high-priority groups. Most conspicuous is the lack of knowledge about how to implement workforce programs. Because so little funding from any source is devoted to the needs of the employed, workforce literacy has not proceeded much beyond the conceptual and early experimental stage.

Finally, the institutional and intellectual problems of literacy programs are reinforced, and in some cases ultimately caused, by their political problems. Literacy instruction is rarely the major goal of the public programs that support it. The Adult Education Act is an exception, but even in that case, literacy programs are managed through state education departments and usually are the responsibility of people at the second or third level of authority within those departments. In the corporate world, literacy instruction is usually either one aspect of a broader corporate human resource program or a small workplace enrichment effort with no clearly determined status. Only among volunteer and CBO programs is literacy the primary focus.

Because adult literacy is rarely the highest priority of either the funding sources that support it or the higher level agencies responsible for administering it, the people who manage literacy programs are at a distinct disadvantage in bidding for resources. And because those programs are fragmented and small, it is difficult for them to demand support from the political system. As a result, there is no effective lobby for literacy, either within the institutions responsible for literacy services or in the larger public policy arena, and there is very little pressure for change.

The Response Required

If the nation's response to the adult literacy problem is manifestly inadequate, it is easy to imagine the form an adequate response should take. The goal must be to build a truly effective, integrated system of literacy instruction from the presently fragmented and pluralistic efforts. An adequate national response must start from the strengths of the programs that now exist and move on to remedy their individual and collective shortcomings in a systematic way.

Toward an Informed Pluralism. A realistic objective for the near term might be described as developing an informed pluralism in the adult literacy field. We must accept that literacy service will continue to be provided under a great many different authorities, both public and private. But we can aspire to overcome much of the weakness of the present system by creating stronger links among those efforts — by finding the common strand of literacy that runs through them and reinforcing it.

Given the nature of the present shortcomings in the adult literacy field, any effort to build an informed pluralism must have at least three key elements: (1) upgrading the quality of service, (2) establishing greater coordination of efforts, and (3) expanding resources.

Building a strong national literacy system along these lines means establishing a solid intellectual base from which all literacy providers can benefit and establishing better ways for them to obtain information about the state of the art. It requires creating cooperative arrangements among programs to share staff, training, and other resources. It also demands a wider acceptance of common statements of mission, standards for instruction and teacher training, and systems of accountability, so that cooperative efforts are possible. And it means more cooperative efforts among public, voluntary, and corporate sponsors, and a greater commitment by everyone involved, to reach underserved groups, particularly the working poor. Finally, it requires more resources, so that the various pieces of the pluralistic system will be large enough to support a more coordinated effort and to reach a larger portion of the population in need.

It is important to realize, however, that resources alone are not enough. Simply providing more resources can at best only increase the numbers of people who receive instruction. In all likelihood, it will not improve the quality of instruction very much: we will simply have more learners registering nominal gains. Unless we seek to strengthen and coordinate the field at the same time — to develop an *informed* pluralism — more resources alone will not do the job.

The Time of Opportunity. The good news about this ambitious agenda is that the early years of the 1990s offer an unusually promising opportunity to bring about fundamental change in the literacy field. Concern about the problem of adult literacy is at an all-time high among both the general public and leaders in all sectors of society. In part, this heightened concern has been stimulated by public awareness campaigns, press reports, and the efforts of farsighted individuals to publicize the issue. At the same time employers and employees are beginning to sense the first pressures placed on the economy by the steadily widening job-skills gap. Finally, the political configuration of the literacy issue has made it easy for politicians of all stripes to enlist in the cause. Adult literacy is a bipartisan, consensus issue that combines humanitarian and civic concerns with a strong economic bottom line. It is one of the few truly safe issues in a very troubled political environment.

In fact, a plethora of bills designed to promote the national literacy effort has been introduced in recent sessions of

Congress, and some substantial progress has been made. At the same time, a number of states and some cities have launched their own efforts to strengthen adult literacy service. The AFL-CIO and individual labor unions have placed adult literacy high on their worker education agendas, and some locals have achieved gains through collective bargaining agreements. And, as noted earlier, an increasing number of companies have begun to devote at least some attention and resources to literacy.

Although most of these initiatives are still fledgling, many appear to have great potential. At the very least, they indicate widespread receptivity to investing in solutions to the literacy problem.

It is by no means foreordained, however, that the nation will take advantage of these opportunities to build a more effective adult literacy system. Will the generalized interest of both the public and national leaders focus on the major issues that must be addressed? Will the fledgling efforts receive the support they need to realize their full potential? Will the nation move beyond these initial stirrings to the more substantial measures required? These are still unknowns.

The Challenge to Leadership. Who will determine whether the nation seizes the present opportunity to come to grips with the adult literacy problem? That responsibility largely rests on the shoulders of leaders within the literacy field itself.

One of the major by-products of the fragmentation and other shortcomings in the literacy field has been the development of a cadre of highly dedicated, talented, and flexible leaders who have come to the fore in recent years. In simplest terms, because there are so few material benefits to be gained from working on the problem of adult literacy at any level, the people who concentrate on the problem must have an unusually high degree of commitment. And because success of any sort is usually achieved only against the odds, those who have been successful in fostering adult literacy have had to demonstrate exceptional political, intellectual, and managerial ability.

Who are they? They are the teachers and program administrators in public, voluntary, or corporate programs who work at the grass-roots level. They are the federal, state, local, corporate, and voluntary sector officials who have some responsibility for literacy. They are legislators, legislative staff, and executives at all levels of government. They include some corporate leaders and some leaders of the voluntary sector outside the literacy field. Finally, they are members of the research community in universities, private research organizations, and corporations who devote their time to literacy.

There are literally thousands of literacy leaders, and they know who they are, although they have no very good way to keep in touch with one another. In the past, they have directed their leadership efforts primarily toward starting, developing, and keeping afloat the often fragile programs under their immediate responsibility. If the United States is to develop an effective system of adult literacy service, they will have to reach beyond their own bailiwicks and devote their energies to that larger cause.

Near-Term Recommendations

The tasks for leaders ready to seize the opportunity to upgrade the adult literacy system are formidable, but they are well within the capacity of the field. Literacy leaders must fully inform themselves about all the pieces of the literacy problem and achieve a solid understanding of how those pieces fit together to form an overall solution to the shortcomings of the literacy effort nationwide. Because public policy plays such a large role in structuring the literacy field, they must become active in the policymaking process at all levels to demand change.

But they should not await political action. There is no good reason why literacy leaders should not begin at once to tackle the key issues of the field head on with the resources available to them, as some have already begun to do. They should develop linkages and cooperative efforts. They should create networks for sharing information. They should tackle questions of standards and accountability both through collective efforts and in their own backyards. And they should join their limited resources for more investments in research, technology, and staff. Finally, they should make a more aggressive effort to expand services in workforce literacy, ESL, and other high-priority areas.

These are the types of responsibilities that leaders in most fields of endeavor routinely undertake. They are the types of activities that are synonymous with leadership. Although not all literacy leaders can be active in all of these ways, there is no literacy leader who cannot make some contribution to upgrading the literacy field. A truly informed pluralism will emerge only if and when literacy leaders conscientiously consider the key issues that must be addressed, when they decide how best to address those issues, and when they take the actions required to lead.

References

Anderson, R. E., and Kasl, E. S. *The Costs of Financing of Adult Education and Training.* Lexington, Mass.: Lexington Books, 1982.

Berlin, G., and Sum, A. *Toward a More Perfect Union: Basic Skills, Poor Families and Our Economic Future.* New York: The Ford Foundation, 1988.

Brizius, J. A., and Foster, S. E. *Enhancing Adult Literacy: A Policy Guide.* Washington, D.C.: Council of State Planning Agencies, 1987.

Carnevale, A. P., Gainer, L. J., and Meltzer, A. S. *Workplace Basics: The Skills Employers Want.* Alexandria, Va.: American Society for Training and Development, 1989.

Cremin, L. A. *American Education: The Metropolitan Experience, 1876-1980.* New York: Harper & Row, 1988.

Diekhoff, G. M. "An Appraisal of Adult Literacy Programs: Reading Between the Lines." *Journal of Reading,* 1988 (Fall), *3,* 624-630.

Finney, M. I. "The ASPA Labor Shortage Survey." *ASPA Personnel Administrator,* 1989, *3,* 6-12.

Foner, E. *Reconstruction: America's Unfinished Revolution.* New York: Harper & Row, 1988.

Hunter, C. St. J., and Harman, D. *Adult Literacy in the United States.* New York: McGraw-Hill, 1985.

Johnston, W. B., and Packer, A. H. *Workforce 2000: Work and Workers for the Twenty-First Century.* Indianapolis, Ind.: Hudson Institute, 1987.

Kirsch, I., and Jungeblut, A. *Literacy: Profiles of America's Young Adults.* Princeton, N.J.: Educational Testing Service, 1986.

Lerche, R. (Ed.). *Effective Adult Literacy Programs: A Practitioner's Guide.* New York: Cambridge University Press, 1985.

Mikulecky, L., and Diehl, W. *Job Literacy.* Bloomington: Indiana University Reading Research Center, 1980.

National Advisory Council on Adult Literacy. *A History of the Adult Education Act.* Washington, D.C.: U.S. Government Printing Office, 1980.

National Advisory Council on Adult Literacy. *Illiteracy in America: Extent, Causes and Suggested Solutions.* Washington, D.C.: U.S. Government Printing Office, 1986.

Pierce, W. F. *A Redefined Federal Role in Adult Literacy: Integrated Policies, Programs and Procedures.* Washington, D.C.: The Southport Institute, 1988.

Sticht, T. *Functional Context Education: Workshop Resource Notebook.* San Diego, Calif.: Applied Behavioral and Cognitive Sciences, Inc., 1987.

Sticht, T. "Adult Literacy Education." In E. Rothkoph (Ed.), *Review of Research in Education.* Washington, D.C.: American Educational Research Association, 1988.

U.S. Department of Education. *Adult Literacy Estimates for States.* Washington, D.C.: U.S. Government Printing Office, 1986.

U.S. Department of Education. "Adult Education Fact Sheet." Washington, D.C.: 1988, unpublished.

U.S. Department of Labor, U.S. Department of Education, and U.S. Department of Commerce. *Building a Quality Workforce.* Washington, D.C.: U.S. Government Printing Office, 1988.

2

📖 Hanna A. Fingeret

Changing Literacy Instruction: Moving Beyond the Status Quo

The field of literacy education is changing. All change is stressful, even if positive and desired; it is difficult to develop a perspective on the central issues and forces of the change process while we remain immersed in our continuing daily routines. Nonetheless, it is important to present a context within which to examine the leadership challenge presented in the chapters that follow. Therefore, this chapter presents a snapshot of the quickly moving picture that is adult literacy education today.

This discussion is organized into four major domains of change. The first is learning theory — specifically, the relationship between skills and knowledge that is drawn from recent cognitive research. The second is the tension around program goals that is created by the present focus on a relationship between individual skill attainment and larger social issues. The third domain has to do with expanded roles for learners in the literacy field today, and the dismantling of old stereotypes that this requires. Issues around control in the field make up the fourth domain, exacerbated by the very changes literacy educators have been seeking for years: increased attention from policymakers and the private sector.

The Major Issue Domains

1. *Theories of learning.* Learning theory is the backbone of an educational program, in many ways. Traditionally the realm

25

of psychologists, the developing field of cognitive science also is embracing anthropologists, sociologists, linguists, and others as the complex relationships between culture and cognition begin to unfold. With this kind of multidisciplinary attention, new research findings point to the importance of students' relationship to the content of the materials they are using to learn how to read and write, and not just to the skills. This pushes educators to respect students' existing knowledge, derived from their ability to read their world, if not print.

2. *Goals of learning.* For many years illiteracy was viewed as a one-dimensional issue affecting a relatively homogeneous group of people. Now that is changing as more sophisticated analyses show that race, class, gender, culture, social structure, and power are all important dimensions for understanding the literacy problem. This is a complex social issue — not only an issue of cognition — intimately related to other social issues. There are increased pressures now for literacy educators, social service providers, and policymakers to work together to create holistic models of comprehensive programs that might have an impact on larger social change. However, the relationship between individual learning and broader social goals remains elusive and complex.

3. *Expanding roles for students.* As the field of literacy instruction matures, students are moving into new roles. They are assisting with program governance, instruction, and management. Students are creating support groups to help themselves and one another, and they are asking educators to involve them more fully in programmatic decisions. These changes create pressures for literacy staff to reexamine their assumptions, preconceptions, and attitudes about adults with low print literacy skills, and to open themselves as learners in some new ways.

4. *Control of the system.* Issues of power and control pervade the field — questions about who controls instruction, program decisions, resources and funds, and the direction of the field. New coalitions are developing at the local, state, and national levels — new partnerships that are necessary to support the range of students' and programs' needs. As these relationships create an expanded potential for power, they also require that the power

be shared. Each of these domains is explored in more depth in the following sections.

Theories of Learning

Traditionally we have assumed that first you "learn to read" and then you "read to learn." In other words, adults must develop general literacy skills, and then they can apply those skills to learn other skills and information. Thus, if nonreading adults want to learn job skills, they are referred to a kind of "generic" literacy program first, in which the content used for instruction is considered only tangentially important. Then—sometimes years later—they are referred to a job-training program.

Now, however, there is growing support for the view that cognitive processes and knowledge cannot be separated (see Sticht and McDonald, 1989, for an overview of recent cognitive research supporting this position). This means that there is a relationship between the content of instructional materials, the instructional tasks, and the literacy skills that will be learned. Therefore, according to this view, materials used to teach literacy skills should reflect the contexts within which those skills will be used, whether an adult's personal life, work life, or community involvement.

Although this is known today as *functional context* and *customized curriculum,* it has much in common with attempts to create a "survival skills" and "coping skills" curriculum in the 1960s and 1970s; indeed, it may be seen as an evolution of those earlier attempts to teach skills in context rather than as abstract principles. However, the survival skills curriculum was based largely on a deficit theory, emphasizing those things that nonreading adults could *not* do. The pedagogy implied by more recent cognitive science developments is based more directly on students' strengths. It starts from the learners' existing cognitive structures that reflect their life experiences and uses those as a foundation upon which to build new skills.

Today, rather than assuming that students are "blank slates," we know that they bring a wealth of knowledge that relates to literacy tasks. Even though their print literacy skills may be minimal, most adults engage in literacy practices every day. They may have to ask someone else for assistance with the technical skills, but they bring an understanding of the meaning, the context, and the function of the task that is equally important (see Reder, 1987, for additional discussion).

For example, adults may want to learn to write a check—a common exercise in coping skills curricula. A teacher grounded in cognitive science would begin by exploring with the students everything they already know about writing checks as a technical skill and a social practice. The technical skills have to do with writing out and knowing where to place numbers, dates, signatures, and notes (like invoice numbers) on checks. The teacher would investigate social practices by discussing topics such as the purposes of checks, the functions of check writing (not carrying around large amounts of cash, presenting a certain kind of image to strangers, providing records of how money is spent, and so on), and the relationship between writing checks and general money management. Another set of questions addresses issues such as who owns banking institutions and whose interests are served by students using checks. Students then approach the task of becoming proficient check writers with an understanding of how much they already know and with the ability to place check writing in the context of their lives rather than to develop it as a discrete coping skill.

Literacy educators always have agreed that relating content to learners' lives and interests is important to increase motivation. Put simply, nobody wants to spend time learning to read and write things that they find boring—although, if the goal of developing literacy is important enough, they may tolerate boredom. But topics that are interesting and meaningful will help students persist through the long commitment needed to see some real change in their literacy ability. For this reason, resourceful programs always have used *realia* (such as local newspapers, restaurant menus, housing leases, and credit contracts) as curriculum materials.

Attention to the content of instructional materials also is important because different types of literacy tasks may require different cognitive processing skills (Mikulecky, 1986). Skills that are learned in one context and for one kind of task do not necessarily transfer to other contexts and tasks automatically. For example, a student who learns to answer the main idea question at the end of a reading passage in a school textbook is not necessarily prepared to apply information contained in a reference book to set the gauges on a technologically sophisticated new loom in a textile mill.

In addition, content is important because it appears that we learn by first relating new information and skills to what we already know; there is an interaction between our existing cognitive structures and the text as we make sense out of what we are reading. For the most efficient reading process, we want to facilitate students' ability to make sense out of the text, which means using content that they can relate to and then building on that foundation as we introduce new concepts and vocabulary.

This makes sense intuitively to all of us who are quite literate and have tried to read a piece of technical material in an area in which we have no previous background. An advanced nuclear physics journal is understandable to a nuclear physicist, but to a humanist with no nuclear physics training, it will be unintelligible—even though that humanist can read and understand extremely sophisticated materials in the humanities. Indeed, much of the success of scientists, such as Carl Sagan, who have popularized technical scientific information results from their ability to relate technical concepts to familiar ones.

For example, Carl Sagan can talk about the age of the universe and the length of humankind's time on our planet with numbers, and the concepts remain too abstract for us to grasp. But then he places it all on a twelve-month calendar. He explains that if the entire year stands for the lifetime of the universe, then the life of human beings occupies only the last day in December (Sagan, 1977). Now we can attach very concrete meaning to that. Accordingly, embedding skills instruction in content that is relevant to an adult's background knowledge appears to facilitate learning.

Most educators agree that content is important, whether its importance is related to motivation or cognitive processing. Typical programs continue, however, to be based on the assumption that literacy skills can be taught in the abstract, and that relevant content is nice but not necessary. Programs that integrate literacy skills instruction with instruction in other subjects, such as job skills, parenting education, or health care, remain few and far between. Little systematic research has been conducted on the development of such programs.

It is also important to remember that there always will be a need for general literacy programs that differ from the traditional prepackaged curriculum; they can provide a place in which adults come together to discover their common ground as partners in learning and teaching basic skills. Learners and teachers can work together to create curricula for adults who do not feel that their jobs or family responsibilities require additional literacy skills, but whose dreams include writing poetry, reading letters, or leading Bible study classes.

Our developing understanding of the relationship between knowledge and skills raises a host of questions and issues. Much more work needs to be done on the conceptual complexities of the term *context* and its relationship to literacy skills development, values, and culture. For example, Auerbach's (1989) analysis of the prevailing model of family literacy provides an example of how a curriculum that uses the family as a context promotes a set of attitudes — specifically, "transmitting the culture of school literacy through the vehicle of the family" (p. 169). She cautions that, when left unexamined, the assumptions upon which prevailing practice is based "will justify a model that blames the victim by attributing literacy problems largely to family inadequacies" (p. 169). Rather than building on parents' knowledge, family literacy programs attempt to transfer school practices into the home.

When we advocate a curriculum content that is meaningful to learners, it is important to understand that this implies that learners must be involved in the process through which content decisions are made. For example, many guides to workforce literacy programs advocate a "literacy audit" in which an educator analyzes the literacy "demands" of the work environment. This process need not necessarily involve workers (see Human Resources Development Institute, in press, for an extensive discussion of these issues). When the curriculum is designed by educators and employers without workers' involvement, the content may not reflect workers' analysis of their own needs and interests. Even though the resulting program may integrate skills and job-related content, it still may be alienating or simply inappropriate.

New concern with the relationship between skills and content raises questions for commercial publishers and for computer software developers. Touted as a supplement to classroom interaction, computers provide opportunities for a range of activities, from self-paced, independent reinforcement of selected skills to group problem solving. There is an increasing emphasis on software development that allows teachers and students to adapt the content to their own knowledge and interests, and that supports group work as well as individual work. Much of the software available currently, however, is little more than "electronic page turning," with the same limitations as those found in print workbook materials. As development continues, questions about the most desirable level of specificity in relation to a student's situation must be confronted by commercial publishers as well as software developers.

Materials chosen and developed for their content imply an emphasis on the construction of meaning as a primary purpose for reading. Within that framework, students still need to develop specific skills, such as phonics analysis. But how do we ensure that skills are not actually sacrificed for content, thereby creating narrow job-training programs rather than literacy education?

Questions also are raised about the role of the world outside the classroom as an arena for instruction. For example, on-the-job training might be necessary as part of a literacy/vocational development program to help apprentices develop their experience in the context that will facilitate their comprehension of print materials. Experiential learning theory now assumes a new relevance in relation to literacy education.

And if we allow that there is a relationship between skills and knowledge—that the facility with which someone can be said to use literacy skills has to do with the tasks to which those skills are applied—then our approach to testing and evaluation of learning is called into question. Traditional tests, like the dominant mode of instruction, have assumed that there is a set of abstract skills that can be tested without regard to specific content. New approaches to assessment are now being developed that attempt to take into account a relationship between the learner, skills, and content. For example, the Adult Literacy Evaluation Project at the University of Pennsylvania involves students in many ways in the assessment process. The Initial Planning Conference provides an opportunity for students to "describe and assess their own experiences, interests and abilities with regard to literacy and to begin planning for their own learning" (Lytle, Marmor, and Penner, 1986, p. 28). Learners' existing knowledge is valued as they work with literacy program staff to plan ways of using and building on their skills. Many gaps remain, however, in our attention to the range of evaluation issues.

On another level, the issues raised by new cognitive science research are part of a long-standing debate about the relative merits of inductive or deductive teaching, about presenting principles in the abstract to be applied or presenting them embedded in practice to be discovered. The resurgence of attention to contextualized literacy education has renewed that age-old debate, which is challenging the literacy field to respond in creative ways.

Goals of Learning

From the outset the Adult Education Act of 1964, the enabling legislation for the federal literacy program, contained language supporting literacy development as a means toward other ends—predominantly individual economic self-sufficiency. Conceived of as part of the larger War on Poverty, the individual development of literacy was supposed to contribute to the eradication of poverty in America. However, literacy programs traditionally have focused on meeting individual learners' goals, including reading for pleasure as well as more utilitarian goals. Attempts rarely have been made to translate policymakers' concerns with larger social issues directly into practice. Thus, a tension always has been apparent between a program's desire to meet students' personal goals and its responsibility to meeting goals defined by the larger society.

For many years, programs had to confront this tension only minimally, as federal attention was focused elsewhere. Now, however, the tension is being heightened as policymakers enter the literacy arena. As social issues, such as economic competitiveness, overcrowded prisons, high school dropout rates, adolescent pregnancy, and dysfunctional families, gain prominence, policymakers are focusing on literacy education as part of their response.

In the past, educators have made the point that if the program simply focuses on the development of "generic" literacy skills, adults will naturally apply those skills in ways that will affect larger social issues. For example, they will read to their children, get better jobs, have an improved sense of self-esteem that will decrease their involvement in crime, and so on. The assumption of a causal relationship between individual change and larger social change is quite controversial, however (see authors such as Scribner and Cole, 1981, and Graff, 1979, for further discussion of this point).

Nonetheless, the current widespread support for the development of family literacy and workforce literacy programs attests to policymakers' belief that literacy education can influence larger issues. Analyzing these programs provides some insight into how we are trying to resolve the tension between individual and social goals today.

Let us begin with family literacy programs, which are designed to meet a range of goals, from increasing the pleasure of reading to improving national economic productivity (Nickse, 1989). If a mother wants to learn to read to her children, there are a number of ways a literacy program can respond. First, it can simply enroll her in the program's general curriculum with the assumption that as she learns to read the texts used in the program, she will develop skills that can be applied to reading children's books aloud. Or, the program could teach her to read to her children, using children's literature as texts and modeling good story-reading techniques.

In the past, this is where most adult literacy programs would stop. Now, however, there is pressure to intervene in the "cycle" of illiteracy; and so this mother is viewed as a part of a family network that includes her children, her spouse, and others. Thus, programs now work directly with children as well as with parents. Some programs are teaching parents how to help their children learn to read—even when the parents' reading skills are quite low. Push Literacy Action Now in Washington, D.C., for example, provides a kit for parents that contains samples of literacy-related activities they can learn to do with their children. Literacy Volunteers of America has recently published a guide for teaching parents with low-level literacy skills a range of activities they can do with their children that will improve their children's reading skills.

A family literacy program also may involve mothers and children in direct instruction. For example, the Parent and Child Education (PACE) program in Kentucky asks that children and their parents board a school bus every day and attend a school-based program together. Some activities are provided for them separately, and some for them together. In addition, parents volunteer in the schools, becoming more comfortable with school buildings, procedures, and staff. The MOTHEREAD program in North Carolina creates cooperative arrangements with agencies, such as Head Start and public schools, which already have a relationship with the children. MOTHEREAD provides complementary activities for the children and their parents.

Nickse (1989) proposes that what is new in these latter models is the increased amount of intervention in the family system, designed to have an impact on the children's school performance and on the school system itself in some cases, as well as on the parents' literacy abilities. Programs with a broad intervention approach remain in the minority, but pressure for change is mounting as preliminary research points to the apparent effectiveness of the interaction of all of the components of these programs (Hayes, 1989).

The spectrum of workforce literacy programs shows some similarities and some important differences. Workforce literacy programs abound that are simply situated in the work environment and use a general, prepackaged curriculum. Evaluation and impact studies attempt to document results, such as the number of students who attribute a new job or job promotion to their increased literacy competency, but the shortcomings of those studies are well known (see Darkenwald and Valentine, 1984, for a discussion of the strengths and limits of impact studies). It is only with the influence of cognitive science research, and the work of researchers such as Sticht (1987) and Mikulecky (1985), however, that direct integration of literacy and vocational education is beginning to occur.

Union programs have begun moving away from literacy models that are predominantly individually oriented (Fingeret, 1984) and concerned primarily with individual social and economic mobility. They are attempting to respond to individual needs within the context of the larger community. With their traditional orientation to improving the quality of life for their members and their communities, union programs often define workforce literacy broadly. For example, the Consortium for Worker Education in New York City and the California Immigrant Workers Association project in Los Angeles provide a range of educational programs that are developed in consultation with workers to respond to their needs and their situations. The programs often include workers' families as well, and create relationships with the larger community.

Unions understand that community development requires leadership, and historically they have been a forum for indigenous leadership development. Unions attempt to influence the curriculum for workforce literacy development by emphasizing the needs of the workers rather than simply training workers to respond to needs as defined by employers. They are more experienced than most literacy educators at attempting to negotiate responses to workers' and employers' perceptions of need.

Some community-based literacy programs try to address community development issues even more directly (Association for Community Based Education, 1983). These programs are primarily community-oriented. They try to encourage collaborative efforts rather than continuing to isolate students, and the curriculum is built around community issues that the group members want to address, such as housing, drug abuse, or health care. Staff in these programs see themselves as working toward broad social change as well as assisting in students' literacy and skill development. Theoretically these programs are activist in nature; they do not assume a relationship between literacy and community development, but try to implement the relationship, to involve themselves in the community's struggles. Community-oriented programs are seen as an important alternative to other kinds of programs, but they also remain in the minority. They are difficult to develop and labor intensive; and research documenting effective approaches to developing community-oriented programs remains scarce.

Evaluation research has to reflect the range of goals that programs attempt to meet, and it must somehow come to grips with the tension between individual skill development (enhanced by attention to learners' unique goals) and policymakers' and funders' concerns with larger social impact. Frequency counts of the number of students who received promotions while in literacy programs will not suffice. There is a general understanding now that evaluation must be multifaceted; no one source of information can respond to policymakers' and funders' needs for data while also respecting learners' personal goals and reflecting the range of their experiences in programs.

Most workforce literacy programs — whether general literacy programs that happen to be situated in a workplace or programs with a functional context curriculum — still directly address change only at the individual level. Community development efforts that integrate attention to literacy skills may offer some potential for more directly addressing the social issues as well. But we must remember that educators can influence only one small piece of the picture. National and state economic policy must support the availability of jobs and development capital. Real progress on the broader social issues will require the involvement of a wide range of organizations, comprehensive social policy committed to equity and social justice, national as well as local leadership, and an infusion of funds.

Another approach is to focus directly on the larger social issues as the goal of programs and to integrate attention to literacy skills as appropriate. Examples of attempts at this kind of activity can be found in programs such as Project Uplift in Greensboro, North Carolina. A comprehensive services program for poor families in a housing project, Project Uplift tries to help families learn to address their needs in areas such as drug abuse, employment, parenting, child care, preschool, adult literacy, and so on. It is a natural evolution from earlier programs of community action agencies; as Project Uplift evolves, it is attempting to create a coherent internal philosophy and a relationship among the services it provides, rather than simply being a "supermarket" of services. Literacy has its place within the spectrum of services, but the emphasis primarily is on helping families take control of their lives by confronting social and economic issues.

Similarly, the Family Support Act of 1988, known as welfare reform, is an attempt to confront a social issue by developing comprehensive programs that include a range of educational, training, and support services. Literacy is to serve the larger end of economic self-sufficiency as one component of a multifaceted program. This legislation does not address the economic, social, and political forces influencing poverty, but it is an important early attempt at federal legislation that acknowledges the interrelatedness of educational, social, and economic issues.

Implicit in all of the conversations about interventions in family systems, in workplaces, or in communities are values, assumptions, and beliefs that rarely are made explicit and often reflect the norms of middle-class professionals. In most literacy programs today, professionals are in power and making decisions about the vision of the "good life" to which programs aspire. Students' knowledge and world view usually are not respected, and students participate in creating programs only to a small extent.

Although there is a lot of talk about literacy as a means of addressing broader social issues, this means different things to different people. For some, it means developing a work force that is literate enough to sustain the present economic system. Workers with the least skills and the lowest paid jobs would become slightly more literate, but the basic status quo would remain. For other analysts, however, addressing broader social issues means social change—and on a relatively grand scale. It implies a redistribution of the wealth of the society so that the conditions creating poverty, drug abuse, and other social ills are changed.

A tension exists between these two possible outcomes of literacy education. For example, employers who have problems related to workers with low-level literacy skills may nonetheless be ambivalent about supporting literacy education. They may view literacy as potentially threatening to their position of power in relation to their workers and as the first step toward workers demanding better pay and working conditions for themselves. These employers may support a narrow program in which workers are trained in the use of new machines that are specific to their jobs, but are not provided with instruction in broader literacy skills. In community development efforts as well, community leaders may be threatened by citizens' increased literacy skills, which could lead to more critical participation and demands for shared leadership in the efforts.

Viewing literacy education as a means to address broader social problems raises a host of ethical, political, and social issues. Programs have the potential for helping either to reinforce or to transform the conditions that support the development of literacy problems in the first place.

Role of the Learner

Literacy programs traditionally have placed great emphasis on "meeting the needs of the learner," but only in a framework in which the learner is viewed as the relatively passive focus, target, and recipient of services that are actively planned, provided, and evaluated by staff. Community-oriented programs have attempted to break from this mold; they have tried to develop a model in which power is shared among program participants and staff. Now other programs are beginning to create new models as well. Although these are still largely undeveloped, there is more interest than ever before in ways of involving students in instruction (for example, in curriculum development or peer tutoring), program management (for example, in student and teacher recruitment and training), and governance (such as sitting on boards).

Literacy Volunteers of New York City, for instance, has a student representative to its governing board and students on the staff. Students are involved in setting educational policy and in a range of program management and public relations tasks. The program also provides group instruction in which students are involved in peer teaching, and it supports a student group in which leadership is developed, fund-raising activities to support student projects are organized, and a general forum is provided for student communication and involvement. This broad process of collaborative work among students and staff is being called a participatory model (see Fingeret and Jurmo, 1989).

Participatory literacy programs are still in the minority. Sharing the power among learners and staff remains threatening to many, and it is a difficult goal to achieve. Research on the process of developing participatory programs is scanty, and their strengths and limits are not well documented.

National volunteer organizations, which have more flexibility than federal Adult Education Act programs, have been particularly active in promoting student involvement. For example, Laubach Literacy Action has a student on its national board, and it conceptualized the first National Student Congress, an opportunity for learners to come together from all over the country to discuss and develop a set of recommendations for literacy education. Laubach Literacy Action and Literacy Volunteers of America also are developing training materials to support local programs' efforts to involve students more fully.

Participatory curriculum development, representing a natural outgrowth of literacy educators' traditional concerns for responding to students' goals, represents the most widespread area of student involvement right now. It is a process in which students work together with teachers and program staff to develop curricula; materials may include students' writing or information students have dictated to teachers for transcription. A participatory process can result in a meaningful learner-centered curriculum that addresses students' relationships to literacy in specific contexts (such as work or family).

Jurmo (1987, 1989) describes three main reasons given by supporters of this participatory approach. First, they believe it can promote learning (efficiency); this is closely tied to the arguments presented in the preceding sections. Students' involvement ensures that content is meaningful, context-related, and interesting. Second, participatory programs appear to provide opportunities for personal development as students move into new roles, experience their own authority, and develop critical thinking and leadership skills. Finally, participatory approaches are heralded as promoting social change. As students move into leadership positions in the literacy program, they develop skills and understanding that can be more broadly applied. They also can bring their community's concerns to the literacy program for incorporation into a curriculum that helps them address their aspirations for an improved quality of life.

Expanding learners' roles depends on replacing old stereotypes with images that are more respectful of adults' status and accomplishments. Learners must be viewed as capable of meaningful participation. This is often difficult because we have inherited a *deficit perspective* in which the skills, world view, and attitudes of adults with low print literacy abilities have been dismissed or downgraded. Even worse, our society has inherited a *literacy mystique* that implies that adults with low print literacy skills are unable to develop good moral character as well. This image of nonreading adults as fundamentally incompetent has become deeply embedded in our conventional wisdom, even though it is not supported by critical examination of its underlying assumptions or by current research and theory development (see Fingeret, 1989).

In addition, although the media have made tremendous contributions to furthering literacy education, present media attention to literacy unfortunately often frames the literacy "crisis" at students' expense. Nonreading adults are pictured as dependent, responsible for serious social ills, unable to grow and learn, and barely able to cope with daily life. Although these stereotypes are grossly unfair, nonreaders internalize these images, believing that they should feel ashamed of themselves and losing touch with their own strength and power. In addition, educators internalize these images and do not view nonreading adults as capable of participating in program decisions.

Unfortunately, nonreading adults have rarely been invited to influence how their struggle is portrayed by the media. They are usually asked to provide testimonials, but they could be involved in the more fundamental program decisions, helping to shape the public's perceptions of them and their issues, rather than continuing to have to cope with those images as they are fashioned by others.

Adults with low-level skills in print literacy are not a homogeneous group; their experiences, motivations, aspirations, and circumstances vary. Many nonreading adults have been consistently productive workers, family members, and in some cases community leaders. Nonreading adults are the creators of their own social lives, and they participate in the ongoing creation and maintenance of the social world in which they live.

Adults with poor literacy skills often are viewed as being isolated, alienated, and largely inarticulate because that is how they appear to middle-class researchers who visit their classrooms and judge them in this often alienating environment. If we try instead to understand their culture on its own terms, a very different picture emerges (for example, see Fingeret, 1982; Fingeret, 1983; Heath, 1980; Reder, 1987; Reder and Green, 1985; Weber, 1975).

Nonreading adults do not depend upon print for learning, communicating information, or accomplishing tasks; instead, they rely on talk and interpersonal interaction. They learn with one another, watching and telling one another how to do things. They develop systems for gathering and preserving information, controlling the flow of information, and assessing the truthfulness of information. They also develop the capacity for dealing with required literacy tasks. These systems depend on talk, interaction, and mutual exchange. Folks help one another out, are proud of their common sense, and learn from experience. They see themselves as collaborators in social networks in which others contribute technical reading or writing skills

(Fingeret, 1983). At the same time, however, nonreading adults are aware that the larger society views their poor literacy skills negatively, and they feel the stigma of illiteracy.

New images of nonreading adults are slowly replacing the old stereotypes as students become more active and visible nationally, making presentations at conferences and developing public statements, such as those from the National Student Congresses. Their experience with the social and functional aspects of literacy as well as their broader knowledge of oral cultural patterns, their life experience, and their personal goals provide a rich resource for literacy education and, indeed, for our entire society.

In the last few years new literature by new writers—adult literacy students—is becoming more widely available, providing another source of insight and understanding about learners' lives and culture. Many local and state programs are creating anthologies of student writing, and the Adult Literacy Resource Institute in Boston and the teachers of the Invergarry Learning Center in British Columbia, Canada, publish literary magazines that are more widely available (see *Focus on Basics,* 1989, for a longer discussion). These publications are a source of validation for the writers, relevant reading material for the readers, and leadership opportunities for student editors. They also are a source of insight for the larger society. New writers have an authentic voice that speaks of their experience to a society that is not used to hearing them. Their literature may fill a need for readers with low-level skills in print literacy, but it also now is accessible to those with many years of schooling who may be moved by its eloquence. It profoundly challenges the prevailing stereotypes of adults with low levels of literacy skills.

Several complex issues still must be negotiated in this arena. Much more action research is needed, in which students work with researchers and literacy staff developing research projects in which their questions (rather than only the questions of researchers) are addressed and a more complex, respectful image of their lives is developed and portrayed. And if literacy education is ever to reach the status of a "social movement," it must go through a transition in which students provide increasing amounts of leadership. The power in the field still remains largely in the hands of a small group of professionals and policymakers. Just as this transition is difficult for individual programs, it will be difficult for the field as a whole.

In addition, as students move into leadership roles, a tension may develop between students' and staff's perceptions of what is good. For example, students may believe that individual tutoring is the "best" kind of instruction, based on their positive experience with a tutor or on a negative experience they may have had in a large class. On the other hand, the staff may believe in small groups, for ideological or pedagogical reasons. Since they are operating from different domains of knowledge, the two groups may find it difficult to resolve these conflicts.

Also, as new leaders appear there may be a tension between their assessment of their own interests and the needs of the larger society. This is a classic tension in a democratic society. With the exception of some notable social philosophers and activists, such as Paulo Freire, most literacy educators have yet to confront issues of their responsibility to their students when it appears that their work may lead to conflict with larger social expectations.

Control of the System

For many years literacy educators focused their energy primarily on developing their local programs. With very scarce resources and a high degree of commitment, they struggled with issues such as student recruitment, instructional materials, diagnosis and testing, tutor and teacher training, and program evaluation. Unstable funding made long-range planning difficult and, together with small staff size and other factors, precluded involvement in a range of program and policy development activities.

Over the past quarter-century, literacy programs have been concerned with linking to other organizations. Social service organizations provided student referrals and assisted with a range of students' related needs, such as health care, child care, transportation, and legal assistance. Other literacy organizations were

a source of support in a shared struggle; talking with other teachers or administrators helped literacy staff feel less isolated and
provided stimulation and new ideas. However, literacy educators
often assumed that their cause was considered so marginal by
policymakers that they could have little influence over resources
once the heydey of funding in the 1970s was behind them.

Now some literacy educators are adopting a more proac-
tive stance about their situations. They are turning informal
associations of literacy programs into formalized collaborative
efforts. Members of these do not necessarily all trust each other,
but they have found ways to work together toward goals that
they all value and that they cannot achieve individually (Williams, 1989).

The purposes of these collaborative efforts vary. They may
have been created to develop and distribute new funds, like the
Boston Literacy Fund. Or they may provide training, technical
assistance, or an information clearinghouse, like the Houston
READ Council. They also provide an open forum for sharing
information, providing support, and engaging in advocacy activities, like the New York Coalition of Adult Education Providers.

Still other literacy educators are creating organizations
specifically designed to meet the need for additional training
resources. For example, the Literacy Assistance Center in New
York City, set up as a nonprofit organization with the support
of the mayor's office, provides technical assistance, information,
research, training, and advocacy. The North Carolina Center
for Literacy Development, another nonprofit organization, was
created to promote participatory literacy education through
training, technical assistance, and research.

In addition, university involvement seems to be increasing. For example, the Adult Literacy Resource Institute in
Boston, providing training and technical assistance, is jointly
supported by Roxbury Community College and the University
of Massachusetts. There also is a growing number of university
centers dedicated to research on literacy, including those at the
University of Tennessee, Pennsylvania State University, and
the University of Pennsylvania.

At the national level, literacy educators have come together to create the National Coalition for Literacy, an organization of and for national organizations that have literacy as a primary focus. And the coalition has been the foundation for an ad hoc group called the Working Group on Adult Literacy, which formulated a policy paper during the last presidential election and has been promoting national literacy legislation.

Educators understand that effective and widespread literacy education requires stable funding and support mechanisms at the local, state, and national levels. In addition, in order to respond to students' complex needs, literacy programs need help providing assistance with services such as transportation, child care, health care, personal counseling, legal assistance, and job training and placement.

In response to these needs, a wide range of organizations has made an increasing commitment to literacy work in the last decade, in addition to institutions funded under the Adult Education Act (such as public schools and community colleges) and volunteer literacy programs. These include libraries, unions, United Way organizations, mass media (especially print and television), and community-based organizations. They also include public offices, such as those of mayors and governors; public institutions, such as state library systems and federal and state corrections systems; and federal agencies, such as the Department of Labor, Department of Education, and ACTION. Mayors and governors are mandating task forces and other collaborative efforts in which literacy providers are only one of a number of types of organizations that come together to promote comprehensive policy initiatives, agency coordination, or public awareness on a large scale.

All of this activity remains fragile. Funding is often on a year-to-year basis, and the leadership base in the field is small. Literacy teaching is rarely considered a career option by professional educators; there are very few full-time teaching positions, few or no fringe benefits, and almost no opportunities for promotion. Thus, as new leadership positions are created on the local, state, and national levels, relatively few experienced, qualified persons are available to fill them. In addition, students' leadership roles are still largely undeveloped in relation to the overall system. Students are only marginally involved as literacy educators struggle with their relationship to others with an interest in the field. The challenge exists to move outside the relatively small group of those already in leadership positions to bring in new leadership and share power.

As the range of organizational involvement increases, literacy educators often have to deal with new players — sometimes from organizations with values, beliefs, and goals that are quite different from those of the literacy community. For example, as business and industry leaders become increasingly involved in literacy, they want to participate in shaping the field's responses. They often have strong ideas about what they will fund and for what purpose, ideas developed in consultation with but not under the control of literacy educators. As the number of players increases, the tensions around negotiating roles and authority increase as well.

There is a lot of talk about the present as a time of opportunity, because attention to literacy, like attention to other social issues, is cyclical. In the past, literacy educators have taken advantage of a period of high attention primarily to build local programs. Now there is an attempt to institutionalize responses, to create larger structures and systems that will outlast the fickle attention of the general public or policymakers. This involves creating new alliances and cooperating as an equal partner, at the least. It will be a few years before we can know if this process of transformation will have lasting effects, or if the slowly emerging literacy education system will dissolve as educators become burned out and policymakers and funders turn their attention elsewhere.

Near-Term Recommendations

An understanding is emerging that an instructional program is only one piece of the large network of persons, organizations, and relationships that must be established if there is to be a major improvement in literacy in the United States.

There also is increasing consensus that the system must be pluralistic, including organizations whose approaches and goals may differ from one to the other, while demanding high quality. Furthermore, we are coming to understand that the response to the need for literacy development must be integrated with responses to a host of other social issues, including poverty, housing, vocational training, economic development, crime, and health care. And underlying everything is a commitment to learners, to creating opportunities that respect and respond to students' needs, aspirations, and experiences.

The field remains far from this ideal, however, as forces for change compete with strong tendencies toward the status quo. Assessment of the progress made so far must be done carefully. For example, new coalitions are emerging at the local, state, and national levels, but their value will depend on the extent to which they can accomplish goals that their constituent members are unable to achieve independently. Coalitions are not ends in themselves.

In addition, new funds are available today, but many of them are narrowly targeted in areas such as workforce literacy. Therefore, a simple aggregate analysis of funds available for literacy misrepresents the resources available for purposes such as program development, research, training, and services in other areas. The field continues to require additional resources that can be used to meet the wide range of needs.

A number of recommendations emerge from this analysis. First, research in cognitive science and its applications must continue. In addition, research and training in collaborative work should be supported. And policymakers should spend more time with literacy staff and learners exploring the relationship between individuals' objectives and larger social goals. We need forums for citizens' debate about the greater good and their personal relationship to those goals.

As issues around learning theory, program goals, learners' roles, and control become clearer, policymakers' responses must promote constructive change that is informed by and built upon the foundation laid over the past two decades. After a long period of slow, evolutionary change, now the pace is quickening and the challenge is clear: Will we, as a society, support literacy development for all, with everything that entails? The choice and the opportunity are open to us all.

Acknowledgments

I would like to thank the following people for generously donating their time to respond to previous drafts of this manuscript: Page McCullough, Jean Hammink, Jacqueline Cook, Sondra Stein, Peter Waite, and Paul Jurmo. I also would like to thank Robin Britt, Tom Sticht, Tony Sarmiento, Ruth Nickse, Eli Zal, Marilyn Boutwell, Nancye Gaj, Carolyn Dickens, Meta Potts, Susan Lytle, and Lee Weinstein for their assistance with my representation of their important work. And my deep appreciation goes to Brent Snow, Annette Laico, Tom Valentine, Dianne Ford, O'Neal Jones, and Jim Elliot for their continuing support, Jonathan Estes for his production assistance, and Forrest P. Chisman, Wendy L. Campbell, and Alan B. Knox for their invaluable assistance as editors and colleagues in the writing process.

References

Association for Community Based Education. *Adult Literacy: Study of Community Based Literacy Programs.* Washington, D.C.: Association for Community Based Education, 1983.

Auerbach, E. R. "Toward a Social-Contextual Approach to Family Literacy." *Harvard Educational Review,* 1989, *59* (2), 155–181.

Darkenwald, G., and Valentine, T. *Outcomes and Impact of Adult Basic Education.* Research Monograph No. 6. New Brunswick, N.J.: Center for Adult Development, Rutgers University, 1984.

Fingeret, A. "The Illiterate Underclass: Demythologizing an American Stigma." Unpublished doctoral dissertation. Syracuse, N.Y.: Department of Adult Education, Syracuse University, 1982.

Fingeret, A. "Social Network: A New Perspective on Independence and Illiterate Adults." *Adult Education Quarterly,* 1983 (Spring), *33,* 133–146.

Fingeret, A. *Adult Literacy Education: Current and Future Directions.* Columbus, Ohio: ERIC Clearinghouse on Adult, Career, and Vocational Education, 1984.

Fingeret, A., and Jurmo, P. *Participatory Literacy Education.* New Directions in Continuing Education, No. 42. San Francisco: Jossey-Bass, 1989.

Focus on Basics, 1989, *2* (2).

Graff, H. *The Literacy Myth: Literacy and Social Structure in the 19th Century City.* New York: Academic Press, 1979.

Hayes, A. *Keenan Trust Family Literacy Model — Breaking the Cycle of Illiteracy: The System of Influence.* Louisville, Ky.: National Center for Family Literacy, 1989.

Heath, S. B. "The Functions and Uses of Literacy." *Journal of Communication,* 1980 (Winter), *30* (1), 123–133.

Human Resources Development Institute. *Worker-Centered Learning: A Union Guide to Workplace Literacy.* Washington, D.C.: AFL-CIO Human Resources Development Institute, in press.

Jurmo, P. J. "Learner Participation Practices in Adult Literacy Efforts in the United States." Unpublished Ed.D. dissertation. University of Massachusetts, Amherst, 1987.

Jurmo, P. "The Case for Participatory Literacy Education." In A. Fingeret and P. Jurmo (Eds.), *Participatory Literacy Education.* New Directions in Continuing Education, No. 42. San Francisco: Jossey-Bass, 1989.

Lytle, S. L., Marmor, T. W., and Penner, F. H. "Literacy Theory in Practice: Assessing Reading and Writing of Low-Literate Adults." Unpublished manuscript. Philadelphia: Graduate School of Education, University of Pennsylvania, 1986.

Mikulecky, L. "Literacy Task Analysis: Defining and Measuring Occupational Literacy Demands." Paper presented at the annual meeting of the American Educational Research Association, Chicago, 1985. ERIC Document Reproduction Service No. ED 262 206.

Mikulecky, L. "Job Literacy Research: Past Results and New Directions." Paper presented at the annual meeting of the International Reading Association, Anaheim, Calif., 1986.

Nickse, R. "The Noises of Literacy: An Overview of Intergenerational and Family Literacy Programs." Unpublished mimeograph. Washington, D.C.: U.S. Department of Education, 1989.

Reder, S. M. "Comparative Aspects of Functional Literacy Development: Three Ethnic Communities." In D. Wagner (Ed.), *The Future of Literacy in a Changing World*. Volume 1. Oxford: Pergamon, 1987.

Reder, S. M., and Green, K. R. *Giving Literacy Away*. Portland, Ore.: Northwest Regional Laboratory, revised Nov. 1985. ERIC Document Reproduction Service No. ED 253 775.

Sagan, C. *Dragons of Eden: Speculations on the Evolution of Human Intelligence*. New York: Random House, 1977.

Scribner, S., and Cole, M. *The Psychology of Literacy*. Cambridge, Mass.: Harvard University Press, 1981.

Sticht, T. G. *Functional Context Education: Workshop Resource Notebook*. San Diego, Calif.: Applied Behavioral and Cognitive Sciences, Inc., 1987.

Sticht, T. G., and McDonald, B. A. *Making the Nation Smarter: The Intergenerational Transfer of Cognitive Ability*. San Diego, Calif.: Applied Behavioral and Cognitive Sciences, Inc., 1989.

Weber, R. "Adult Illiteracy in the United States." In J. B. Carroll and J. Chall (Eds.), *Toward a Literate Society*. New York: McGraw-Hill, 1975.

Williams, M. "Collaboration: Why, Who, What, Where and When." Presentation to the National Forum on Literacy Collaboration and Policy Issues. Minneapolis, Minn.: Literacy Network, Inc., 1989.

3

📖 Karl O. Haigler

Building Ties Among Literacy Programs: Achieving Strength Through Cooperation

What constitutes a proper definition of *linkages* largely depends on who is doing the defining. For instance, when literacy advocates speak about the need for better linkages among literacy programs, they usually mean the formal or informal ties established among programs to strengthen their individual efforts through cooperation. In this context linkages result from networking activities or, more broadly, from efforts to increase collaboration. Policymakers in literacy are more likely to stress the need for better coordination among publicly supported as well as nonprofit programs serving adults needing improved literacy or basic skills. Policymakers and members of the corporate community also stress the importance of developing partnerships, specifically between the public and private sectors, around such issues as workforce literacy. In its broadest definition the term *linkages* includes all of those efforts that have as their aim increasing the ability of literacy providers to serve the needs of adult learners through cooperation with other organizations, whether other literacy providers, private corporations, or public agencies.

Building effective cooperative relationships among literacy programs and interested agencies is important because literacy programs by and large exist on the margin—the last to be funded and first to be cut. They are primarily staffed by part-time teachers and administrators, paraprofessionals, and volunteers,

51

and they often lack adequate funds for teacher training, student recruitment, support services, or program administration. Affiliations with other programs in collaborative efforts at the community, city, or state levels can often bring needed resources, however scarce or short-lived, to literacy programs that might otherwise cease to operate. In addition, many literacy programs that are community-based reach adults whom the more established, regularly funded programs have difficulty in attracting or retaining. To the extent that linkages can remain fruitful—providing more access to programs that not only reach adults but also teach them the basic skills they need to pursue their own goals and those of society—linkages provide a fragile web of community literacy education for those most in need.

Barriers to Effective Linkages

As desirable as it may be for literacy programs to gain strength by combining their efforts and seeking support from interested public and private sources, a number of factors act as impediments to such linkages. These barriers include the following:

1. *The tendency to view a linkage strategy as an end in itself—a way of satisfying some externally imposed mandate.* While cooperative agreements, formal or informal, may serve short-term interests, long-term collaboration must be based on goals or ends rather than means. Linkage is a *means* to some goal, not an end in itself. Moreover, such agreements often serve as substitutes for action on a broader scale, which requires involvement with groups outside the literacy community—for example, political involvement or "marketing" literacy to the private sector.

2. *The relative ineffectiveness of requirements for coordination and collaboration that exist in federal legislation.* Public agencies may not act as their own monitors or may view mandates as burdensome; they therefore do not actively seek such linkages. Nonpublic literacy providers tend to be intimidated by the format and language of federal requirements, particularly if there is no perceived countervailing power at the state or local levels to enforce mandates upon reluctant public agencies.

3. *The idea that what needs to be done is to link literacy programs — the "coalition approach."* Forming coalitions at the local and state level may be a necessary first step, but the programmatic emphasis may preclude a more "client centered" approach that is called for in providing comprehensive services that adults need.

4. *The view that real philosophical differences between literacy programs can and should be ignored in order to overcome the "fragmentation" of the literacy field.* What appears to outsiders as "turf protection" among literacy groups may in fact reflect important differences in their views of how to best serve adult learners as well as competing political agendas. Attempts to ignore such differences may take the shape of common referral systems, recruiting, or consciousness-raising campaigns — activities that are least likely to emphasize distinctions among programs that may be vital to the adult learner.

5. *The lack of sophistication in defining literacy in more policy-relevant terms.* The relative insularity of the literacy "community" from public social service or job-training networks has prevented literacy providers from developing contacts or vocabulary that would connect literacy services to comprehensive intervention programs for adults "at risk." Literacy providers have not been at the forefront in connecting literacy to state or local political agendas.

6. *The view that self-interest has no place in collaboration.* Literacy as a social cause seems at times to require sacrifice and other forms of selfless behavior (such as voluntarism) that tend to run counter to bottom-line, results-oriented approaches of business or, increasingly, public demands for accountability. This assumption colors collaboration efforts, which need to be informed by calculations of what each group can gain by joining with others and what benefits thereby accrue to the adult learner.

7. *The absence of politically supported offices to promote a linkage or coordination strategy, such as a state office of literacy.* Responsibility for translating mandates into action steps is typically diffuse in literacy efforts. The ability to provide incentives for collaboration and to ensure oversight in linking public and private literacy and literacy-related programs is best carried out by offices with political clout.

8. *The real power that publicly supported programs have and exercise over nonpublic programs in matters affecting policy development and funding decisions.* The primary advantage held by public programs in literacy education is their presumptive right to funds coming through the state from the federal government; therefore, public programs have few incentives to build linkages to nonpublic programs.

9. *The tendency to build linkage strategies around available "status quo," school-based solutions.* The marginal nature of most literacy and adult education programs tends to make them more reliant on available, familiar educational materials and approaches. School-based programs are characterized by the use of grade-level measures in testing and student placement, with credentialing (high school equivalency) as a typical outcome. With few resources for adapting materials and instruction to the needs of adults, many literacy educators in public *and* nonpublic programs tend to mimic typical grade school methods for the teaching of reading and mathematics.

Although this list does not exhaust the factors that may influence particular instances, it includes the ones that seem formidable to leaders who seek to promote linkage strategies. The fallacy of the linkage prescription needs to be avoided in any case—the idea that all that we need to do is to strengthen the bonds among programs, develop stronger networks, expand collaborative efforts, and build more partnerships in order to solve the adult literacy problem. A focus on linkages might even obscure a grander vision that would better serve the needs of adult learners and the nation as a whole. Such a vision may begin to emerge from a closer examination of specific barriers to linkages and opportunities to overcome those barriers at the national, state, and local levels. Any view of linkages ultimately depends on how they are defined in practice by policymakers and practitioners and evaluated in terms of their ability to improve and expand the delivery of services to adult learners. In other words, we need to remember that our efforts finally point past linkages as an end of literacy policy and toward the establishment of permanent routes of access for adults that will survive the competing interests in the literacy community and the competition for resources among public agencies.

The Current Situation

As a point of departure in considering almost any policy issue in adult literacy, an examination of the Adult Education Act (AEA) programs run by the U.S. Department of Education is crucial. In the 1980s many of those who became involved in literacy were surprised to find out that a federal program existed that was specifically designed to help undereducated adults. Although meagerly funded since its enactment in 1964, as part of the Great Society effort, AEA provides a vehicle for building stronger linkages among literacy programs. An examination of this act, including how it has operated in the states and as a vehicle of national literacy policy, offers important lessons in the promise of, and the barriers to, the implementation of federal legislative mandates.

For those who aspire to influence policy or operations of the adult education system, AEA is required reading. In many ways it answers the concerns of those who are interested in serving the adults most in need of literacy service, those who want to see nonpublic groups (those which do not receive government funds directly) included in literacy efforts at the state and local levels, and those in the private sector who advocate greater accountability in federal programs. However, when the funds provided by the act find their way to the state and local levels, it becomes clear that much of what Congress intended has been lost by a system that is only beginning to discover the difference that collaboration, linkages, and partnerships can make in reaching those most in need.

Proponents of collaboration can take their bearings from the language of AEA: It requires each state education agency (SEA) to describe how agencies, groups, and individuals outside the system of public education have been involved in developing the state's four-year plan for adult education and how they will be involved in implementing the plan. The State Advisory Council on Adult Education, although optional, is supposed to be broadly representative of groups interested in adult education but clearly not members of the adult education establishment. The council would thus provide a mechanism for expanding the base of support for adult education in the state.

And the local applications requesting funding of programs under AEA are required to show coordination with other federal programs, such as the Job Training Partnership Act (JTPA), the Carl D. Perkins Vocational Education Act, and the Domestic Volunteer Service Act (VISTA).

Moreover, in the AEA amendments of 1988, Congress gave a clear indication that it wanted more funding to go to groups serving "educationally disadvantaged adults," as opposed to those serving adults who want a high school equivalency diploma. The latter group of adults, in the consensus of the field, are easier to motivate and not as costly to serve. The act calls on the SEA to give "preference" to those local programs that have demonstrated or can demonstrate the ability to serve educationally disadvantaged adults—defined as those adults functioning below the sixth-grade level or who are placed at the lowest level of adult programs not using grade-level equivalents.

The requirement to give preferential treatment to such applicants appears to open a back door for Congress to influence funding decisions without mandating or setting aside funds for particular literacy groups, typically volunteer literacy and community-based groups that see the low-functioning adults as their particular clientele. Congress also may have been responding to complaints of volunteer and community-based groups that they were being excluded from AEA funding, in spite of the collaborative language and intention of the law.

The allocation of funding at the local level supports the perception of nonpublic programs that, whatever linkages may have appeared in state plans, these were not the ties that bind when funding decisions were made. In fiscal year (FY) 1987 the Division of Adult Education found that 62.7 percent of AEA funds went to local education agencies (LEAs); 28.4 percent went to community colleges; 3.7 percent went to community-based organizations (CBOs); and 1 percent went to volunteer organizations. The remainder went to libraries, institutional programs, and other unspecified groups (U.S. Department of Education, 1988). Funding for non-LEA or non-postsecondary institutions tended to be limited to a few states; for instance, South Carolina, with $567,222, accounted for almost half the total funding to support volunteer organizations, and New York was far and away the leader in funding community-based organizations, with 33 grants totaling $1,423,976. To put these allocations data in perspective, it is important to remember that FY 1987 reflects federal funding allocations during the first year of the national literacy campaign of Project Literacy U.S. (PLUS). It is safe to assume that, in making their funding decisions that year, SEAs should have been highly sensitive to the funding needs of those groups most involved in recruiting volunteers and adults targeted by the PLUS campaign (educationally disadvantaged adults). Instead, the practices of funding allocations under the AEA undercut the intent of Congress for a system that mandated participation of nonpublic groups in the planning and implementation of the states' adult education programs. The rhetoric supporting linkages and collaboration apparently broke up on the shoals of institutional jealousy, whereby volunteer efforts in particular were encouraged by SEAs to demonstrate the feasibility of the Reagan administration's contention that volunteers could solve the literacy problem through a united, national effort—but without the support of additional federal funding.

The Adult Education Act and its actual operation at the state level illustrate a number of the barriers to building stronger linkages among literacy providers. First, they show the real power that publicly supported programs have and exercise over nonpublic programs (eighth barrier). Second, reinforcing the institutional bias that adult education systems in public schools and community colleges have against other agencies in their local area is the reality of the philosophical differences that often exist between public and nonpublic programs (fourth barrier). Another issue implicit in the use of public adult education programs as the institutional base of literacy efforts is their operating program philosophy, which is typically more "individually oriented" than "community oriented." As Hayes and Snow (1989, p. 14) point out, it is highly questionable whether programs with such differing philosophies can be linked or brought into collaboration, all in the name of networking or coalition building:

Ultimately, therefore, the two approaches cannot be merged, nor can the best qualities of each be combined. The different mission of each will necessitate that they remain separate and distinctive. However, another possibility is that educators in each type of program can cooperate, serving perhaps different clientele, to attain their goals. Unfortunately, this cooperative relationship is, in the end, impossible. The goals of each program are not complementary; they are radically opposed. The programs can, as they do now, coexist, but as one type of program succeeds in attaining its goals, it will lead to the obstruction of the goals of programs with the other orientation.

In attempts to paper over the real differences that exist at the local and state levels between public adult education programs and nonpublic programs, coalitions are formed at the state, regional, or local levels, and the roles of nonpublic providers are duly reported to fulfill legislative mandates for "coordination" and "collaboration" (first barrier). The emphasis on linking programs through a coalition approach (third barrier) not only interferes with building linkages that last but also has had little impact on funding decisions or on policy development at the state level.

The tendency to build linkage strategies around "status quo," school-based approaches to literacy (ninth barrier) comes most clearly to light when discussions about literacy move to policy levels and involve issues such as workforce preparation, training, or retraining. An obvious example is the concern over workforce literacy, a matter that appears to transcend the confines of state departments of education and suggests broader based strategies that involve both vocational training and job-training agencies. Approaches called for in the teaching of basic skills in the context of particular occupations run counter to the broader educational approaches used by typical adult education and volunteer literacy groups. Closer ties with job-training programs under JTPA tend to threaten the inclusion of status quo, school-based models in the delivery of services.

The inability or unwillingness of literacy providers to present the issue of weak basic skills as integral to a governor's or a state's concerns for economic development or welfare reform illustrates the fifth barrier—the lack of sophistication in defining literacy in more policy-relevant terms. Although state planning agencies, including the National Governors' Association (NGA) and the Council of State Planning and Policy Agencies (CSPA), have recognized the role of literacy as an integral part of governors' economic development strategies, little advocacy for such an approach came from the literacy field itself as a policy issue. NGA's report, *Making America Work: Bringing Down the Barriers* (1987), made adult literacy an issue that governors needed to consider in helping their states develop economically.

In addition to, and to some extent as a result of, the NGA emphasis on literacy, a number of states issued reports and formulated recommendations in 1988 on the issue of adult literacy. Those reports dealt with a number of common concerns, including the call for closer coordination, collaboration, and cooperation among all parties involved in literacy or literacy-related activities. With its particular emphasis on economic development as a key policy issue, the North Carolina Governor's Commission on Literacy (1988, p. 7) illustrates this point:

> To serve this broad cross-section of citizens [adults needing literacy service] effectively, we *must* mobilize a wide array of resources cutting across many traditional organization boundaries. To accomplish this, one of the overriding elements of the North Carolina strategy *must* be that of *coordination and cooperation*—among agencies, between state and local governments and between public and private sectors. [Emphasis added.]

To the imperative tone of the North Carolina report could be added that of Missouri, Arkansas, and many other states. The absolute necessity to cooperate, coordinate, and collaborate is echoed in recommendations concerning what needs to be done;

what is most often left out is who has clear responsibility for the doing. The general silence of the reports on this point is indicative of two barriers: the absence of a politically supported office to promote a linkage strategy (seventh barrier), and the relative ineffectiveness of the legislative requirements for coordination that already exist in federal legislation (second barrier).

The final report of a state literacy policy academy (Chynoweth, 1989) shows that ten participating states all saw the same need to build stronger interagency operating plans or strategies as a key policy "intervention." At the same time the academy staff noted, among the "lessons learned" during the academy process, "team unwillingness to work on details." "Interagency collaboration is hard work. . . . Detailing a two-year action plan is . . . more precise than defining the problem" (p. 36).

The experience of the planners in the state literacy policy academy has been replicated many times over at the local level, where efforts at collaboration founder upon issues of turf. Lay members of local, regional, and state coalitions lament the fragmentation of the literacy field, without appreciating the philosophical and institutional differences that may be operating implicitly and that serve to undermine cooperative efforts. What is likely to occur under such circumstances is the raising of the rhetorical banner that "we all ought to put our differences aside and work together for the people we are trying to serve." This exemplifies the sixth barrier—the view that self-interest has no place in collaborative efforts.

Anyone seeking evidence of self-interested behavior on the part of literacy programs need go no further than an evaluation of Project Literacy U.S. done by COSMOS Corporation. The PLUS outreach effort on the national, state, and local levels brought various organizations into the literacy issue and into association with literacy service providers, with some very interesting results. Among the COSMOS report's most important observations on the issue of linkages and collaboration, based on a survey of representative task forces, was the following:

A task force whose membership consists primarily of literacy service providers, especially from one delivery system, is likely to focus in-

itially on awareness-raising, recruitment, and service delivery activities, rather than on developing linkages with non-service provider organizations. These types of task forces found it useful to have a non-service provider convener, who can mediate *the vested interests of the various service providers* [Alamprese and others, 1987, p. 83; emphasis added].

The literacy field stands now where many advocates for change and for the development of more effective solutions have stood before. We want to unite, yet we have real differences that divide us. With few resources to go around, it is little wonder that those who have been systematically excluded harbor resentment toward those who have been more fortunate, more connected to the "powers that be," and more represented in vital decisions concerning funding. As a result, what follows as the next stage in building stronger linkages may not appear to be a linkage strategy at all. In fact, the paradox may be that the goal of literacy policy may have to be something other than building linkages if we are to succeed in building linkages that last.

Building Linkages That Last

The primary reason to consider any strategy to expand and improve literacy education is the effect it will have on the adult learner. It follows that we must keep in mind the self-interest of the adult, specifically, his or her reasons for engaging in literacy education. Linking adult literacy programs in a series of networks may serve in the short run to help providers continue in operation, but such an approach inevitably will fail if support services, such as child care and counseling, are not in place as well. Building linkages with social service and job training agencies suggests, in turn, a comprehensive approach that is more centered on adults as clients in a system that includes literacy education but is not limited conceptually, philosophically, or institutionally to literacy provider networks.

Such an approach is clearly envisioned in the Job Opportunities and Basic Skills Training (JOBS) Program of the Family Support Act of 1988 (welfare reform). Until recently, however, we have lacked an understanding of adult basic skills that has policy relevance at the federal and state level to an ambitious program such as JOBS. Since the publication in 1986 of the young adult study by the Educational Testing Service (Kirsch and Jungeblut, 1986), literacy professionals and policymakers have had to come to grips with a view of literacy that is more contextual, that is, defined by how adults actually put their basic skills to use in a variety of life contexts, including their occupations and their roles as parents. The Educational Testing Service research report and the contextual view of literacy that it embodies clearly influenced policy at the federal and state levels, leading to unparalleled federal program coordination and to a series of contextual literacy initiatives.

One of the positive outcomes of this controversial report was the development of a close working relationship between the U.S. Department of Education's Adult Literacy Initiative (ALI) and the U.S. Department of Labor's Employment and Training Administration (ETA), which oversees JTPA and contributed significantly to the Secretary of Labor's literacy strategy. ALI and ETA developed a public-public partnership that resulted in one major publication, *The Bottom Line: Basic Skills in the Workplace* (U.S. Department of Education and U.S. Department of Labor, 1988); an interagency agreement among Education, Defense, and Labor on a civilian version of a military program of computer-based training in basic skills; and the previously mentioned policy academy for states (in concert with NGA and CSPA) (Chynoweth, 1989). The partnership between ALI and ETA was informed by a strategic view of the literacy issue that went beyond the rhetoric of collaboration or linkages: The coordination of the federal departments was aimed at promoting a more contextual view of the literacy issue that linked basic skills improvement to policy goals of the federal administration (for instance, increased private sector involvement) and those of the states.

In approaching the issue more contextually, the departments were guided by the research of literacy experts, such as Tom Sticht and David Harman, both of whom advocated approaches to literacy that were more functional and less school-based. The involvement of adult educators in the projects undertaken by this partnership (as in the adult literacy policy academy) set the stage for an increased emphasis on workforce literacy, an emphasis underscored and supported by a new national discretionary grant program in 1988 (in P.L. 100-297). And while the efforts of the federal departments were often criticized for focusing on the narrow, functional view of literacy, it is clear that the coordinated strategy — the linkage — achieved more than the two departments could have done separately.

This federal case study of interagency coordination serves as a positive illustration of how linkages that last have to avoid a number of the barriers outlined in the previous section:

- Both departments focused on *serving the interests of the private sector and states through advancing a more contextual rather than a school-based view of literacy.*
- *AEA programs and JTPA are required to coordinate by law,* but such a requirement had never clearly been expressed in policy at the federal level in real initiatives.
- Both ETA and ALI *carried administrative, political mandates to cooperate, and doing so brought recognition to the political actors involved.*

The experience of this collaborative initiative also shows that federal departments cannot assume that the states or the private sector, without support at the federal level, will seek either to develop policy strategies that better integrate literacy services or to build public-private partnerships. Activities in technology transfer, state policy academies, and program coordination provide opportunities for federal agencies to become agents for change — for instance, to promote the translation of research into practice. And the key to this role is a proper appreciation of the state policymaker and the potential of private-sector support for policy initiatives.

In order for the federal government to exploit its role as an agent for change, federal mandates for coordination in existing laws — in adult education, job training, and welfare reform — can serve as a foundation. However, strategies also must be informed by an awareness of what some states are already doing to integrate public programs and partnerships into a more comprehensive system of literacy service. A few states are developing policy strategies along these lines. The State of Mississippi may serve to illustrate a number of strategies that address barriers to linkages and, more broadly, point the way to opportunities to exploit educational, economic development, and welfare reform initiatives for the benefit of literacy.

Mississippi benefited, as did many other states, from the support of the Gannett Foundation Literacy Challenge grant program, which provided over $3.5 million for building literacy coalitions. One of the first and most pressing recommendations of the Mississippi Coalition for Literacy was the creation of an office charged with the coordination of the state's literacy initiatives, including public and nonpublic programs. The main sticking points on the establishment of such an office were how it should be funded and to whom it would be accountable. Nonetheless, it was the governor's wife, Julie Mabus, who chaired the coalition, and her suggestions for addressing these problems carried much weight. Mabus's program knowledge of AEA and JTPA was derived mainly from an initiative of the U.S. Departments of Labor and Education, working with NGA: a national conference for state literacy initiatives. The governor, Ray Mabus, decided to allocate discretionary funds under JTPA (from the 8 percent education/coordination set-aside) for the new Office for Literacy; he located it in a visible place in his offices; and he gave it a prominent role in major policy initiatives that affected adults as parents, as employees, and as welfare recipients.

In both its establishment and the responsibilities with which it has been charged, the Governor's Office for Literacy is designed to address several of the barriers to building effective linkages:

- There is now a politically supported office that has a mission to promote partnerships, collaborative efforts, and program coordination.
- One primary mission of the Office for Literacy is to utilize existing federal mandates for coordination in policy development, which means in practice defining literacy in more policy-relevant terms.

- The office also acts as an advocate for *adult learners* in its relationship with state agencies, literacy providers, and the private sector, rather than being an advocate for *literacy programs*.

The Office for Literacy, working closely with the governor and the office of the first lady, has identified a number of funding sources for basic skills development and has begun to implement a grants program, working with the state Department of Education, involving the governor's entire 8 percent discretionary funds under JTPA — about $2.7 million. It has been instrumental in developing four demonstration programs, built along contextual lines, educating adults who want to be more involved in the education of their children or to improve their own abilities to perform better on the job. On the legislative front the Office for Literacy has worked with the Department of Economic and Community Development in formulating and implementing a 25 percent income tax credit to businesses that invest in basic skills training and retraining for their employees. The governor's new educational reform package, to be considered by the next session of the legislature, includes as one of its seven goals a two-thirds reduction of the illiteracy rate over the next ten years. It also emphasizes the need to deal with out-of-school adults for reasons of economic competitiveness and building a quality workforce.

The role, visibility, and experience of an Office for Literacy makes it uniquely suited to be at the center of any efforts to reform the welfare system — particularly given the requirements for education and training present in the JOBS program. This program is replete with legislative mandates for coordination, which must be incorporated in the state's plan for implementing Family Support Act requirements. The governor plays a crucial role in this program, as in JTPA. A recent publication of a number of groups interested in the implementation of the Family Support Act emphasized the point:

At both the federal and state level the AFDC [Aid to Families with Dependent Children] agency is required to consult with the education agency. This mandate, together

with the leadership of the Governor, is intended to promote the coordination of JOBS planning and programming
with other education and training programs in the state.
The mandate also points to the importance of providing
comprehensive services to meet the multiple needs of AFDC
recipients trying to bolster their future employability [*New
Partnerships,* 1989, p. 9].

The JOBS program offers many opportunities for building
stronger linkages around the needs of adults learners, but without
advocacy for the welfare recipient with limited literacy skills,
the ambitious aims of the program may founder. And elements
of the JOBS program may lead to the wrong prescription, yet
again, for these targeted adults. Prescriptions that are school-
based will not necessarily lead to educational gains that make
recipients more employable. And, most important, such basic
skills programs will need to appeal to the motivations and real
literacy practices of the adults they intend to serve — particularly
since JOBS mandates participation for "nonexempt" welfare
clients (as defined in the legislation).

Developing the JOBS program calls for nothing less than
a comprehensive contextual literacy policy at the state level.
Among other benefits, such an approach addresses the barrier
involving the roles of individually oriented, public basic skills
programs and community-oriented programs. Community-
oriented literacy programs may form the vital link to this particular target population, because they are generally in better
touch with the existing social networks of undereducated adults
than are individually oriented programs. The latter, however,
offer access to the broader system of education and job training
that welfare recipients will need as their literacy skills improve
and as their reasons for learning become more centered on meeting the demands of the world outside their community.

Using the strengths of both the individually and community-oriented programs requires a third party that can develop
a division of labor between these typically competing interests.
An Office for Literacy or some other coordinating body outside
the educational and welfare establishments appears to be ideally
suited for this task. Such an approach under the JOBS program

can overcome the three problems that normally prevent the establishment of such linkages:

- The view that real philosophical differences between literacy programs can and should be ignored (fourth barrier).
- The real power that publicly supported programs have and exercise over nonpublic programs in policy development and funding decisions (eighth barrier).
- The tendency to build linkage strategies around available status quo, school-based solutions (ninth barrier).

As an advocate for adult learners, an Office for Literacy can advance strategies that are clearly linked to the goals and purposes of the Family Support Act, but go beyond the building of stronger linkages among literacy programs. Such an advocacy role appears to be needed when the typical communication between a Department of Public Welfare and welfare recipients is written at a level that makes comprehension by an adult reading at relatively low levels difficult, if not impossible. Since the new act requires welfare recipients to understand their new obligations (as possible mandatory participants in education and job training), advocates for adult learners can use this opportunity to develop client-centered literacy programs. Such programs can begin by using the existing social networks in communities of undereducated adults to recruit and perhaps to provide some rudimentary literacy training. This particular approach uses the *social contexts* of welfare recipients that educational research has identified as crucial to literacy development, particularly in "at risk" populations.

Relying upon existing state agencies and traditional, school-based approaches to literacy development may be the path of least resistance in welfare reform programs, but it will not build better access to literacy programs that will make a difference. Nor can the mandated literacy instruction or job training provided be reinforced in "at risk" communities if they are not understood more positively by the persons they are intended to help. Success in welfare reform may ultimately depend on the social meaning that is attached to literacy and basic skills development by communities of educationally and economically disadvantaged adults. As one critic of "overselling literacy" has aptly stated, "Literacy is good for several things, all of which have to be demonstrated personally; they are not compelling if simply talked about. No one learns to be literate on promissory notes of what literacy will do for them" (Smith, 1989).

Near-Term Recommendations

Adult literacy and basic skills improvement is beginning to find its way into the parlance of policymakers now as never before. As a result of sustained public awareness campaigns such as PLUS, the development of state literacy initiatives in a majority of states, and more serious policy-relevant activities at the federal and state levels, we are now poised to begin building a national system for the provision of basic skills service. The outlines of such a system can be inferred from much of what has been advanced as ways to build stronger linkages for literacy. But building linkages is but one particular strategy in the development of a national system, not a goal in itself.

Suggestions for next steps in linkage strategies depend on a view of literacy that is contextual, centered on the functional needs of adults, concerned with comprehensive provision of related services, and informed by the knowledge and experiences adults bring with them to any formal learning activity. This view underlies all of the following suggestions of what we can do in the next two years to make the Family Support Act's JOBS program the beginning of effective basic skills development.

What the Federal Government Can Do. There is a clear need to develop policy and program coordination among the U.S. Departments of Health and Human Services, Labor, and Education by advancing specific policy initiatives, which should include the following:

- Establish ongoing policy academies for states and technical assistance for literacy programs involved in welfare reform and economic development.
- Continue to support technology transfer initiatives with the private sector and the states that translate federal research

and development activities into useful tools for functional literacy.

- Publish readable translations of basic and field research in the teaching of reading, writing, mathematics, and reasoning in adult literacy contexts.
- Support state literacy coordinating activities with incentives to states to establish offices for literacy, such as grants developing workforce or family literacy partnerships with the private sector, schools, and universities.

What States Can Do. States have become increasingly important as critical links in literacy policy development and program innovation. Recommendations for and models of state literacy activities are more numerous than ever before, with the major involvement of organizations such as NGA and CSPA. Working within these organizations around specific policy issues such as welfare reform, states should also consider undertaking the following steps:

- Establish a politically supported office for literacy as an integral component in policy development and program coordination.
- Through an office for literacy provide grants to basic skills programs as incentives for developing new curricular approaches and teacher training in the context of building linkages with nonprovider social service and job-training agencies.
- Develop interrelated policy initiatives around education, economic development, and welfare reform that have measurable goals and specific outcomes.
- Establish standards of performance across funding sources for literacy programs that are system-neutral and do not discriminate against nonpublic providers of basic skills instruction.
- Support local demonstration projects in a variety of settings that illustrate comprehensive, client-centered approaches to contextual literacy instruction.
- Involve state universities and private foundations in research, evaluation, development, and assessment projects around

specific problems identified by policymakers and literacy providers.

- Develop and support teacher training, curriculum development, and technology initiatives that involve personnel from public and nonpublic programs as well as job-training, vocational, and welfare programs.

What Local Programs Can Do. It is easy and typical for decision makers to praise the efforts of those hard-working folks on the "front lines of literacy," but the fact is these knowledgeable individuals are the least listened to when it comes to developing specific initiatives, state plans, or funding justifications. Local programs often are at fault because they are too overwhelmed by their own work to be active at the state level, much less the federal level. This situation must change. A first step in the process is for local providers to become more conversant with the variety of funding sources for literacy, especially the JOBS program. Most important, local programs can act as the "conscience" of the coordination mandates that exist in federal legislation. This means that they must become more astute in the relation of literacy to national and state policy agendas.

At the local level, literacy programs should consider the following suggestions as they apply to building linkages that will best serve them and their clients:

- Build literacy networks by way of community coalitions around needs of the adult learner, to include support services, such as child care, counseling, and transportation.
- Act as advocates for adult learners in negotiating the welfare, job-training, and education bureaucracies.
- Activate "social networks" in "at risk" communities, and support literacy development outside school-based, individually oriented contexts.

What the Private Sector Can Do. As community leaders whose interest in literacy might most clearly support a state or local economic development agenda, business leaders can act as a third column in advancing the cause of literacy. All the major pieces of federal legislation mentioned in this chapter provide an explicit or implicit role for private sector representatives. More broadly, business leaders can represent the community at large in advocating a literate workforce.

Representatives from the private sector should consider the following specific suggestions for building linkages:

- Become conversant with the literacy demands in job-training and retraining programs.
- Learn more about the operations of the State Job Training Coordinating Council and the Private Industry Council at the local level.
- Become an advocate for accountability in "real world" terms for education—elementary, secondary, postsecondary, as well as adult literacy education.
- Support the establishment of pilot community literacy programs that are employment-related or that help parents become more involved in the education of their children.
- Explore the relevance of publicly developed basic skills technology for business and vocational training and retraining programs, and encourage state agencies to develop an awareness of technology transfer.

Building linkages that last must, in the final analysis, involve the successful integration of all levels of government—"vertical integration" as well as strong "horizontal integration" at each level, national, state, and local. And, at each level, this process must be informed by the needs of the adult learner as well as society as a whole. In examining the bases for building stronger linkages, we must all become more literate about literacy.

References

Alamprese, J. A., Schall, R. L., and Brigham, N. *Project Literacy U.S. (PLUS): Impact of the First Year's Task Forces.* Washington, D.C.: COSMOS Corp., 1987.

Chynoweth, J. K. *Enhancing Literacy for Jobs and Productivity.* Washington, D.C.: The Council of State Policy and Planning Agencies, 1989.

Hayes, E., and Snow, R. B. "The Ends and Means of Adult Literacy Education." *Lifelong Learning: An Omnibus of Practice and Research,* 1989, *12* (8), 12–18.

Kirsch, I., and Jungeblut, A. *Literacy: Profiles of America's Young Adults.* Princeton, N.J.: Educational Testing Service, 1986.

National Governors' Association. *Making America Work: Bringing Down the Barriers.* Washington, D.C.: National Governors' Association, 1987.

New Partnerships: Education's Stake in the Family Support Act of 1988. Washington, D.C.: American Public Welfare Association, 1989.

North Carolina Governor's Commission on Literacy. *Literacy for the 21st Century: Recommendations of the Governor's Commission on Literacy.* Raleigh, N.C.: Office of Policy and Planning, 1988.

Smith, F. "Overselling Literacy." *Phi Delta Kappan,* 1989, 353–359.

U.S. Department of Education. "Adult Education Delivery System: Subgrants/Contracts under Section 306, Fiscal Year 1987." Washington, D.C.: U.S. Goverment Printing Office, 1988.

U.S. Department of Education and U.S. Department of Labor. *The Bottom Line: Basic Skills in the Workplace.* Washington, D.C.: U.S. Government Printing Office, 1988.

4

Susan E. Foster

Upgrading the Skills of Literacy Professionals: The Profession Matures

Thousands of people today are engaged in the task of helping adults improve their literacy skills, but very few of them are able to help learners realize significant learning gains. Programs are isolated from one another, lack adequate resources, have little in the way of standards for quality programs, lack incentives or resources for staff development, and lack goals or direction for improvement. The purpose of this chapter is to clarify the steps needed to build an adult literacy profession capable of helping adults attain significant improvements in literacy skills.

Mapping the Problem

Literacy is best represented as a continuum of skills. The task of a literacy instructor is to help individuals progress along this continuum. In too many cases, we are not giving literacy staff the benefit of existing knowledge that could improve their skills. We are not providing literacy instructors with a professional structure, which implies continuing research and the application of research to practice on an organized basis.

With few exceptions, literacy programs today can demonstrate only very limited gains in literacy skills. Reviewing the work of many others in the field, Diekhoff (1988) found that the majority of participants in adult literacy programs do not achieve

73

meaningful, practically significant reading improvements, and that they leave the programs without having achieved "functional literacy," however one may choose to define the term.

Darkenwald (1986) has indicated that the most successful instructors — those working with learners who experience the greatest gains — seem to be those who are willing to abandon traditional teaching methods and to adopt methods and materials that are relevant to the learners. Yet we persist in assuming for a major part of our adult literacy system that adequate preparation for adult literacy instructors or facilitators consists of traditional teacher training.

Part of the problem in both instruction and assessment is that we have not settled on a meaningful way to measure improvements in literacy skills. Most leaders in the field agree that we need both a better way to evaluate literacy gains and a system of measuring improvement in literacy skills that is predicated upon the types of skills that will be required in the labor force and everyday life.

In addition to the problem of limited learning gains, virtually all types of literacy programs experience very high dropout rates. Reviewing the retention rates of basic skills instruction programs, Diekhoff (1988) reported that the majority of students in such programs stay with literacy training for less than one year, with only 20 percent maintaining enrollment for longer than that.

As Mikulecky suggests (pers. comm.), experience has shown that instructors whose students experience the highest learning gains seem to be those who have holding power — that is, they seem to be able to match personal and program goals and encourage students to stay with the program. We need to set standards for literacy practice related to these abilities.

There is ample evidence of the need for more training, but there is no evidence suggesting that this training should follow the traditional academic model as used in grades K–12. To the contrary, research and practical experience show the compelling advantages of nontraditional approaches (Fingeret, 1984).

We need to question what instructors are teaching, how they are teaching, and how the content and methods of instruction are tailored to the needs, expectations, and culture of learners. These are the questions related to the preparedness of the teachers.

We also need to evaluate the resources available for staff preparation and development, information-sharing opportunities, and the performance expectations of funding agencies. These are the questions related to the infrastructure needed to support increased professionalism.

The State of the Field

All literacy programs operate from some common ground. The major types of programs operating today, however, do have substantial differences in the importance they grant to these elements of common ground.

Programs vary in terms of their approach to the content of instruction and the support structure available for teacher preparation. In adult literacy programs, the range of qualifications of the instructors currently is very wide (Harman, 1985).

In-service training and other forms of staff development are most often undertaken on the instructors' own time and at their own expense. Because of the historical lack of agreement on the proficiencies required for adult literacy instruction and because of the lack of standards imposed by federal or state governments, adult literacy instructors often tend to be chosen more for their characteristics as concerned, caring individuals than for specific instructional proficiencies or training (Cranney, 1983).

Training and Approaches to Instruction. While the training required of staff varies greatly among local programs, some generalizations can be made.

Volunteer tutoring programs usually require minimal formal educational attainment and focus instead on a commitment to the program. Typically, fourteen to twenty hours of preservice orientation are provided to a tutor. There are no formal in-service training requirements. The volunteer tutoring approach has been predicated on the assumption that, with a modest amount of preparation, anyone can teach any other adult to read. This approach has been modified somewhat recently, as many volunteer programs have begun to work in close association with trained staff. Persons involved in volunteer tutoring programs are beginning to voice their conviction that literacy training is no job for volunteers alone.

The assumption behind most federally funded adult basic skills programs has been that an instructor should be trained in helping learners acquire academic skills, culminating with acquisition of a high school equivalency diploma. The skills needed to pass the examination for this diploma are thus assumed to be the skills needed to function adequately in the workplace. Adult basic skills programs generally accept credentials of teaching in elementary and secondary schools. Approximately 60 percent of instructors in adult basic skills programs operating in local education agencies and community colleges are moonlighting after elementary or secondary education teaching jobs. In nineteen states, prerequisites for instructors are the same as those for elementary and secondary education. The remaining thirty-one states enforce no particular certification requirements for adult educators (Widen and Kightlinger, 1987).

In most states, in-service training requirements are minimal and largely consist of voluntary attendance at group discussions, lectures, or seminars. These sessions are episodic in nature and are offered as freestanding programs rather than as part of a continuum of training. Few standards exist to specify qualifications for those providing instruction in such programs. Released time is rarely provided for attendance. Minimal requirements are often met by offering conferences that can be attended on a voluntary, nonreimbursable basis by the staff of local adult literacy programs.

Several states have taken decidedly different approaches. California, Connecticut, New Mexico, and Virginia, for example, have used Section 353 (formerly Section 310) of the Adult Education Act (AEA) to address staff and development needs on a more formal basis. Several states have used AEA funds to create resource centers for adult literacy. In other states, such as Illinois, considerable effort has been made to sensitize staff to the needs of adult learners. More of this type of activity is needed.

Community-based programs have been built around the belief that the lack of literacy skills is just one of many problems facing individuals as they seek to become self-sufficient. Advocates of the community-based approach insist that literacy staff be sensitive both to the family and community environment and to the personal goals of the learner, and be skilled in providing literacy services in the context of the life circumstances of the learner. No specific set of preservice or in-service training requirements exists for community-based programs. Training opportunities provided for staff members of these programs are often directed toward helping staff "unlearn" formal training they may have received in favor of an approach as facilitators and advocates (Fingeret, 1984). Selection requirements for community-based programs tend to be more academically flexible than those for federally funded adult literacy programs, and more rigorous than those for volunteer tutoring programs.

Workplace literacy programs have been predicated on the dual assumptions that (1) the best motivation for skill enhancement is job retention or promotion and (2) instruction must be provided in the context of the learner's job environment by someone who is knowledgeable about that environment. Employers offering workplace literacy programs frequently establish liaisons with community colleges or public schools, so they are in most cases dealing with the same orientation and talent pool as federally funded adult basic skills programs. While the prerequisites for instruction are typically those required for elementary and secondary education, the orientation required by the firm is highly contextual and job-related. As in federally funded adult basic skills programs, participation in in-service training programs is voluntary and done on the time and at the expense of the instructor.

A special type of workplace literacy program is found in the military. In this type of program, rigid, job-specific curricula have been developed to enhance skills. The military approach has been to control the content of instruction to such an extent that virtually anyone with a college degree could become an instructor with little or no additional training. The only prerequisite for adult literacy instruction in the military is the possession of a college degree, in part because of the rigid curriculum used. In-service training is limited to informing the instructor of any changes made in the curriculum.

While education and training prerequisites and in-service training requirements are minimal for most literacy programs, prerequisites for administrative staff are rare. Program administrators of federally funded adult basic skills are often vocational educational directors or federal program directors in local educational agencies or community colleges. They are sometimes more poorly prepared than instructors. Because responsibility for the adult literacy program may have been added on to a large array of other responsibilities, administrators may be more committed to other programs or may lack the time or resources to become fully aware of program training requirements for adult literacy service.

Conditions for Reform. Recent research shows that there are elements of a productive approach in all of the types of programs operating today — elements upon which standards should be based. There are instances of exemplary practice in literacy programs across the country that should be shared with other programs. Taken individually, these *best practices* constitute necessary but not sufficient conditions for practical learning gains by adult learners. Information is also available both from research in adult learning and from evaluations of literacy programs that can help us reorient programs and improve their effectiveness. Information has been compiled on the types of skills needed to function in our economy, which can help us to clarify and target instruction (see Chapter 7). To create the sufficient conditions for reform, we must join what we know about the best practices from the field with the knowledge gained from research and evaluation, to form the basis for a set of standards for literacy professionals.

To implement these standards and encourage instructors

to exceed them, we need to provide support and assistance to programs and staff. We will have to make resources available for preservice and in-service training. We must provide incentives for professional development. We should develop mechanisms for information sharing. We must also encourage staff to view self-evaluation and accountability as key components of a literacy system.

Programs now exist in some states that should serve as models for other states. The Commonwealth Literacy Campaign in Massachusetts is developing uniform standards for program effectiveness and client outcomes, standards of practice for literacy staff, and a model for training of adult literacy staff. The State of Michigan is working on training and technical assistance materials for adult training and educational providers. Michigan is also developing model assessment tools for programs to use with adult learners. Virginia is targeting federal AEA funds to provide technical assistance to local literacy programs. This assistance will focus on improved administration, curriculum design, and instruction. Across the country, literacy programs are developing new techniques and better practices that could guide the development of standards.

The lack of a support structure for enhancing staff proficiency has been a major contributor to a slow pace of advancement in the state of the field. Despite several decades of activity, adult literacy is still a fledgling field. We can proceed if we have a better understanding of the extent and scope of structural problems in the field today. These problems can be grouped into two categories: those related to the teaching process itself, and those related to a support system for the advancement of the profession.

The Missing Standards of Practice. For the quality of education and training for adult literacy instructors to be improved, agreement must be reached on the common elements of proficiencies needed by instructors. A foundation for agreement can be derived from the literature on adult literacy and from practitioners in the field, but in the past no mechanism has existed to translate this information into practice. We need to develop standards of practice that will guide instructors in what to teach, how to teach, how to be responsive to the goals, needs, and culture of the learner, and how to improve accountability.

In many literacy programs today, the material being taught is not linked directly to either the goals of the state or those of the learner. Literacy programs are often generic in nature, rather than being directed to a specific and quantifiable program goal that is shared by the learner. Research has shown that learners do best when they see a clear relationship between what is being taught and achievement of their own goals. According to Mikulecky (pers. comm.), programs with the best holding capacity seem to be those in which completion of a literacy or skill improvement program is directly related to a personal goal, such as employment retention or job advancement — that is, where learners clearly recognize the need for skill improvement and where they have an incentive to improve their skills.

Clarification of goals is one important dimension of standards of practice. Others include clarification of the types of skills that are being taught and their relationship to the goals of the learner or the state, ways of approaching instruction to capture the interest of and demonstrate learning gains for the learner, and ways to improve accountability. (A proposed set of interim standards will be discussed in the next section.)

The field will have to define standards of practice for both instructors and administrators. This can and should be done in steps, starting with the establishment of interim standards derived from common elements of good practice in the field and from the existing research base. This task could be taken on by national membership organizations and by state-level groups representing the gamut of providers and policymakers. At the same time, a concerted effort should be applied to the longer term development of more formal standards of practice for the field. This is a task well suited to a national membership organization and one that could be informed by state experience and national research results. The adoption of even interim standards of practice would do much to establish a common goal toward which adult literacy programs could move without sacrificing important and valuable differences in approach.

The Missing Infrastructure. Literacy programs lack the infrastructure to support the improvement of the proficiencies of literacy staff. There are few incentives built into the existing system of service provision to advance the state of the field. Consequently, each institutional approach to basic skills instruction builds itself up without serious questioning, overemphasizes its successes, and struggles to provide more of the same with limited resources. Literacy programs are a bastard of the educational system—isolated from the mainstream and deprived of adequate resources for health, growth, and development.

Few programs engage in systematic program evaluation. To make adult literacy programs more effective, funding organizations and program providers need to build evaluation into every phase of literacy program operation. Further, it is crucial to instill a culture of self-evaluation and self-improvement in all adult literacy staff.

Compensation levels for adult literacy program staff are lower than in comparable fields of education, and no career path exists for advancement. The current rate of pay for literacy instructors is between nine dollars and twelve dollars per hour. In some areas, the rate is as low as six dollars per hour, and in some urban and suburban areas the rate approaches twenty dollars per hour. In most cases, this rate applies only to in-class teaching time, not to preparation time. Jobs are overwhelmingly part-time with few or no fringe benefits and with limited opportunities to build a career. If salaries were made commensurate with other, comparable jobs, and if more full-time positions were made available, career paths could be developed and support could be provided for improving proficiencies.

Administrators are rarely required to be trained in the field of adult basic skills education and are frequently unaware of the increasing knowledge base which could guide the operation of their programs. This lack of orientation and training in the subject of adult literacy education further compounds the isolation and low status of some of these programs.

Adult literacy programs suffer from a limited network for information sharing. In its 1986 report, the New York City Adult Literacy Initiative indicated that the single most common technical assistance request related to staff development was for more networking (Literacy Assistance Center, 1986). The New York City program is not alone in its perception of this need. Because of limited resources and lack of attention to the professional development needs of the field, the concept of building a network for information sharing is only beginning to be realized. Without such a resource, each program operates essentially on its own.

Building a Literacy Profession

To make significant advances in the performance of adult literacy programs, we need to change the culture of literacy providers. Literacy practitioners need to become major contributors to an action-based research agenda that will result in the development of more informed training practices. We must encourage experimentation and creativity. Once adopted, standards of practice must be refined. We must devise contextually based models for many different situations and learning goals. We must initiate programs to increase public awareness of the need for basic skills enhancement and create incentives for participation in literacy programs. Above all, the level of performance must be the taskmaster.

Changing the Culture of Literacy Providers. Changing the culture of literacy providers means exposing the staffs of all existing adult literacy programs to current knowledge and goals in order to improve the teaching-learning process. It also entails holding staff and programs accountable for meeting minimum standards of quality and achieving learner and program goals. Perhaps the most important prerequisite for advancing the state of the field is understanding that adult literacy instruction is an evolutionary process. Much information is available that should now be translated into practice, but there is much yet to be learned by examining practice and determining the causes of success and failure.

The practice of basic skills education should not be constrained to the development of one pedagogy. Various approaches are appropriate and necessary, depending on the context in which skill improvement is to occur. If we have learned one thing about literacy instruction for adults, it is that it must be contextually based.

A set of standards or specifications for practice for adult literacy staff can be developed that will apply to all adult literacy programs, regardless of orientation. That is, based on research and practical experience, we can extrapolate from what works in adult literacy programs to standards for adult literacy staff. These standards can be grouped into four areas: (1) what is being taught; (2) how basic skills are taught; (3) the goals, needs, and culture of the learner; and (4) accountability.

1. *What is being taught.* All levels of literacy staff should be knowledgeable about the latest information available that suggests what approach should be used in helping people upgrade basic skills. Over the years, three different approaches to instruction have been developed. The first is the traditional approach to literacy education, as taken in the elementary and secondary schools. Reading is viewed as one skill, writing as another, and history as a separate subject from geography or health. This approach is based on the assumption that each subject represents a block of knowledge or information that can be separately transferred to the learner. The unstated assumption of this approach is that these skills can be learned and then applied by the learner in other aspects of life. The unfortunate aspect of this approach is that it has already failed with most of the adult population with limited literacy skills. Further, adults with low levels of literacy skills appear to have a very limited ability to generalize knowledge from one skill to a related skill area (Kirsch and Jungeblut, 1986).

In response to the concern that *literacy* should be defined as including the ability to perform certain tasks as well as possession of specific bodies of knowledge, many programs began to focus all or part of their instruction on the second approach — functional or competency-based education (Lerche, 1985). This approach involves teaching specific literacy skills needed to solve the problems of daily life. This approach seems to retain more people in the programs than the traditional academic approach, but some critics argue that a focus on the acquisition of particular functional skills may not provide adequate training in basic encoding and decoding. The major criticism of this approach is that it simply extends the academic approach to literacy to a broader array of individual and specific tasks, without providing the basic problem-solving skills that would enable the learner to generalize to situations not anticipated in the classroom. In sum, the skills learned are not really portable (Venezky and others, 1986).

Research and experience have pointed out a third approach — one that orients instructors through experimentation to the development of a curriculum that teaches the underlying skills and strategies required in everyday literacy tasks. This is called the *portable skills approach* and was developed as part of the National Assessment of Educational Progress, a study conducted by the Educational Testing Service in 1986 of the literacy skills of adults twenty-one to twenty-five years old (Kirsch and Jungeblut, 1986).

The portable skills approach is based on the assumption that to be literate in today's society means not just the ability to encode and decode or perform separate and discrete tasks, but rather includes problem-solving or information-processing skills.

Elements of this approach might include skills in three different types of literacy, as defined in the National Assessment of Educational Progress survey — prose literacy, document literacy, and quantitative literacy. *Prose literacy* includes the knowledge and skills needed to understand and use information from texts, such as editorials, articles, letters, poems, and other similar types of written material. *Document literacy* involves the knowledge and skills required to locate and use information contained in job applications or payroll forms, bus schedules, maps, tables, indexes, and other charts. *Quantitative literacy* is defined as the knowledge and skills needed to apply arithmetic operations, either alone or sequentially, that are embedded in printed materials, such as balancing a checkbook, figuring out a discount, completing an order form, or determining the amount of interest from a loan advertisement (Kirsch and Jungeblut, 1986).

Implementing the portable skills approach will be an

evolutionary process. Many programs have already rejected or modified the traditional academic approach to basic skills instruction for adults and have adopted the functional competency approach. Building on these changes, literacy professionals can train instructors and program administrators in methods of instruction that teach a set of underlying skills through practice on a number of functional problems relevant to the real lives of adults.

Just as literacy staff should be conversant with the portable skills approach to literacy instruction, adult literacy program administrators should be knowledgeable about management practices and techniques. They should be familiar with various funding sources for basic skills instruction activities and know how to combine program funds to create a local program. Finally, they should be conversant with technologies that can assist in skill acquisition and should know how to plan and allocate costs to ensure that the necessary technologies are acquired.

2. *How basic skills are taught.* The second issue to be addressed is that of how the information is to be conveyed to the learner — that is, what skills or techniques the instructor should possess in order to afford the greatest advantage to the learner.

Best practices in the field and research results show that all literacy instructors, aides, and volunteers should possess good communication skills and should be able to orient them to specific groups of adults. Like all teachers, persons involved with helping others upgrade their literacy skills should be able to communicate effectively, should possess good listening skills, and should be able to select and organize material for presentation to the learner so as to build upon the learner's existing knowledge base.

Several different methods of instruction are now used in the field — phonics, sight-word, look-say. Different methods may be more effective with different adults. For this reason, literacy program staff need to be acquainted with various methods of instruction and should be able to match the method to the needs of the learner.

There is much ado these days about computer-based or computer-aided instruction. It is wise to remember, however, that the computer is a valuable tool for self-paced instruction, not an end in itself. Computer-aided instructional materials should be developed to provide a broad range of experiences in which problem-solving and information-processing skills can be learned. Instructors should be knowledgeable about various computer-based or computer-aided instructional materials and be able to evaluate them in terms of how well they can contribute to the learning goal.

Assessment is a critical area of expertise for literacy staff — for the adult learner, the program, and the funding agency. Literacy staff should be able to assess the skill level of the learner in the context of what is to be taught and how far the individual needs to progress. To do this effectively, staff must know the range of assessment tools available and their relationship to the content of and approach to the instruction given in the particular program. The choice of an assessment tool is dependent on a decision about what to measure. Literacy program staff members must be able to specify where an individual fits on the literacy continuum and to select an assessment tool that can measure and document progress in moving along the continuum toward the individual's goal.

3. *The goals, needs, and culture of the learner.* The third issue to be addressed in the teaching-learning process is the relationship of the first two issues — the content and methods of instruction — to the goals, needs, and culture of the learners. Teaching adults involves taking into account the particular needs, problems, and life circumstances of the learners in tailoring programs to meet individual needs. Research and practical experience have taught us that adult basic skills educators must be particularly aware of the barriers to adult learning, and that they must be trained in techniques of motivating adults to continue in what may be a long and arduous process of learning.

Cultural awareness and appreciation of the backgrounds and ethnicity of learners appear to be essential parts of good practice. According to most researchers, the ability of adult literacy instructors to relate to the culture and background of adults is very important both to communication with adult learners and to improving motivation. Respect for how learners see their world and what they can contribute as well as what they may wish to learn is an essential basis of education (Lerche, 1985). Literacy staff should be familiar with the culture and values of the learners, should tailor programs to learners' life experiences, and should appreciate and build upon the existing base of knowledge and skills adults bring to the program.

Good practice is also concerned with the relationship between the environment where learning takes place and the comfort and motivation of learners. The setting of literacy programs is important both as it relates to proximity and access and as a symbol of the relationship of the program to learners' personal goals. Literacy staff should be aware that the setting of the program can be used as a tool to support and reinforce learners.

4. *Accountability.* Setting standards for literacy providers also involves holding programs accountable for meeting minimum standards of quality based on this knowledge and the goals of the funding agency and the learners. We must help literacy staff build into their curricula the ability to judge effectiveness. Literacy staff must be able to assess routinely the progress of learners, to determine when they have acquired the needed skills, and to evaluate the effectiveness of individual program components, including their own individual and programmatic efforts.

Accountability in training must be linked directly to accountability in teaching and skill acquisition. Performance standards for teachers must be related directly to movement of learners along the literacy continuum. We must turn the entire field of basic skills instruction into a research base for effective programs. All programs should be required to build a strong capability for self-evaluation that examines all elements of program operation and learner performance, including staff performance.

Different programs have embraced selected elements of these standards. The Commonwealth Literacy Campaign in Massachusetts has adopted a complete set of standards which includes all of these elements and more. If the field of adult literacy would adopt standards like these for instruction as a starting point, a significant step could be taken toward the building of a common framework for advancement of the profession.

Creating an Institutional Infrastructure. To build an infrastructure we need to take five important steps. We need to (1) change the rhetoric of adult literacy, (2) create training and support programs for literacy staff, (3) create national organizations to support a growing profession, (4) increase compensation for literacy staff, and (5) help learners take advantage of skill improvement programs.

1. *Change the rhetoric of adult literacy.* To create the necessary infrastructure and an environment that stimulates progress, we must first exert leadership at all levels of government and in the private and voluntary sectors to change the rhetoric of adult literacy. Myths related to the ease of instruction and acquisition of skills, as well as the nature of literacy itself must be dispelled and replaced by a frank admission and discussion of the state of the field. Policymakers must avoid the trap of simplistic "solutions" that eventually waste public funds and dash the hopes of millions needing help. It is time to speak out about the complexity of the problem, the fact that literacy skill improvement takes a long time, and the fact that it will cost more to do it right.

2. *Create training and support programs for literacy staff.* To create the conditions wherein staff training becomes an essential element of any literacy program, we should work for legislative and regulatory changes that would build requirements for preservice and ongoing in-service training into federal, state, and local grant programs for all instructional, facilitative, volunteer, and administrative staff. This training should be focused, at a minimum, on the standards of practice discussed earlier in this chapter. Federal programs should further require that responsibility for providing such training and assuring competence in meeting those standards belong to the states.

These same federal programs should include in their funding allocations additional funds to enable programs to meet these training requirements, including released time for attendance at training programs and conferences, coverage of participation costs, funds for the development of good trainers, and differential pay for trained staff. State and local governments should be strongly encouraged to include such requirements in their programming as well.

Community-oriented and volunteer tutoring programs also should be encouraged to adopt up-to-date criteria for facilitator or tutor preparation, and they should be required to demonstrate the proficiency of literacy staff in order to receive federal or state funds. States should also encourage employers to adopt current criteria in preparing instructors for workforce literacy programs.

Training programs should include both paid and volunteer instructional staff and administrative staff. Programs might be modeled after principals' academies that have been created for elementary and secondary school principals. They should be designed to improve instruction in the field through a range of experiential and innovative practices.

States should either develop such training programs themselves or contract for them. If states choose not to provide these services directly, they should identify and approve those training programs that will provide the requisite training for adult literacy staff.

Training should be based on the interim standards already discussed, until basic and applied research permits the development of a better informed set of criteria. Until more is known about the prerequisites for effective staff, formal certification should not be granted. States should, however, work toward the development of standards of practice that might be an appropriate basis for certification in the future.

In the interim, the states should keep the system for advancing the state of the field as flexible and as outcome-driven as possible by linking continued designation as an approved training program to the outcome of learners in the programs for which they have provided training.

To develop the institutional capacity to foster staff development and training, federal support should be made available for the development of state staff development and training centers for adult literacy in each state. These centers would function as the primary institutional resource at the state level for technical assistance and technology transfer for purposes of staff development and training. They would serve as state clearinghouses for new approaches to staff development and training, and they would provide some of the training required by staff in existing and new programs.

Centers should be supported primarily by state funds and should focus on the development of resources for staff development and training in many different settings and based on many different goals. They should operate as a freestanding entities rather than under the auspices of existing institutional structures.

To assist states in building an infrastructure for staff development and training, grant assistance should be provided by the federal government. Incentives should be provided for states to form multistate centers so that a critical mass of resources might be amassed to serve two or more states. These centers should work closely with a national institute for basic skills (described below).

State university systems can also contribute to the advancement of the field of adult literacy. To add to the credibility of the profession, state universities should be challenged and encouraged to develop more adult education programs oriented to the literacy skills of adults. The creation of additional university centers for adult literacy could bolster development in the field and direct talent to needed research related to practice in the field. The approach taken by these centers should not be tied to that taken by the current elementary and secondary education system and should not be used as barriers to entry into the field.

3. Create national organizations to support a growing profession. National associations can play valuable roles in the development of a profession, such as networking and information sharing, advocacy for legislative and regulatory changes to strengthen the profession, and standards development.

Existing national associations for adult literacy should be strengthened and supported, and new associations should be created to meet these needs. A national association should study the issue of certification of adult literacy staff as a means to further advance the professional levels of adult basic skills education practitioners.

The function of conducting basic and applied research and development must be assumed by a national organization.

A national center for basic skills should be created and, as part of a much larger set of responsibilities, should assume a leadership role in developing models and materials for training literacy instructors, facilitators, and administrators. It should commission studies on successful methods and materials in all sectors of adult literacy instruction and should widely publish the results. It should develop training materials and make these available to states in the establishment of their training programs. It should also function as a national clearinghouse on staff development and training for adult literacy.

4. *Increase compensation for literacy staff.* To attract high-quality personnel to the field, compensation levels must be made competitive with those in other, related parts of the economy. A necessary condition to creating and advancing a profession is providing competitive pay and the potential for increased remuneration as skills are advanced.

5. *Help learners take advantage of skill improvement programs.* Advancing a profession involves reaching out to the persons it serves. An important part of building an infrastructure is helping learners take advantage of skill improvement programs. Even if all the steps outlined here were taken, we would still have no guarantee that significantly more people would take advantage of literacy programs.

Different incentives are now being tried to increase the literacy skills of those with very low levels of basic skills. Virginia has instituted a "no read, no release" program, offering differential parole opportunities for incarcerated persons who participate in literacy programs. Florida has enacted a program that requires teenage mothers who receive Aid to Families with Dependent Children (AFDC) to participate in basic skills education programs as a condition of receipt of the grant. No data are available on the effects of these programs on the level or rate of learners' skill acquisition.

Other incentive programs could be tried. Tax incentives could be provided to businesses to work with persons who need to upgrade their basic skills. Learners could receive payment while participating in literacy programs. Stipends could be provided for the literacy training of parents to work with their children. Higher unemployment compensation benefits might be provided to persons who engage in basic skills training. By envisioning a full list of reasons why people need to increase their skills and by considering incentives and obstacles to accomplishment, one could develop a wide range of incentives that would encourage and support the improvement of the literacy skills of our population.

The Task Ahead. Improving the literacy skills of our population is an important national goal. The literacy programs of today, for the reasons discussed, need a "jump start" to meet the challenge of the future. Public policy must prepare the way for major advances in literacy service so that significant gains in skills can be realized.

Part of this preparation will require that public policymakers support the creation of a literacy profession in order to attract and retain more full-time staff and to provide incentives for improving the quality of instruction. This job requires both national and state leadership. It demands a federal presence for purposes of leadership, research and development, capacity building, and funding for staff development and training. It requires state intervention to establish and maintain professional standards, create a climate of practice-based research to advance the field, encourage and support local staff development and training efforts, and drive the development of a performance-based accountability system.

But responsibilities are not limited to state and federal governments. The problem is too large and the resources too scarce. Cooperative efforts between government and the private sector must be expanded, and full use must be made of the resource of trained volunteers. All sectors and interests must contribute cooperatively toward the advancement of the adult literacy profession in order to reach the common goal of basic skills improvement.

Near-Term Recommendations

The job of helping individuals improve their literacy skills is a formidable one, which cannot be accomplished by a national cadre of untrained workers, no matter how good their intentions, or by volunteers alone. It cannot be accomplished simply by extending the responsibilities of our elementary and secondary education system, or solely by infusing the existing system of literacy providers with additional funds. But it is a task that can be accomplished.

Effective basic skills education will require a thorough understanding of the motivations for and roadblocks to adult learning. Making significant gains in the literacy skills of adults will require a critical assessment of the performance of existing programs and approaches to literacy instruction as well as a commitment to advancing the state of the field. This task will require training and institutional support for the development of a literacy profession.

The development of a profession will require time, creativity, experimentation, and determination. States, public officials, private employers, volunteers, providers, and learners will have to work together to accomplish the agenda outlined above. But the steps taken in the near term will be crucial in setting the stage for achievement of longer term goals. To start out on the road to upgrading staff proficiencies, we should take five key steps:

1. *Adopt interim standards of practice.* States should develop standards of practice to guide the development of the profession and offer assistance to providers in meeting these standards. The standards would inform providers of a research and practice base for instruction, would signal concern for performance, and would provide a basis for the development of more formal standards over the longer term.

2. *Adopt training requirements at the state level for literacy programs receiving funds through the state, and allocate funds to cover these costs.* States should require all providers to participate in preservice and in-service training programs if they are to receive funds through the state. Training should be based on the interim standards of practice. This requirement will certify the importance of training to providers and the public. States must make funds available to support costs associated with training.

3. *Create staff development and training centers for adult literacy.* To provide the technical assistance and technology transfer needed to build a profession and provide clearinghouses for infor-

mation exchange, states should begin to establish training and development centers, either individually or in concert with other states.

4. *Develop performance standards for literacy programs.* To help move the existing system of literacy programs in line with state goals and standards of practice, the states should develop performance standards for quality programs.

5. *Support the development of national literacy organizations.* In the short term, the creation of national literacy organizations can do much to urge state and federal program reforms to support literacy. They should also assume the role of developing a national literacy network to share best practices, promote research, and help states in the development of interim standards of practice. Already groups as diverse as Laubach Literacy Action, Literacy Volunteers of America, State Literacy Initiatives Network, and the Urban Literacy Network have begun to work together on literacy issues and to discuss the need for a national coalition.

References

Cranney, A. G. "Two Decades of Adult Reading Programs: Growth, Problems, and Prospects." *Journal of Reading,* 1983, *26,* 416–422.

Darkenwald, G. "Effective Approaches to Teaching Basic Skills to Adults." *Sociology of Education,* 1986, *48.*

Diekhoff, G. "An Appraisal of Adult Literacy Programs: Reading Between the Lines." *Journal of Reading,* April 1988, *13* (7), 624–630.

Fingeret, A. *Adult Literacy Education: Current and Future Directions.* Columbus, Ohio: ERIC Clearinghouse on Adult, Career and Vocational Education, 1984.

Harman, D. *Turning Literacy Around: An Agenda for National Action.* New York: Business Council for Effective Literacy, 1985.

Kirsch, I., and Jungeblut, A. *Literacy: Profiles of America's Young Adults.* Princeton, N.J.: Educational Testing Service, 1986.

Lerche, R. *Effective Adult Literacy Programs: A Practitioner's Guide.* New York: Cambridge Book Company, 1985.

Literacy Assistance Center. *New York City Adult Literacy Initiative: Final Report for Fiscal Year 1985.* New York: Literacy Assistance Center, 1986.

Venezky, R. L., and others. *The Subtle Danger: Reflections on the Literacy Abilities of America's Young Adults.* Princeton, N.J.: Educational Testing Service, 1986.

Widen, S., and Kightlinger, P. *A Report on Adult Education Certification.* Worcester, Mass.: Adult Education Center, Worcester State College, 1987.

5

⌇ Judith A. Alamprese

Strengthening the Knowledge Base in Adult Literacy: The Research Imperative

A critical step in solving the adult literacy problem is to expand our knowledge regarding the improvement of adults' skills, knowledge, and abilities. Our success in meeting adults' educational needs through a coordinated, quality system of basic skills instruction depends in part on our capacity to undertake research that can guide the design of instructional programs and professional development activities. Data also are required to assess the progress that is being made in addressing the literacy issue and to formulate more responsive educational and social policies. This chapter highlights the factors that have contributed to our limited investment in building an intellectual base in adult literacy, and it suggests key initiatives in research and program development that are essential to an improved system.

The Problem

Increasing knowledge is vital to the progress of any field. In adult literacy, systematic inquiry into the factors affecting the motivations and learning capacities of educationally disadvantaged adults has lacked direction and support. Furthermore, research efforts that have been undertaken have not been well utilized, and the results of those efforts have not been adequately disseminated.

96

Inadequate Data. The complexity of the adult literacy problem is quickly revealed when one attempts to categorize and count programs, learners, and expenditures. Adult literacy programs — broadly defined to include literacy, basic skills, English as a Second Language (ESL), and adult secondary education — are designed to achieve different learning outcomes and are targeted at different types of learners. The category of *adult learner* is not homogeneous but encompasses subpopulations of adults, who have differing levels of education and income, possess varying levels of literacy skills, and function in a variety of social and cultural environments. Funding sources and costs for adult literacy research, development, and program operations also are not uniformly reported or aggregated at the federal level, resulting in an imprecise and somewhat confusing numerical picture of adult literacy.

The variations in programs, learners, and accounting of literacy-related expenditures have posed challenges at all levels of government in the attempt to describe the magnitude of the literacy problem and the impact of literacy services. While individual federal programs may require funded agencies to submit data concerning participants and services offered, no single source exists that captures information across all programs. The data reported are often based on different program definitions and learner categorizations. At the state and local levels, data are also not always readily available. Although states may ask local programs to submit information about learner participation and outcomes, the instruments used to collect such data often are not uniform.

Equally problematic is the financial information provided about literacy services. For example, state monies that are used in conjunction with federal funds to support basic skills programs often are not accounted for in the federal reports. Also absent from any aggregate reporting procedures are local government and private funds that are used to finance literacy programs. The result is that the data compiled about literacy programmatic efforts are, for the most part, only gross estimates of the national effort.

Inadequate Financial Investment. Historically, the federal government's support of adult literacy research and development efforts has been neither substantial nor consistent. This lack of investment reflects both the perceived unimportance of the problem by policymakers and government officials, and the relatively low status of the adult basic skills program in the federal system. During the late 1960s and early 1970s, a primary source of funding for literacy research and development was federal monies authorized under the Adult Education Act, Section 309. During that period, basic skills projects were undertaken by university faculty and, to a lesser extent, by local education agency staff. A few of the projects were significant in size and impact, such as the Adult Performance Level (APL) study (Northcutt and others, 1975) and Mezirow, Darkenwald, and Knox's (1975) national study of adult basic skills education programs. By and large, however, most of the Section 309 projects were of limited scope and were not intended to serve as models for other programs. In some cases, the quality of the projects was questionable; in other instances, the results had limited potential for transferability (Radwin, 1984).

Funding under Section 309 ended in 1974, after which no targeted federal support for research and development in adult literacy existed until 1988, when monies for research were appropriated under Section 384 of the Adult Education Amendments of 1988 (P.L. 100-297). Currently under way are studies to investigate topics such as the use of technology in basic skills instruction and demonstration programs for workforce literacy partnerships. While these projects address issues critical to the improvement and expansion of adult literacy programs, they represent a minimal investment in solving a major need.

The states' research and development efforts have centered on activities supported under Section 310 (now Section 353) of the Adult Education Act. State education departments have authority to set priorities for expenditures of Section 310/353 monies, and past projects have included the development of curricula, assessment systems, and staff-training programs. In some instances, the Section 310 projects have been multiyear efforts resulting in the creation of model programs. In most cases, the funds have been expended on short-term projects intended to address a specific need within a state, such as the provision of specialized staff-training workshops or the creation of program materials (Parker, 1988). States have made little effort to coordinate the priorities for their Section 310 projects or to fund joint projects, in order to create products that transcend the needs of an individual state.

Although the primary funding for research and development in adult basic skills has come from the U.S. Department of Education's Division of Adult Education, other parts of the agency have supported limited efforts. During the late 1970s, the National Institute of Education's Teaching and Learning program sponsored the publication of several reports concerning adult development, adult literacy, and analyses of the APL study (see Lasker and Moore, 1980; Simpson, 1980; Eberle and Robinson, 1980; Fisher, 1980; and Haney and David, 1980). The early 1980s saw an increase in the Department of Education's activity in adult literacy with the publication by the Basic Skills Improvement Office of a set of papers discussing critical issues in adult literacy and community-based organizations (Mercier, 1981). The department also sponsored an assessment of the state programs funded under the Adult Education Act (Development Associates, 1980) and a study of the evaluability of the federal adult education program (Russ-Eft, Sisk, and Haberle, 1981). Those efforts illustrated the difficulties involved in describing the range of adult literacy programs and participants and in determining the effects of the programs.

The mid-1980s saw a renewed federal interest in literacy with Secretary of Education Terence Bell's Adult Literacy Initiative. Although much media attention was focused on the adult literacy problem, the funding for research and development did not increase accordingly. The major federal effort resulting from the Adult Literacy Initiative was the National Adult Literacy Project (NALP), sponsored by the Office of Educational Research and Improvement (OERI). NALP produced policy papers that discussed various aspects of the literacy issue and also identified key characteristics of effective adult literacy programs (Lerche, 1985). Although no new literacy research was undertaken as part of NALP, the project engendered discussion among researchers about the nation's adult literacy problem and helped to focus their attention on possible actions for improving practice. During the same period OERI funded an assessment of the literacy skills of young adults through the National Assessment of Educational Progress (NAEP). The NAEP study has broadened our understanding of literacy to include not only reading but a more complex array of skills, such as information processing and reasoning (Kirsch and Jungeblut, 1986) (see Chapter 1). In addition to NALP and NAEP, OERI has funded a few modest literacy studies and policy papers that have investigated such topics as the efficacy of family literacy programs (for example, see Nickse, 1989; Nickse and Paratore, 1988; Darling, 1989).

Further federal efforts have included the Office of Vocational Education's sponsorship of a series of monographs, in which workforce basic skills programs and community-oriented literacy efforts were reviewed. The production of issue papers and monographs has been helpful in stimulating thinking about the adult literacy problem, but more efforts are needed to build a strong intellectual base.

Federal agencies other than the Department of Education are funding basic skills activities in varying degrees. Most of these monies, however, have been used to support direct service rather than research and development. Some recent exceptions are the Department of Labor's funding of the American Society for Training and Development to examine workforce skills, and of the Educational Testing Service to conduct a two-stage assessment of workforce literacy. Those projects, along with the Department of Education's new adult literacy study, represent major initiatives in literacy research.

The gap in federal support for literacy has not been filled by private efforts. Although foundations' interest in the topic has increased gradually since 1970, their monies have been used primarily for community-based literacy programs to improve operations, staff training, and networking. The grants programs sponsored by the Gannett Foundation, B. Dalton Bookseller, and the John T. and Catherine D. MacArthur Foundation exemplify these efforts. Only minimal foundation funding — less than 2 percent of the total effort — has been spent on literacy research and development (The Foundation Center, 1970–1988).

The lack of a sustained and targeted federal program for research has greatly impeded our progress in addressing the adult literacy problem. Without stable support, the task of building a cumulative knowledge base that can be used to improve literacy service will remain difficult.

Inadequate Research. Literacy research has been hampered not only by the limited availability of funding, but also by the nature of the literacy problem and the methodologies used to study it. Publications in the field have tended to be program descriptions and "how to" articles, rather than reports of systematic research with empirically derived conclusions (Fingeret, 1984; Darkenwald, 1986). This lack of research is partly due to the complexity of the literacy issue, since the field is not well bounded in terms of theory or subjects. To investigate literacy issues, researchers must draw from sociology, psychology, and cognitive science. Theories in these disciplines concerning the underclass, social change, personal motivation, problem solving, and critical thinking provide frameworks for understanding the contexts in which adults learn, as well as adults' motivations and capacities for learning. Furthermore, the adult learners who are the subject of study consist of subpopulations with varying socioeconomic and cultural backgrounds, needs, and expectations. While most of the adults who are involved in literacy programs are educationally disadvantaged, they are not necessarily economically disadvantaged. As a result, designing literacy research tends to be neither simple nor straightforward.

Another impediment to literacy research has been the types of methodologies traditionally employed. Because of the nature of the questions, the structure of literacy programs, and the fluidity of the program participants, the use of experimental designs often is inappropriate or even impossible. Rather, qualitative methods — such as participant observation, case histories, and case studies — may be better suited for understanding issues like the learning contexts of undereducated adults and the long-term effect of participation in literacy programs (Fingeret, 1983; Merriam, 1989).

Inadequate Dissemination. One purpose for conducting research is to help improve the practice of a discipline. In adult literacy, two factors have deterred the improvement of classroom-based and volunteer programs: (1) a lack of data about effective practice and (2) insufficient mechanisms for disseminating the information that has been produced.

While literacy practitioners' and policymakers' interest in program accountability has grown during the recent past, the implementation of data collection systems has not kept pace with the growth in interest. Numerous factors have accounted for this delay, including (1) the difficulty of instituting statewide procedures for program evaluation, (2) the dissatisfaction among service providers with the quality of learner assessment instruments, and (3) the lack of agreement about our national goals for literacy and how they should be evaluated. Some states have initiated projects, such as the California Literacy Campaign's Adult Learner Progress Evaluation Process and Connecticut's Adult Performance Program. However, more efforts are needed to systematize the collection of data for assessing program impact and identifying effective practice.

When successful programs or practices are identified, the options for dissemination are limited. While the U.S. Department of Education's National Diffusion Network (NDN) has been a primary vehicle for disseminating information about a small number of exemplary literacy programs — including adult diploma programs, competency-based instructional and assessment systems, and volunteer programs — this system is used by only a small number of literacy service providers. Access to the NDN also has been limited because of its evaluation requirements, which few literacy programs attempt to meet.

To encourage dissemination of good practice within states, two state systems modeled on the NDN were developed during the early 1980s. Although the systems no longer exist, they did provide a forum for peer exchange among literacy practitioners. This interaction seemed to be a key factor in promoting program improvement.

Another way to improve programs is to use the information generated from research studies. The field of adult literacy is rife with unpublished research and evaluation reports, produced primarily by consulting firms and universities. The main access to this information is through the Educational Resources Information Center (ERIC) Clearinghouse on Adult, Career, and Vocational Education. In the past, ERIC has published reports, such as a review of literature on adult literacy education (Fingeret, 1984). However, although the entries in ERIC's comprehensive data base are categorized to facilitate retrieval, the reports are often of minimal utility for practitioners. The problem lies more in how research findings are presented than in the quality of the dissemination mechanism. Greater attention needs to be given to improving the presentation of research results to make them more relevant to service providers.

Research and Development in Adult Literacy Learning

In spite of the marginal financial support for adult literacy research and the impediments to undertaking systematic study of a complex issue, some advances have been made in understanding the types of adults who seek literacy services and the programs that can best meet their educational needs. Other areas of research, including the nature of the learning process and the assessment of skills and knowledge, are less developed. In all cases, additional investigation is required if we are to meet the demands for a better trained and more informed citizenry.

One of the most important areas of research in adult literacy concerns adults' capacities to learn. Four topics are of particular concern: the development of critical thinking skills, learning in context, the development of beginning reading skills, and acquisition of English by speakers of other languages.

Critical Thinking Skills. As the demands of the American workplace increase, it becomes imperative to have a qualified workforce capable of carrying out the changing requirements of jobs. A recent survey of manufacturing plants in the rural

South found that automated technology requires *more* skills on the part of production workers rather than fewer (Mendel, 1988). Other research has indicated that the workplace requires that workers have the ability not only to read, write, and compute but also to use these basic skills to communicate with other employees and to solve problems on the job (U.S. Department of Education and U.S. Department of Labor, 1988). Changing expectations about job requirements also have stimulated states to identify the categories of skills that will be demanded of workers. In Michigan, for example, a task force of business, labor, education, and community representatives was convened to specify the abilities and behaviors that are necessary across a broad range of business, service, and industrial job sectors. The task force identified academic, personal management, and teamwork skills — including computation, reasoning, and information processing — as those workers will need to be considered "employable" (Employability Skills Task Force, 1988).

An important part of addressing our need for an increasingly skilled population of workers is investigating the processes that adults with skill deficiencies use to acquire reasoning and other higher order thinking skills. For example, new research in the area of cognitive science, particularly concerning the transfer of cognitive ability from parents to children (often called *family literacy*), suggests that previous studies did not take into account the role of different types of knowledge in intellectual development (Sticht, 1989). Further inquiries about the nature of intelligence and the factors that influence individuals' cognitive development are essential to broaden our knowledge base in adult learning theory. Issues that particularly warrant further study and development are:

- processes used by adults with low levels of basic skills to acquire reasoning and other thinking skills in the context of specific domains of knowledge (such as verbal and mathematical)
- strategies for helping adults develop content knowledge and problem-solving skills
- types of information and processes used in the transfer of cognitive ability in families

Learning in Context. The question of whether adults learn more effectively when material is taught in a "real world" context is one that is discussed frequently by both practitioners and researchers. Since the early 1970s, basic skills programs across the country have adopted a competency-based, *life skills approach* for delivering services. For many programs, such as those funded under the Adult Education Act and the Comprehensive Employment and Training Act (followed by the Job Training Partnership Act), implementing this approach has meant identifying a list of life skill competencies that serve as program outcomes, and using instructional materials that emphasize the applications of basic skills in "real life."

The life skills approach also has been effective in ESL programs, where participants' goals often involve learning to accomplish a "real world" task. The success of these programs is shown in increased learner retention and learners' progress in mastering life skills (Alamprese and others, 1987). The life skills approach has influenced the development of adult student assessment systems and external high school diploma programs, as well as the organization of adult basic skills materials.

One important issue in the implementation of competency-based, life skills programs is the extent to which the basic skills learned in these programs are transferable across life skill areas. Often, instruction focuses on applying a specific life skill, rather than on integrating life skills and basic skills. For example, an instructor may teach learners how to read a bus schedule without giving them multiple life skill applications to ensure that they understand the underlying basic skill (reading a matrix). In such a case, it is not clear whether a learner has grasped the basic skill and can apply it across different areas of "real world" applications. The teaching of basic skills in the context of life tasks may be an effective method for relating instruction to learners' needs, thereby motivating their participation in programs and enabling them to acquire critical life skills. Further investigation is needed, however, to determine the utility of this approach for increasing learners' abilities to apply a core set of skills across various domains of knowledge.

Studies of functional education programs have focused

on the development of literacy skills in different contexts, such as the workplace. Analyses, such as those conducted by Sticht (1975), Mikulecky and Diehl (1980), and Guthrie and others (1984), have shown that higher levels of general reading ability are associated with higher levels of job-related literacy. Some research has indicated that learners in programs that integrate literacy with development of job knowledge are likely to show gains in job-related reading that are two to three times greater than the gains they make in general literacy skills. In addition, learners in these programs improve their general literacy as much as or more than learners in general programs. However, learners in general literacy programs make almost no progress in job-related literacy (Sticht, 1988). These findings provide initial evidence about the "generalizability" of skills from one specific domain to another, more broadly defined domain. Further information is required to assess the utility of the functional approach for developing both specific and general literacy skills and the content knowledge that adults need to function successfully in society.

A related topic of study concerns the contexts in which adults can develop literacy skills. Recent research by Fingeret (1983) and Reder and Green (1985) has identified the importance of the community context and the roles of social networks in facilitating adults' acquisition of reasoning and problem-solving abilities. Further inquiry is needed to understand how "literacy helpers" can serve as mediators for adults who have low literacy skills.

The development of a systematic knowledge base about the contexts in which adults can improve their literacy and basic skills is critical to the overall improvement of our basic skills education system. Issues that should be considered for research and development include:

- effects of the use of a functional competency approach for developing adults' literacy and basic skills across different content domains
- identification of generic skills that are transferable across different contexts, and of processes for teaching these skills

- the role of social networks in the development of adults' literacy skills

Beginning Reading Skills. Many of the adult learners enrolled in classroom-based and volunteer literacy classes are at the initial stages of developing their reading skills. Literacy instructors take various approaches to teach reading, which reflects gaps in our understanding about how beginning readers become literate and acquire greater proficiency.

Studies by researchers such as Sticht (1982) have found differences in information processing between child and adult literacy learners. For example, Park's (1983) work on semantic structures and Boraks and Schumaker's (1981) examination of reading strategies indicate that adult literacy students process written information differently from children — suggesting that the same instructional strategies may not be appropriate for adults and children. Other differences have been found in the speed with which adults and children learn to read. The work of Chall (1987) and Bowren and Zintz (1977) suggests that adults in the early stages of acquiring reading skills may learn more rapidly than do children in the same stage, because adults have higher levels of oral language and knowledge. Another difference concerns adults' and children's *reading potential,* which is defined as the difference between their oral and written vocabulary recognition and comprehension ability. Our knowledge about adults' reading potential is still in the formative stage and requires more in-depth study.

To improve the quality of efforts to develop adults' reading skills, existing theories about adults' acquisition and expansion of reading skills need to be validated and new hypotheses tested. Topics for study include:

- differences in processes used by adults and children to acquire reading skills, such as vocabulary recognition, comprehension, and information processing
- the reading potential that adult new readers can be expected to have, and the conditions under which this potential can be developed

Acquisition of English as a Second Language. The population of adults who desire to learn English as their second language continues to increase at a significant rate. While many of the adults enrolled in ESL classes are literate in their native language, others lack literacy skills in any language. As with the research on adults' beginning reading, ESL instructional theories are a focus of debate among professionals engaged in practice and research. Increasingly, ESL programs are using a competency-based, life skills approach to deliver instruction (Rickard and others, 1984). Some teacher training programs have combined a competency-based approach with the use of specific ESL instructional techniques, such as dialogues, language experience, and drills (Savage, 1987).

Only limited systematic research has been undertaken to determine the efficacy of these instructional approaches. Further study is needed to understand the influence that adults' motivation, circumstances of immigration, and type of occupation can have on their learning processes. Topics for further research and development include:

- the integration of ESL and literacy instruction for adults with low levels of literacy in both English and their native language
- the effectiveness of different instructional approaches in adults' development of language skills

Research and Development in
Adult Literacy Programming

Related to our need for a better understanding of the processes involved in adults' acquisition of literacy skills is the need to improve our knowledge about the delivery of instruction in literacy programs. Several aspects of this research topic warrant immediate attention: staff development, instructional strategies, performance standards, learner assessment procedures, program evaluation, and program models.

Professional Development for Literacy Staff. Our ability to improve our literacy education system depends on the quality of the professional staff who support the system and on the utility of the system's structure. Currently, the majority of the instructors who teach basic skills work either part-time or as volunteers. Furthermore, most instructors have had only minimal formal training in teaching methods for literacy and basic skills. While a few states, such as California, Maryland, and Connecticut, have initiated statewide training efforts to improve the proficiencies of their basic skills instructors, most provide staff development on a less systematic basis. Thus, the present system neither prepares instructors to perform at maximum levels of productivity nor provides ongoing support to sustain their performance.

Several steps must be taken to create a structure for the professional development and ongoing support of staff in adult basic skills education. The following research and development activities exemplify how to improve the present state of practice:

- identification of the academic knowledge and methodological proficiencies that should be required of instructors in literacy programs
- development of teacher training programs for preparing and upgrading literacy instructors
- examination of the differential effects of voluntary and mandated certification programs on the creation of an adequate pool of literacy professionals
- development of a mechanism for the ongoing support of literacy professionals

Instructional Strategies. The strategies used to deliver instruction in adult basic skills programs have evolved over the past two decades. They have included the traditional group lecture, individualized instruction, and cooperative learning. In many instances, ESL programs have maintained the group format but have used an interactive instructor-learner process to develop language skills. In basic skills classes, the shift from group to individualized instruction has been an attempt to meet the specific needs of learners and, in many cases, has assumed that the adult is an independent learner. The more recent use of cooperative learning methods has combined an individualized format with team-building processes. Although these approaches appear to be effective in developing adults' skills, little systematic research has been conducted to identify the conditions under which these methods can be used with different types of learners to teach different skills.

In addition to the methods just described, the use of computers has been introduced slowly to literacy programs. Computer-based learning systems hold promise for literacy instruction, since computers provide economies of scale and permit self-paced instruction. Still, few adults are taught through computer-assisted methods. Some of the factors that account for the limited use of computers are the lack of access to hardware, the quality of the available software, and basic skills instructors' reluctance to learn the technology.

Several topics should be considered for further study and development in the area of instruction. They include:

- examination of the conditions under which a variety of instructional techniques can be used effectively with different learners
- development of classroom management strategies that can be used successfully in various learning environments
- evaluation of the potential of all forms of computer-assisted instruction, especially interactive systems, for basic skills education

Performance Standards. The efforts to evaluate our progress in addressing the adult literacy problem have been greatly hampered by a lack of data at all levels — federal, state, and local. Restrictions at the federal and state levels regarding information collection account for part of the situation. Other factors include local programs' difficulties with assessing learner outcomes and program impact because of limited resources or lack of expertise in evaluation. The development and implementation of improved assessment and evaluation procedures will allow us to be both more accountable and more knowledgeable about our efforts.

A critical step in the design of any service delivery system is the creation of standards against which the performance of participants can be judged. Historically, no single set of standards has existed for the adult literacy education system. Rather, individual states and local programs have specified the desired outcomes for participants in adult literacy programs — such as the life skills identified in the APL and subsequent studies undertaken in the 1970s, or grade-level gains traditionally associated with elementary education. In other instances, programs have allowed learners to set their own goals and have used the reported accomplishment of those goals as evidence of program success.

Some standards have been specified for programs, such as those funded under the Job Training Partnership Act, which considers a program's success in placing participants in jobs. The work undertaken by Michigan's Employability Skills Task Force exemplifies new state efforts to specify skill requirements. The overall result of these efforts is that where standards exist, different sets of criteria are being used to assess learner performance. The difference in standards can be counterproductive for learners who wish to move from one program to another, and it makes the collection of national data on program effectiveness nearly impossible.

With the press for program accountability and the need to provide a basic skills system that can better upgrade and "retool" the American workforce, the creation of performance standards for the system becomes imperative. Thus, steps should be taken to:

- create performance standards for basic skills programs that are relevant to the goals of the program, are measurable, and are interpretable
- ensure that standards cover the basic skills that are required across different occupational categories

Learner Assessment Procedures. An essential component of program standards is the measurement of learner performance. In many literacy programs across the country, no formal instruments are used to measure learners' acquisition of skills. Programs that do undertake some form of assessment usually rely on instruments such as the Tests of Adult Basic Education (TABE) or Adult Basic Learning Examination (ABLE), which many program instructors believe do not adequately measure participants' learning. Even when instruments are used, problems occur with their administration and interpretation. For example, program instructors sometimes do not follow the time requirements of tests, or they make no attempt to control for or adjust gain scores for regression and warm-up.

The usefulness of the outcomes specified by these instruments has been called into question. Sticht's review of thirty-two different studies involving the U.S. Army, Navy, and Air Force programs, the national reading academies, the Job Corps literacy programs, and computer-assisted or computer-managed literacy programs shows grade-level gains of from 6 months to 3 years, with hours of instruction ranging from 2 to 141. The average gain was 1.5 years in 48 hours of instruction (Sticht, 1987). It is not clear what these gains represent in terms of learners' skills or overall effects of programs.

The implementation of competency-based assessment systems, in which the attainment of specific life skills is measured, represents an alternative to traditional grade-level tests. Another promising alternative is the use of applied performance measures in competency-based high school diploma programs, where a spectrum of adults' skills is assessed by multiple measures (Alamprese, 1979; Shelton, 1979). The General Educational Development (GED) program's incorporation of a writing assessment component into its testing program represents an attempt to examine a broader range of adults' skills. Finally, the Educational Testing Service's project to identify and measure the core basic and higher order thinking skills needed by adults should provide new directions for basic skills assessment.

The efforts under way to provide alternative forms of assessment for basic skills programs appear promising. Nonetheless, more work is needed if we are to have a system in which the majority of programs assess learners' gains routinely. Activities that should be taken to meet this goal include:

- design of reliable and valid measures for assessing learners' acquisition of basic and higher order thinking skills

- development of model projects that demonstrate the use of new technologies for assessment
- creation of mechanisms for training instructors and tutors in the proper administration and interpretation of assessment instruments

Program Evaluation. Literacy program staff rarely evaluate the impact of their services. Several factors account for this, including the lack of staff who are trained in evaluation methodology and the unavailability of monies for third-party evaluations.

With the increased emphasis on accountability from the federal level in the Adult Education Amendments of 1988, as well as with the requirements in the welfare reform and job training legislation, more systematic efforts are needed in program evaluation. The conduct of formative as well as summative evaluations can provide valuable information to improve programs and also can provide data about the transferability of these programs.

Activities that could enhance program evaluation and encourage the conduct of evaluations include:

- development of evaluation models that can be used by classroom-based and volunteer literacy programs — especially those that utilize technology
- creation of mechanisms for training staff to implement data collection procedures that can be used in formative evaluations

Development of Program Models. Our pluralistic system for delivering adult literacy service involves a variety of organizations attempting to meet the needs of a diverse group of adult learners. As the population of adults who could benefit from this service expands, new efforts are required to attract adults to enroll in programs, and to encourage their participation. The research on barriers to participation in literacy programs is extensive and has contributed to our understanding of the subpopulations of adults who seek literacy programs.

Research results indicate that an undifferentiated approach to program recruitment and planning is not appropriate for attracting the heterogeneous population of literacy students who range in economic success and educational level (Hayes and Darkenwald, 1988).

Developing typologies of adult literacy students also has improved our understanding of the differences in students' motivation and the importance of building students' self-esteem (Darkenwald and Valentine, 1985; Hayes, 1988). Further research is needed to identify the unique combination of factors that inhibits and facilitates learning among the various subpopulations of adult learners.

Because of the diversity of adult learners and organizations involved in literacy, no one program model can meet all needs. Rather, it is critical to document a variety of organizational structures and instructional approaches that can help guide literacy practice. The initiatives undertaken by the U.S. Departments of Education and Labor to disseminate information about basic skills and workforce literacy programs represent useful first steps in creating an improved system.

Any process for identifying effective program models also should include the various emerging types of public and private partnerships in basic skills education. In an effort to upgrade the workforce, private industry is forming collaborative partnerships with educational agencies to facilitate the delivery of basic skills programs. These efforts, which are being encouraged by the U.S. Departments of Education and Labor as well as by business and labor organizations, appear to have great potential for success. The transfer and use of partnership models will depend in part on the steps that are taken to identify and document the critical processes involved in their implementation.

Further developmental efforts are needed to encourage the adoption of proven practices and to improve the overall functioning of literacy service providers. These should include:

- identifying key factors associated with learner gains and positive program outcomes
- creating an interactive system for facilitating exchange of program information

Strategies for Change

The success of our efforts to develop a system that meets the pluralistic literacy needs of our society will require the commitment and involvement of individuals from all sectors and institutions. While the conduct of research may be a priority for universities and consulting firms, literacy practitioners and adult learners are also key players. The true value of research is not just the production of knowledge for its own sake, but the creation of knowledge that can be used to solve real problems.

Researchers, practitioners, and learners must form new alliances, and new roles must be created for institutions. Federal and state governments as well as foundations must step forward to support studies in critical literacy issues and to disseminate the results from research and development. While the funding of initiatives is important, funding agencies also have a responsibility to distribute the information that is collected.

Finally, business and labor must broaden their involvement in solving the literacy problem both by continuing to support literacy programs with financial and in-kind services and by taking on new roles in development and evaluation. The increasing importance of workforce literacy requires higher levels of participation across all sectors.

Near-Term Recommendations

The goal of establishing a coordinated network of federal, state, and local entities engaged in the production and distribution of knowledge about adult literacy will require the development of new structures and a greater investment by both the public and private sectors. The minimal literacy research efforts in progress today are splintered across a few federal agencies. No centralized planning exists at the federal level, and there is no mechanism for aggregating the results of the research. State efforts remain uncoordinated, and the potential for duplication of effort is great. Furthermore, the research that is conducted is not being used to our best advantage. An integrated system of research, development, and technical assistance is critical if we are to improve the quality of literacy service offered to adults.

To achieve this goal, action must be taken by all levels of government, foundations, the private sector, and professional associations.

Creation of a National Center for Adult Literacy. Current efforts to secure funding for a national center for adult literacy represent a major step to create an infrastructure for research and development. Such a center would be a not-for-profit, quasi-governmental corporation with a mission to carry out three main functions: research, policy analysis, and technical assistance and training. The integration of research and technical assistance is particularly important, since one of the greatest barriers to the improvement of literacy programs has been limited use of the knowledge we have acquired about adult learners. Furthermore, the connections among research, practice, and policy are vital, so that the guidelines that are created will reflect the best of what we know both from empirical investigation and from implementation in local programs. Without a central organization that both sponsors and conducts work, our ability to make substantial progress in adult literacy will be significantly hampered.

Federal Funding of Research and Development Activities. To encourage the support of literacy research and development by federal agencies, the Departments of Education, Labor, and Health and Human Services should be authorized to spend up to $7 million from their existing research budgets for research and policy analysis. The departments could use these funds to contract with the national center or to support appropriate activities.

Expansion of State Efforts. State agencies involved in the support and delivery of literacy services should establish interstate consortia to address common literacy issues, using either existing or new sources of funding. The U.S. Department of Education should provide incentives to states to work together in supporting cross-state developmental and research activities, using funds such as those provided under Section 353 of the Adult Education Amendments of 1988. A series of coordinated state efforts that address national priorities in literacy research and development could result in an enriched knowledge base.

States should broaden their efforts in strategic planning to address long-term as well as near-term adult literacy needs. California's Adult Education 2000 Project exemplifies the action states can take to plan for systematic research, development, and technical assistance.

Foundation Support. As catalysts for change, foundations should establish literacy research and development activities as a top priority for funding. Projects could include the support of university research centers to undertake basic research in adult literacy, as well as program development activities. Foundations also should continue their support of community-oriented literacy programs to expand our knowledge concerning literacy practice.

Private Sector Support. Business and labor should encourage and support the development of private-public partnerships for basic skills programs, particularly in the context of the workplace. Such partnerships could include the funding of a literacy provider to develop a model program that could be disseminated within a corporate sector. Business, labor, and the research community could collaborate to assess the utility of workforce literacy approaches and to develop new strategies based on the evaluation results. The active involvement of the private sector in the development of literacy programs, evaluation, and dissemination is essential if we are to create a system that can address our needs in the next decade.

Association Activities. The professional associations concerned with literacy education should expand their activities in professional development. They should conduct regional workshops in teaching methodologies and substantive topics for literacy practitioners. These workshops, along with specialized sessions at national conferences, could help meet the training needs of literacy service providers. Professional associations also should investigate the roles they might play in setting standards for literacy professionals. The associations' work can be a vital support to the literacy initiatives undertaken by other organizations.

References

Alamprese, J. *The New York State External High School Diploma Program: Submission Prepared for the Joint Dissemination Review Panel.* Syracuse, N.Y.: Syracuse Research Corporation, 1979.

Alamprese, J., and others. *Investing in Change: Competency-Based Adult Education in California.* San Francisco: CBAE Staff Development Project, San Francisco State University, 1987.

Boraks, N., and Schumaker, S. *Ethnographic Research on Word Recognition Strategies of Adult Beginning Readers.* Richmond: School of Education, Virginia Commonwealth University, 1981.

Bowren, F., and Zintz, M. *Teaching Reading in Adult Basic Education.* Dubuque, Iowa: Brown, 1977.

Chall, J. "Developing Literacy in Children and Adults." In D. Wagner (Ed.), *The Future of Literacy in a Changing World, Volume I.* London: Pergamon, 1987.

Darkenwald, G. *Adult Literacy Education: A Review of the Research and Priorities for Future Inquiry.* New York: Literacy Assistance Center, 1986.

Darkenwald, G., and Valentine, T. "Factor Structure of Deterrents to Participation in Adult Basic Education." *Adult Education Quarterly,* 1985, *35,* 177–193.

Darling, S. *Family Literacy Education: Replacing the Cycle of Failure with the Legacy of Success.* Washington, D.C.: U.S. Department of Education, 1989.

Development Associates. *An Assessment of the State-Administered Programs of the Adult Education Act.* Arlington, Va.: Development Associates, 1980.

Eberle, A., and Robinson, S. *The Adult Illiterate Speaks Out: Personal Perspectives on Learning to Read and Write.* Washington, D.C.: U.S. Department of Education, 1980.

Employability Skills Task Force. *Jobs: A Michigan Employability Profile.* Lansing, Mich.: Employability Skills Task Force, 1988.

Fingeret, A. "Social Networks: A New Perspective on Independence and Illiterate Adults." *Adult Education Quarterly,* 1983, *33,* 133–146.

Fingeret, A. *Adult Literacy Education: Current and Future Directions.* Columbus, Ohio: ERIC Clearinghouse on Adult, Career, and Vocational Education, 1984.

Fisher, J. "Competencies for Adult Basic Education and Diploma Programs: A Summary of Studies and Cross-Reference of Results." In *APL Revisited: Its Uses and Adaptations in States.* Washington, D.C.: U.S. Department of Education, 1980.

The Foundation Center. *The Foundation Grants Index.* New York: The Foundation Center, 1970–1988.

Guthrie, J., and others. *Reading Competencies and Practices.* Newark, Del.: International Reading Association, 1984.

Haney, W., and David, L. "The APL Study: Science, Dissemination, and the Nature of Adult Education." In *APL Revisited: Its Uses and Adaptations in States.* Washington, D.C.: U.S. Department of Education, 1980.

Hayes, E. "A Typology of Low-Literate Adults Based on Perceptions of Deterrents to Participation in Adult Basic Education." *Adult Education Quarterly,* 1988, *39,* 1–10.

Hayes, E., and Darkenwald, G. "Participation in Basic Education: Deterrents for Low-Literate Adults." *Studies in the Education of Adults* (U.K.), 1988, *20* (1), 16–28.

Kirsch, I., and Jungeblut, A. *Literacy: Profiles of America's Young Adults.* Princeton, N.J.: Educational Testing Service, 1986.

Lasker, H., and Moore, J. "Current Studies of Adult Development: Implications for Education." In *Adult Development and Approaches to Learning.* Washington, D.C.: U.S. Department of Education, 1980.

Lerche, R. (Ed.). *Effective Adult Literacy Programs: A Practitioner's Guide.* New York: Cambridge Books, 1985.

Mendel, R. *Meeting the Economic Challenge of the 1990s: Workforce Literacy in the South.* Chapel Hill, N.C.: MDC, Inc., 1988.

Mercier, L. (Ed.). *Outlook for the 80's: Adult Literacy.* Washington, D.C.: U.S. Department of Education, 1981.

Merriam, S. "Contributions of Qualitative Research to Adult Education." *Adult Education Quarterly,* 1989, *39,* 161–168.

Mezirow, J., Darkenwald, G., and Knox, A. *Last Gamble on Education.* Washington, D.C.: Adult Education Association of the U.S.A., 1975.

Mikulecky, L., and Diehl, W. *Job Literacy.* Bloomington: Reading Research Center, Indiana University, 1980.

Nickse, R. *The Noises of Literacy: An Overview of Intergenerational and Family Literacy Programs.* Washington, D.C.: U.S. Department of Education, 1989.

Nickse, R., and Paratore, J. *An Exploratory Study into the Effects of An Intergenerational Approach to Literacy.* Washington, D.C.: U.S. Department of Education, 1988.

Northcutt, N., and others. *Adult Functional Competency: A Summary.* Austin: University of Texas, 1975.

Park, R. "Language and Reading Comprehension: A Case Study of Low Reading Adults." *Adult Literacy and Basic Education,* 1983, *7,* 153–163.

Parker, J. *Analysis of FY-1988 310 Projects.* Washington, D.C.: U.S. Department of Education, 1988.

Radwin, E. *Promoting Innovation and Controversy in Adult Basic Education.* San Francisco: National Adult Literacy Project, Far West Laboratory for Educational Research and Development, 1984.

Reder, S., and Green, K. *Giving Literacy Away: An Alternative Strategy for Increasing Adult Literacy Development.* Portland, Ore.: Northwest Regional Educational Laboratory, 1985.

Rickard, P., and others. *CASAS Project: Submission Prepared for the Joint Dissemination Review Panel.* San Diego, Calif.: San Diego Community College, 1984.

Russ-Eft, D., Sisk, C., and Haberle, J. *Evaluability Assessment of the Adult Education Program.* Palo Alto, Calif.: American Institutes for Research, 1981.

Savage, J. L. *The ESL Teacher Institute.* Burlingame, Calif.: ACSA Foundation for Educational Development, 1987.

Shelton, E. *Adult Performance Level Project: Submission Prepared for the Joint Dissemination Review Panel.* Austin: University of Texas, 1979.

Simpson, E. "Adult Learning Theory: A State of the Art." In *Adult Development and Approaches to Learning.* Washington, D.C.: U.S. Department of Education, 1980.

Sticht, T. *Reading for Working: A Functional Anthology.* Alexandria, Va.: Human Resources Research Organization, 1975.

Sticht, T. *Evaluation of the Reading Potential Concept for Marginally Literate Adults.* Washington, D.C.: Office of the Assistant Secretary of Defense, Manpower, Reserve Affairs, and Logistics, 1982.

Sticht, T. *Functional Context Education: Workshop Resource Notebook.* San Diego, Calif.: Applied Behavioral & Cognitive Sciences, Inc., 1987.

Sticht, T. "Adult Literacy Education." In E. Rothkpf (Ed.), *Review of Research in Education.* Washington, D.C.: American Educational Research Association, 1988.

Sticht, T., and McDonald, B. *Making the Nation Smarter: The Intergenerational Transfer of Cognitive Ability.* San Diego, Calif.: Applied Behavioral & Cognitive Sciences, Inc., 1989.

U.S. Department of Education and U.S. Department of Labor. *The Bottom Line: Basic Skills in the Workplace.* Washington, D.C.: U.S. Department of Labor and U.S. Department of Education, 1988.

6

📖 Arnold H. Packer
Wendy L. Campbell

Using Computer Technology for Adult Literacy Instruction: Realizing the Potential

Today's computer technology holds great potential for the adult literacy field. In fact, it is as if the capabilities of computer hardware and software in general had been designed with the special needs of adult literacy learners, providers, and funders in mind.

Computers promise adult literacy learners several distinct advantages over paper, pencil, and blackboard. The technology makes it easier to schedule courses on an open-entry, self-paced, open-exit basis — a boon to adults with work, child care, or elder care responsibilities. In addition, some evidence suggests that the content of a curriculum can be taught more quickly with computers than with the traditional tools of the field. But most important, at a computer workstation learners can receive much of their instruction on a private, individualized basis, with immediate feedback on their performance at each step of the way. Literacy learners are reluctant to reenter the traditional setting of a teacher-led classroom or tutorial, and once there they often fear the embarrassment of slowing the pace or, worse, continually making mistakes. Computers put the adult learner in control; they reduce the fear and stigma adult learners associate with literacy instruction (Turner, 1988, pp. 643–646).

An important benefit, from the providers' standpoint, is that through a single software package, the best teaching of superior instructors can be multiplied over a virtually unlimited number of learners. At the same time, the teachers on site have more time to serve in the many other, often more demanding roles required of them in their work with educationally and economically disadvantaged adults: assessing learners' skills at the start, assigning them to an appropriate educational plan, counseling and encouraging them, monitoring their progress and adapting the curriculum accordingly, and referring them to other service providers for such needs as child care and transportation.

Together these potential benefits of the technology promise *lower unit costs,* or a reduction in the costs of providing instruction *per learner* who successfully completes the course of study. In other words, the provider can effectively serve more learners within a given budget.

Beyond these potential benefits to learners and providers, the technology could provide funding agencies and policymakers with a level of accountability not possible using traditional instructional and evaluation methods. The record-keeping capacity of computers makes it possible to design courseware (educational software) that can track learners' performance automatically at each step in their progress through a curriculum. The tracking mechanisms can also record data relevant to an agency's standards for program performance.

Thus, the promise of computer technology is not only as an instructional tool but also as a means to help address many of the serious problems identified in other chapters of this book: too many adults in need of basic skills; too few trained teachers; inadequate funding to meet the demand; a lack of systematic data on learner, program, and system performance; and the resulting dearth of accountability and rigorous research to improve literacy instruction in the field. The most compelling promise lies in the ability of the technology to help serve the sheer number of adults in need — some 25 million now and tens of millions more over the next two decades — with greater economies of scale, that is, again, with lower unit costs. Indeed, it is inconceivable that we will be able to serve this number *without* the technology; we simply do not have the wherewithal to recreate the K–12 educational system on the scale necessary to serve the adult population.

Yet at a time when so much is at stake for the nation, the promise of the technology remains but a promise. For one thing, the literacy courseware developed to date does not yet fulfill the potential of today's hardware and software. And while the 25 million wait, the three parties that could be investing in, developing, and disseminating better technology — the funding agencies, courseware vendors, and service providers — are stymied by a variant on the chicken-and-egg riddle, each waiting for the other to take the first step toward progress.

The first purpose of this chapter, then, is to resolve the riddle. The second is to take an honest look at the question whether we should invest in a new technology that we are reasonably sure does work, even though we are not precisely sure how it works or how well it works. The chapter will make the case that, if we *can* set aside artificial barriers to investment, a rational economic argument in fact demands a stronger commitment to the technology. Finally, the chapter also identifies several steps that, if undertaken simultaneously, should allow the field to begin realizing the potential of the technology for better basic skills instruction.

Resolving the Chicken-and-Egg Debate

Three unresolved arguments form the chicken-and-egg debate. From one corner, literacy providers and funders argue that the literacy courseware available is not in widespread use and remains unvalidated. "How can we justify its adoption?" they ask. The vendors, on the other hand, argue that institutional barriers to long-term investment are preventing providers from even considering purchasing the technology, while the lack of consensus on yardsticks for measuring learner performance has prohibited meaningful evaluation of this, or any other, instructional tool in the field. "How can we test and improve the courseware if we have neither a market nor performance standards?" they ask. At the same time, both literacy leaders and vendors would agree that the courseware has not kept pace with the capabilities the hardware promises.

A decade ago personal computers could display only white letters and simple graphics on a green screen, and they made no sound but beeps of varying tones. Most of the courseware available for adult literacy instruction still suffers from these limitations. This computer-assisted instruction (CAI) software is interactive, has record-keeping capacities, and can be flexibly scheduled. But it is usually deadly dull (referred to in the trade as "drill and kill"), especially for those with limited literacy.

During the 1980s interactive videodisc technology (IVD) made multimedia presentations — on the new color and touch-sensitive screens — possible. Added to the advantages of CAI was the drama of realistic simulations of workplace and life experiences. More specifically, IVDs offer moving video, the human voice, and sophisticated graphics superimposed on high-quality slides. The IVD hardware now available allows access to videodiscs that can hold 54,000 still frames or a half-hour of moving video. (IBM's InfoWindow is the most prevalent example.) IVD and other forms of multimedia hardware are expected to become commonplace in businesses in the 1990s. Compact disks are already available with digital sound and extensive graphics.

As yet, very few IVD software packages have been designed for the adult literacy market, and all of them suffer from one drawback or another: little or no record-keeping capacity, the teaching of only the most basic of basic skills, or a context that definitely could be improved upon. In short, the courseware itself does not yet deliver the full potential of the hardware.

The riddle, therefore, is which *should* come first: a longer, broader based track record for the technology; removal of the institutional barriers to investment by providers; or better courseware. If we look at each of these options in turn, it should become clear that all three options must be tackled simultaneously, and soon.

Lags in Evaluation. Ideally, performance standards should guide the development and testing of all forms of teaching materials. But as several of the previous chapters have shown, the adult literacy field has reached no consensus on yardsticks to define whether an adult has achieved *functional* competency in the five aspects of literacy on which there is agreement: reading, writing, and communicating in English, and math and problem-solving skills.

As a result, it is no wonder there have been so few evaluations of literacy courseware; and those few conducted to date generally conclude with the caveat that no evaluation will be adequate until the field does create performance standards. Moreover, with few exceptions, those studies were themselves poorly funded, yielding inadequate sample sizes and no strictly assigned control group.

One exception was conducted at Fort Benning, Georgia, where 100 soldiers of the U.S. Army were randomly assigned to IVD instruction with Applied Learning's Fundamental Reading for Electronics, while 100 control group members were assigned, also randomly, to the Army's more traditional basic skills program, receiving both classroom and computer-assisted (but not IVD) instruction with PLATO. By three measures — a standardized grade-level reading test, a test referenced to performance criteria developed on an ad hoc basis, and an Armed Forces entrance exam — the group of IVD users scored gains equal to the control group's *in 60 percent less time* (Raaen, 1988).

Several studies of two other literacy courseware packages — IBM's PALS and Interactive Training's Skillpac (the latter developed by author Arnold Packer) — have been conducted. Taken together, these studies suggest that adults using IVD courseware post higher learning gains than the average under traditional instruction and have better attendance and improved attitudes such as motivation and self-esteem (see, for example, Reissman and Jean, 1988; Arterburn, 1989). The researchers in one external evaluation of PALS and Skillpac concluded, "The best evaluative measure . . . must come in follow-up studies in the workplace" — in a life situation that tests learners' *use* of the skills they have acquired (Lutz, Di Vito, and Staczek, 1989, p. 13). One preliminary study did look at workplace performance, albeit with a very small sample; there Skillpac users obtained, on the average, better-paying jobs with more benefits than did the comparison group (Packer and Grognet, 1988). But all of these studies were only suggestive, because they had either very small samples of users or no control group.

The anecdotal and survey evidence from these studies has indicated, however, that both learners and teachers had a very favorable opinion of the IVD courseware. Commonly mentioned were the learner's control over the pace of the instruction; the self-esteem derived from this control, from the instant, nonjudgmental feedback, and from the ability to use a computer per se; and the peace of mind stemming from being able to drop in for time at the computer whenever it was convenient. It is also important to note that both PALS and Skillpac continue to be in use with adults some observers might assume would be intimidated by a computer: those at the lower end of the literacy continuum (reading at or below the fourth-grade equivalent), immigrants from less-developed countries, residents of urban ghettos, and low-income adults.

More extensive, and more reliable, evidence can be found in evaluations of IVD instruction in other fields. In a review of thirty such studies conducted between 1980 and 1987 of courses ranging from anatomy to building maintenance, DeBloois (1988) reported that most found significantly higher postinstruction test scores among IVD users than among learners receiving lectures or videotaped instruction; a persistence of the differences in achievement between IVD users and nonusers over time; time savings for IVD users ranging from 25 percent to 50 percent; transference of the learning from the classroom to the job; and learner preference for IVDs over other instructional methods.

The examples of IVD evaluations in the literacy field demonstrate that the evidence is indeed sketchy. Nonetheless, the Fort Benning study, the best of the lot, together with the literature on IVD usage outside the literacy field do suggest that instructional time savings by learners (and concomitant unit cost savings by providers) are as likely as we might assume. Unfortunately, we simply will not know with certainty until *both* IVD and traditional forms of adult literacy instruction can be evaluated using well-established performance criteria, with large numbers of learners, in much more rigorous evaluation designs. But in the meantime — and this task could take several years — literacy providers are forgoing these potential time and cost savings while they wait.

Institutional Barriers to Investment. The decision to encourage the development and testing of better courseware rests in the hands of the federal, state, and local government agencies, employers, and large volunteer organizations now taking responsibility for funding the nation's adult literacy efforts. At the same time, the decision to purchase courseware (and hardware) rests with the local providers, which receive all or part of their budgets from one or more of those funders. Pluralistic in the extreme, this patchwork of funders and providers underlies our meager investments in realizing the potential of the technology. Two examples from the local level will illustrate.

James Figueroa, assistant superintendent of the Division of Adult and Occupational Education for the Los Angeles Unified School District (LAUD), directs a very large provider organization. Figueroa is responsible for over 400,000 adult learners each year and expects that LAUD will still be serving adults well into the next century. LAUD receives Adult Education Act (AEA) and GAIN (Greater Avenues for Independence, California's welfare reform program) funds from the state departments of education and social services, and immigration reform and Job Training Partnership Act (JTPA) funds directly from the federal government. Corporations requesting custom-designed, on-site programs are also LAUD clients.

In Milwaukee, Wisconsin, Abel Ortiz directs a small SER center serving learners referred from a number of other social programs. SER is a national association of affiliated community-based organizations (CBOs) that serve Hispanic Americans and others. Unlike Figueroa, Ortiz is responsible for only a few hundred learners annually, and his organization survives on short-term grants — soft money. But like Figueroa, Ortiz reports to many funders.

How do Figueroa, Ortiz, and other administrators decide about technology? An unfettered administrator (with some background in economics) would want to add technology until the cost of additional hardware and courseware was just equal to a marginal increase in benefits. But in the real world the administrator would also want to avoid bureaucratic hassle, the risk of failure, and other problems. In practical terms, those other problems may be the most crucial considerations. For example, will the purchases appear in the capital budget or the expense budget, and will the funding agency allow additional budget lines for computer maintenance and teacher training?

Indeed, funding agencies set the incentives and many of the rules under which the providers operate. Rules alone can define what "expensive" means. For instance, if capital purchases exceeding $10,000 will invoke a major budget review, then $10,001 is expensive. But if a $10,001 computer motivates an additional 100 students to complete the course of study (at a cost, that is, of $100 per additional completion), the purchase may be inexpensive, especially if the cost per completion under conventional forms of instruction is $500 to $800, as it is in the relatively sophisticated programs run under JTPA.

Moreover, many existing program incentives favor spending for current operations rather than investing in future program improvements. As a result, most adult literacy programs have no capital budget, and so administrators cannot spread out the costs of a purchase over the years in which the technology will be used.

Agency rules can also discourage needed investment partnerships among literacy providers. For example, although some provisions in the AEA and the Family Support Act encourage or even require such partnerships, overly strict accounting rules may prevent a computer lab funded with JTPA monies from serving AEA-funded enrollees or welfare recipients. And federal funding rules may even prevent computer technology purchased for public schoolchildren from being used in evening courses for their parents.

Ironically, even funders' efforts to impose some accountability on providers can inhibit investments in technology. In another example from California, the state education department funds literacy providers on the basis of their average daily attendance (ADA) rates. Under this formula, some providers see no advantage at all in a technology that could reduce a four-month course to three months, even though it would allow them to serve one-third more students annually without an increase in staff or facilities. "We would only increase the cost of instructional materials without increasing our ADA," they say.

Thus, few at the local level can initiate change, but many at higher levels can veto it. For Figueroa and Ortiz's counterparts in other organizations to purchase computer technology, they usually must expend their administrative energies on lobbying against the funders' regulations or garnering unencumbered grant funds from the government or a foundation—funds in short supply. Much of the hardware and literacy courseware purchased for JTPA programs has come from special funds: foundations, governors' discretionary "8 percent" funds, demonstration funds, and other sources.

Finally, although some subdepartmental agencies in the federal government have shown interest in supporting the development and dissemination of literacy courseware (primarily through the demonstration funds just mentioned), there is no evidence that anyone in a top leadership position has seized on the potential of the technology and decided to facilitate, let alone encourage, its introduction.

Lags in Courseware Development. While we have witnessed extremely rapid advances in computer hardware over the past decade, the lack of performance standards, paucity of evaluations, and scant investment in the technology for literacy instruction have effectively prevented accompanying advances in the courseware. Granted, several of the IVD packages do, as noted earlier, live up to some of the hardware's potential. Learners work at their own pace, while the computer "patiently" and privately corrects wrong answers. And several packages present basic skills at least in part in the context of the adult learner's life, teaching how to place an order or fill out a maintenance form, for example. But, again, no package takes advantage of the full capabilities of the hardware; and none carries out the full potential of today's hardware *and* software capabilities to teach literacy side-by-side with occupational and life skills, as envisioned in the next chapter.

Resolving the Debate. In the end, the only possible resolution of this debate over which should come first—better evaluations, more investment, or better courseware—is a reordering of the priorities of the parties involved. If all eyes were on the demographic deadlines presented in Chapter 1, the priority would be to serve as many adults as possible, as soon as possible, as well as possible (based on performance standards), using our best judgments on the potential costs and benefits of adopting or forgoing the technology. If this were the highest priority, the funders, providers, and vendors would have to set aside the debate and could then work simultaneously to pursue all three of these options.

As a nation we simply must cut the Gordian knot in which these options are now entangled. And if policymakers and providers begin to pursue the other recommendations posed in this book — for better linkages, a national center for research, development, and technical assistance, and so on — a more convergent, top-down and bottom-up strategy would prevail, with funders setting performance standards and seeding the market by removing barriers to investment, providers investing in equipment, and vendors (and funders) investing more in evaluation research and product development.

Estimating the True Potential of Computer Technology

Once the parties to the investment decision set aside the chicken-and-egg debate, they should sit down together and develop a reasonable economic argument for the technology. If the courseware were to begin to approach the capabilities of today's computer technology, if it were based on better yardsticks of performance, what might be achieved? How might the technology work in the field? Who would stand to benefit? How much would it cost?

The following discussion addresses these questions from the perspective of making an overall national investment. Thus, while the judgments about the cost and benefits to each party in the literacy system may seem eminently reasonable, it is still important to bear in mind the *total* national cost. If enough adults learn basic skills, the investment will have paid for itself.

The Learners' Cost-Benefit Calculus. Unlike schoolchildren, most adult learners decide for themselves whether to enroll in, and finish, a course of study. Even when sanctions apply (as in welfare reform programs), learners must be motivated to apply their time to the task of learning. Without that motivation, nothing else matters. Unfortunately, the failure of most current approaches to basic skills education is writ large in just these dimensions. Many adults refuse to sign up for classes officially labeled "literacy" but called "dummy courses" by many of the learners for whom they were intended. And as noted in other chapters, many of those who do sign up soon drop out.

Although adult learners may have many reasons for pursuing literacy instruction — to be able to read the Bible, read to their children, manage their family budget — a prime motivator is the desire for better employment opportunities. In this case, the rational learner will compare the instructional costs of tuition, time, travel, child care, stigma, and possible embarrassment to the potential payoffs in a job, a better job, or a higher salary. Our question is whether computer technology will reduce those costs and increase those benefits.

The answer will depend partly on the learner's employment status. Some adults work in large corporations, some in the public sector, some in unionized firms, while others are unemployed. Each group has a different cost-benefit calculus. For instance, some pay tuition, while others are paid to attend courses; some have to travel to courses, while others attend at the work site. For the unemployed, the government often pays the tuition, as in the case of single mothers receiving welfare or prison inmates. Other learners, such as disabled or dislocated workers, may be eligible for government subsidies. Each of these groups has a different calculus as well; among prison inmates, for example, child care, transportation, and opportunity costs (the costs of forgoing other activities or investments) do not even apply.

Funding agencies and providers should be mindful of these differences for particular groups of learners. Nonetheless, if the technology reduces instructional time, as theory and the research evidence suggest, it should reduce *most* of these costs for *most* learners. But even more important, the technology should shorten learners' wait until "graduation," and this in turn will give learners quicker access to expanded employment opportunities. To borrow again from economics jargon, the learners' opportunity costs will be significantly lower with technology than without it.

As important as computer technology should be in reducing learners' costs of instruction, it holds even greater potential to increase their benefits. The DeBloois (1988) literature review pointed to learners' preference for IVD instruction over other forms, while Gold (1989), in a review of the literature on adult literacy courseware, found persuasive anecdotal evidence of greater motivation and self-esteem among IVD users than among other students. Given learners' greater preference for IVDs, their greater motivation and self-esteem, and the convenience of flexibly scheduled, self-paced, and immediately reinforcing individualized instruction, we can reasonably expect that the prime benefit to learners will be their greater tendency to stay with a curriculum until they have mastered it.

It is literacy taught as part and parcel of everyday work and life experiences that is especially relevant and motivating to adults over the duration of their coursework (see, for example, Sticht and Mikulecky, 1984). Yet assembling materials to teach in the context of these experiences has always been a difficult task for the literacy instructor. A second significant benefit for learners, then, will be the amount of contextual information—or, put differently, the breadth of exposure—possible with a single IVD courseware package. Although video and film can also simulate real life, these media by themselves do not have the interactivity or record-keeping capacities of computers. It is only when computers and moving video are combined, as they are in IVDs, that such simulations can be taught interactively on an individual basis.

Finally, as we enter the 1990s, a large number of entry-level jobs, such as bank teller, supply clerk, ticket agent, cashier, machine operator in a factory, will require work at a computer terminal. Thus, a mere by-product of computer-based instruction—computer literacy—may be one of the greatest benefits for adult learners.

In sum, if the learners' cost-benefit calculus were the driving force in the decision to invest in literacy courseware, providers would add computer workstations until the additional cost was just equal to the marginal net benefit. But because tuition is usually subsidized by a government agency or employer, we must translate the learners' calculus into one that makes sense to those who do drive the investment decision, the administrators of the provider and funding agencies.

The Providers' Calculus. For providers, most of the learners' cost-benefit calculus can be translated into the simple terms of recruitment and retention rates. For all the reasons listed above, we can expect that computer technology will make it easier and less expensive for literacy providers to attract adult learners to courses and then to retain them until they have gained the basic skills being taught. But providers still blanch at the total tab for a small computer laboratory. Again we must return to the concept of unit costs.

At today's prices the cost of adding computer hardware and courseware usually works out to about $100 per learner. This is the cost if the hardware is used intensively — say, 6,000 hours over three to five years — and if the provider uses off-the-shelf courseware. For example, an IVD machine, with all the attendant charges for courseware, furniture, maintenance, supplies, and modest teacher training, might cost $12,000, or $2 per learner hour, to operate. If two learners used the machine simultaneously (an effective arrangement even in open-entry, open-exit courses), the cost would be an additional $1 per learner hour. A 100-hour course would cost an additional $100 per learner served.

A more realistic example is the typical arrangement for a PALS lab. With four IVD units and eight word processors, the lab can serve a full-sized class of thirty-two learners. During a four-hour course block, each learner spends two hours with the teacher and paper-and-pencil tasks, one hour alone at the word processor, and one hour with a partner at an IVD terminal. The PALS lab, including PALS courseware, can be purchased for $60,000. Adding $36,000 for the other software, furniture, maintenance, supplies, and teacher training required brings the cost to $96,000. For a course serving thirty-two learners, this works out to $3,000 per learner slot. If the provider uses the lab for thirty courses of this size (30 times 32 equals 960 learners) over 6,000 hours (200 hours per course), the unit cost is, once again, an additional $100 per learner served. The 200 hours would be divided into segments of 100 hours of traditional instruction, 50 hours at the word processor, and 50 hours, with a partner, at the IVD terminal.

The reader must now think hard about unit costs and technology and about the difference between unit costs and total costs. Technology will *not* reduce total costs in a literacy program. The same number of teachers will be required, and more funds will be needed for teacher training. If class size remains unchanged, the *cost per registered learner* — registered, that is, on the first day of class — will only go up. If, however, attendance improves (as the scanty data suggest it will), the *cost per learner-hour of instruction* to those registrants who continue to attend may be less. If learners' attention is improved (because the computer's interactivity commands learner participation), then the *cost per learner's true time at the task* is further reduced. If measures of the competency achieved were available, then one could obtain a truly meaningful unit-cost calculation, namely, the *cost per learner making a given improvement* in literacy. *No economically meaningful statement about costs can be made until the unit is defined.*

In other words, when the measure is the cost per registered learner, no meaningful calculation can be made: One poorly trained teacher's aide can deliver instruction in a football stadium. But if the measure is the cost per learner reaching the competency requirement of the course, then the *potential* of computer technology is indeed one of reducing the unit cost of instruction, where the potential is defined as the ability to recruit more learners, to capture and retain learners' interest, to show them their progress at each step of the way and thereby motivate them to continue, and to give them the benefit of more personal, individual attention from the teacher.

Using the calculations presented earlier, providers should have little trouble justifying, to their own satisfaction, the additional expense of $100 per learner (a figure that should be even lower in the coming years as the price of the hardware continues to fall). The investment in technology should reap benefits in improved recruitment and retention rates. It should reduce the time learners take to reach a given level of competency, allowing the same number of teachers to serve more learners annually. For example, if a provider can teach the same competencies in a three-month course instead of a four-month course, the unit cost of instruction will drop by a third. And finally, the investment should reduce providers' reliance on teachers' schedules, allowing for full-time use of facilities — thereby reducing the unit cost of classroom space as well. But because providers ultimately must justify the cost-effectiveness of their literacy program to their funders' satisfaction, we have one last calculus to specify.

The Funders' Calculus. In theory, funding agencies should encourage investments in the development, dissemination, and evaluation of instructional technology to the extent that they expect the technology to improve program performance per dollar spent, that is, to the extent it promises to yield a "bigger bang for the buck." In reality, however, many administrators in both government and corporations prefer a no-risk strategy, especially during periods, like the present, when both public and private sectors are facing severe budgetary constraints.

Implementing any new technology is an inherently risky administrative decision, and computer technology in particular simply cannot promise to pay for itself in a single year. But business managers, even the risk averse, will accept this risk if they can predict with confidence that the investment is likely to reduce the total cost of each unit of the product or service being produced (and if they are confident the product has a potential market).

To accept this risk in the literacy business, the funder must define both the unit of the service being produced and the time horizon. In fact, defining these two parameters of the unit-cost calculation is *the most crucial decision* the funder must make. Will the service unit be the hours of instruction provided, the functional skills achieved, course completions, or increased employment or earnings among the learners? And will the technology be in use for three years or five? Assume, for example, that a funding agency wants to finance, directly, production of the ultimate IVD courseware for basic skills instruction, at a cost of a million dollars. If the administrator is confident that at least a million learners will complete the course over the next ten years, the unit cost of the investment is only one dollar per learner.

In practice, reaching agreement on a workable definition of unit costs is often difficult (especially if the agency cannot count on receiving reliable data on the program outcome to be measured). It is possible, though, as the experience of the U.S. Department of Defense (DOD) illustrates. This department is a leading investor in computer-based training technology, largely because its administrators place a premium on the ability of the technology to standardize and report on the instructional process. Even in a decentralized agency within DOD, administrators have well-specified training goals for the long term, and they also know they will serve thousands of trainees over that time horizon. Obviously, the DOD experience has little transferability to the literacy field as it is now configured, that is, where providers like Figueroa and Ortiz are reporting up a chain of command that branches in multiple directions.

But if we move up a step, to the cabinet level and Congress, the calculus for literacy courseware is easier to define. From a national perspective, if the federal government were to adopt a goal of teaching basic skills to 25 million adults during the 1990s, software used by 10 percent of that number would be extremely cost-effective even if it cost $25 million to develop and disseminate (at $10 per user). Indeed, it is at this level of the literacy system that one has to ask once more whether successfully meeting the literacy needs of 25 million is possible without the technology.

The task for the administration, Congress, and top leaders of the funding agencies (public and private) is therefore to take the learners' cost-benefit calculus, and the providers', and develop an appropriate calculus for the nation's adult literacy investment. Chapters 9, 10, and 11 will explain in more detail the changes necessary for these leaders to make this calculus, as they are not in a position to do so today. For our purposes here, suffice it to say that federal, state, and corporate programs for adult literacy instruction are hampered by a lack of well-defined performance goals (which makes real accountability impossible), a short-term perspective, a multiplicity of funding sources, and as noted earlier an overabundance of bureaucratic constraints on investment. In fact, the nation's reliance on part-time teachers and makeshift facilities has been a natural result of this short-sightedness.

The good news, though, is that the potential of computer technology may force the issue: To serve the 25 million within a decade, policymakers will have to commit themselves to both a technology that can do the job *and* the long-term, goal-oriented perspective that will make investments in the technology possible.

Near-Term Recommendations

Quality tools require a quality system. Above and beyond the chicken-and-egg debate and the unit-cost estimations, it is crucial that the parties involved in delivering adult literacy instruction in the United States change the way they think about and deliver services. It should be obvious that computer technology by itself will not solve the adult literacy problem. The important, if less obvious, point is that the technology *cannot* help solve the problem if the delivery system remains configured as it is now. Spending money on computers for a program conducted in a sixth-floor walk-up, with untrained volunteers, at a current unit cost (however it is measured) of no more than $200 per learner annually would be a complete waste.

Computer technology will make sense, however, if all the parties in the system commit to creating a high-quality system. The means to that end can be found in the other chapters of this book. That is, we will be ready to promote cost-effective use of the technology when we have committed ourselves to making meaningful investments in adult learners (in Chapter 11 Chisman estimates that the most expensive existing programs cost around $2,000 per learner annually, or less than half of what we now spend on K–12 students); to creating stronger linkages among the organizations serving in and funding the field; to building a more professional, better-paid teaching force;

and to establishing more systematic ways to collect data, conduct basic and applied research, and evaluate program and system performance. While the nation is building this higher quality system, several more specific steps can be taken in tandem to advance the technology itself.

Develop an Investment Mentality. Hand in hand with the notion of quality goes the notion of investment: committing resources with the expectation of a profitable return over a period of years. Business emphasizes accountability, or the bottom line. And no business buys solely consumables; capital purchases, whose costs are depreciated over more than one year, are a part of any business.

Before addressing the issue of accountability, we have to conclude that the artificial barriers to long-term investments in adult literacy must fall. The federal government, as the major funder of the system, must initiate this process; and the other funders are likely to follow suit. First, the federal agencies now funding literacy instruction should earmark a certain percentage (say, between 1 and 5 percent) of their allocations to states and local providers specifically for investments in computer hardware, courseware, teacher training, technical assistance, planning, and the facilities needed to deploy the technology. Second, where agencies require an accounting of the annual costs and outcomes of a given provider, the provider should be allowed to spread out the costs of these investments over several years. Third, Congress should authorize the federal agencies to offer matching funds for state and provider investments on a one-for-one basis, as incentives to invest. Eligibility for the matching funds should, however, be conditional on satisfying *common-use* requirements; that is, states and providers would receive the funds only if they guaranteed that the technology purchased would be made available to registrants in any federally funded program.

It is important to footnote this recommendation with mention of employers. This group generally *has* an investment mentality; in fact, employers are likely to be the strongest potential market for computer-based literacy instruction. They do, how-

ever, need to be convinced to invest in basic skills instruction —
but that is the subject of the next chapter.

Promote Accountability with Performance Measures. Quality, and an investment mentality, demands accountability, and
accountability requires meaningful standards for all levels of the
literacy system. As is emphasized throughout this book, developing measures of learner needs and outcomes, teacher effectiveness, and program and system performance is high on the agendas of all major actors in the system. It will take a dedicated
and ongoing collaboration among all these actors to reach some
workable consensus on appropriate measures, for their own sake,
but they must make a concerted effort to include the courseware
vendors in the process.

The providers, as well, should be given a prominent role
to play in that process, especially in light of the demands of technological innovation. Paul Strausman, a former vice president of
the Xerox Corporation, advises that successful adoption of a new
technology, in any environment, demands changes in the ways
an organization operates. "The system should fit the people, not
the other way around," he cautions (1985, p. 93). Adult literacy
providers, as the experts on the population in need, must be
among the closest of collaborators involved in what is truly an
iterative process: assessing learners' and employers' needs; defining performance standards that will work in evaluating their
programs' effectiveness in meeting those needs; determining what
factors contribute to learner attrition, retention, and success; and
adjusting their organizations to accommodate the technology
and, more to the point, the organization itself to the learners.

Demonstrate the Costs and Benefits of the Technology. The
market for literacy courseware can grow if we can document
a few success stories. The federal government should sponsor
more, and more extensive, demonstrations of the technology in
the field than it now does and require that they be rigorously and
independently evaluated. The evaluations themselves should be
based on a range of the performance measures available, includ-

ing such "ultimate" measures as changes in the employment status, life circumstances, and attitudes of the participating learners.

More important than the evaluations, though, will be the dissemination of their results. The national and state centers for adult literacy proposed in Chapters 5, 9, and 10 would be the logical conduit for this information. Other possible conduits would be national, state or regional, or local technology centers. In recent years the Gannett Foundation has been funding one such effort, a National Clearinghouse for Technology and Literacy, which sponsors an annual national conference on the subject, publishes an annual software guide, and has arranged for technical consultants in ten regions of the country. At the local level, the St. Paul, Minnesota, school district has sponsored a Technology for Literacy Center. Institutions of higher education are another possibility; the Pennsylvania State University, for instance, has served in a variety of capacities to investigate and report on the technology over the past decade.

These examples of fledgling efforts to disseminate information on computer-based literacy instruction have potential. The federal government and states — but also the vendors — could do much more, however, to recognize the importance of dissemination efforts and help support them.

Deregulate the System. Introducing more competition into the adult literacy system would go a long way toward fostering greater quality in the system as a whole. To the extent possible, the federal government should apply similar regulations, standards, and reporting requirements to all the institutions serving adult literacy learners. Investment set-asides and demonstration grants should be available to all public and private providers. And ideally all providers should be able to compete for any portion of the population of learners.

In other words, if we accept the concept of a pluralistic system, we must level out the playing field. Program performance should be the prime criterion for funding. If it were, providers would have fewer constraints on the decisions they must make to adapt their programs to the needs of their learners. But more important, providers would be competing to attract registrants and create the "best" success stories, instead of competing for funding dollars.

We simply will not know the true potential of computer technology for adult literacy instruction until providers in different settings carry out their own unit-cost calculations, put the technology to use, and demonstrate the return on their investment in terms of outcomes for the learners. But once we have based distinctions among programs on good measures of performance, once a few success stories have surfaced, we can begin to put the potential of the technology to use on a scale that can make a difference.

References

Arterburn, S. "Final Report on the Interactive Videodisk Literacy Course," photocopy. Washington, D.C.: Multicultural Career Intern Program, District of Columbia Public Schools, July 31, 1989.

DeBloois, M. *The Use and Effectiveness of Videodisc Training.* Falls Church, Va.: Future Systems, 1988.

Gold, P. "Workplace Literacy and Technology-Based Programs: The State of the Art, 1989," photocopy. Alexandria, Va.: Hudson Institute, September 29, 1989.

Lutz, R., Di Vito, N. O., and Staczek, J. S. "Interactive Videodisc Literacy Course (Skillpac and PALS)," photocopy. Washington, D.C.: Multicultural Career Intern Program, District of Columbia Public Schools, August 30, 1989.

Packer, A. H., and Grognet, A. "An Experiment in the Use of Interactive Videodisk to Teach English for Workplace Problem-Solving." Washington, D.C.: Center for Applied Linguistics, January 1988.

Raaen, M. "Adult Literacy and Computer Assisted Interactive Videodisc: A Six-Month Study with IBM and the United States Army," photocopy. Atlanta: Georgia State University, March 1988.

Reissman, F., and Jean, P. C. "Consortium for Worker Education: Final Report," photocopy. New York: Consortium for Worker Education, December 12, 1988.

Sticht, T. G., and Mikulecky, L. "Job-Related Basic Skills: Cases and Conclusions," pamphlet. Washington, D.C.: National Institute of Education, 1984.

Strausman, P. *Information Payoff: The Transformation of Work in the Electronic Age.* New York: Consortium for Worker Education, December 12, 1985.

Turner, T. C. "Using the Computer for Adult Literacy Instruction." *Journal of Reading,* 1988, *31* (7), 643–647.

7

Forrest P. Chisman
Wendy L. Campbell

Narrowing the Job–Skills Gap: A Focus on Workforce Literacy

The adult literacy problem clouding our nation's future has already let loose thunderbolts in the U.S. workplace. One of the most celebrated examples is the case of the New York Telephone Company, which in 1987 had to test 57,000 job applicants before it could find 2,100 who had the requisite skills to be trained for entry-level positions as telephone operators and repair technicians. This event and others like it continue to make headlines because they vividly illustrate an unprecedented new phenomenon — one that is not only disrupting the workplace but also threatening a lower standard of living for all Americans well into the next century.

The phenomenon is a *job-skills gap* — a mismatch between job demands and worker skills in the lower echelons of the labor market. The changing workplace is demanding higher order skills of entry-level workers, from bank tellers to machine operators, because of innovations in computer technology, robotics, and systems of authority. The growth industries are in the service sector, where computers are doing what were once routine clerical jobs, while "clerks" are now being asked to be customer service representatives. Entry-level jobs in manufacturing are dwindling, but even in that sector, statistical process control and machines that require sophisticated electronic as opposed to mechanical repair are making math, not muscle, a prime job requirement. The "quality movement," "just in time" delivery

144

systems, and a focus on satisfying the customer have pushed decision-making authority down the chain of command, thinning out the ranks of managers and supervisors and making the worker on the line responsible for on-the-spot decisions and participation in teams of problem solvers (Adler, 1986; Hirschorn, 1989). And the demographics of the baby-bust generation mean that we cannot depend on young workers to fill all these jobs (Vaughan and Berryman, 1989). Older workers must be trained and retrained. But at the same time, among the adults who would normally fill these lower tier jobs are 20 to 30 million with very limited skills.

This story is familiar to all who read the headlines, and it has been well documented elsewhere, both in scholarly and practitioner publications (Johnston and Packer, 1987; Finney, 1989) and in the popular press (*Business Week,* 1988; Fiske, 1989). What is not well documented is what the nation is doing and could do about the job-skills gap. In the past corporations and the federal government have been able to close isolated skills gaps in particular regions or higher level occupations by raising wages or subsidizing professional education or training. But this time the skills gap is in all sectors of the economy and most regions of the country. And this time it must be filled by adults who are not only ill equipped for the available jobs but also ill prepared to *learn* the skills required. Indeed, many employers complain that even graduates of high school equivalency programs are not necessarily "trainable" for today's jobs; before they can enter job-specific training, they need to improve their basic skills.

Thus, a new term has entered the lexicon in the 1980s: *workforce literacy,* or the basic skills needed to function effectively in the economy. The term will be used here to include, in addition to the five basic skills (reading, writing, and communicating in English, and math and problem-solving skills), such skills as the ability to work and learn independently, work cooperatively with others, respond quickly and flexibly to new situations, juggle multiple tasks, and decide what one needs to know and then find the information — in other words, many of the abilities and attitudes traditionally considered necessary for managerial and technical jobs (U.S. Department of Labor and others, 1988, pp. 13–18).

More than a half-dozen major federal programs, and many more efforts by other levels of government and the voluntary sector, offer literacy instruction, in the form of basic skills and "employability" services, to the unemployed portion of the labor force. This chapter focuses on what has been called elsewhere in this book the "forgotten half" of the adult literacy population: those who are employed, but whose basic skills do not meet the needs of the economy today and will surely be inadequate in the years to come. By most estimates 10 to 15 million workers have seriously limited basic skills, and most are low-level, marginal workers—the working poor and near-poor.

This group should be a high priority for both government and employer intervention: Its members are already performing their jobs at some level of competence, and retraining them is a better option for their employers—and the economy at large—than hiring replacements. But there is an enormous gap between promise and performance in the nation's response to the problems of workers with limited basic skills.

Promise Versus Performance

The good news about workforce literacy is that awareness of the problem is high, a large number of fledgling efforts to address it have been launched, and the measures required to provide workforce literacy instruction to the employed are within the grasp of the adult literacy field. The bad news is that, with few exceptions, awareness has not been translated into programs that offer the types of advanced workforce literacy instruction that will result in substantial benefits for either employees or employers.

The Promise. In the last few years there has been a great deal of breast-beating about the job-skills gap on the part of both corporate and government leaders. Chief executive officers (CEOs) have vied with one another in ticking off how many job applicants they have had to reject for lack of basic skills or in voicing concern about the skill levels of their own workforce (Fiske, 1989). Political leaders have waxed eloquent about the skills gap, as have leaders of organized labor and some leaders of the education community (U.S. Department of Labor and others, 1988).

In 1989 alone, at least a dozen major conferences sponsored by government, business, labor, and private research institutes focused on one aspect or another of the workforce literacy problem. In rare collaborations, the U.S. Departments of Education and Labor issued two joint publications (one, with Commerce as well) about the skills gap and workforce literacy, adding to the growing stream of print material that includes newspaper stories, a special edition of *Business Week* magazine (1989), and publications by unions, business groups, and literacy leaders (see U.S. Department of Labor and others, 1988; U.S. Department of Labor and U.S. Department of Education, 1988). The Business Council for Effective Literacy (BCEL), established by retired McGraw-Hill chairman Harold W. McGraw, Jr., has provided invaluable assistance in tracking these and other developments in the literacy field.

A 1987 survey sponsored by the American Association for Adult and Continuing Education (AAACE) found more than 100 basic skills programs for employees scattered across the country (Mark, 1987), and many more have sprung up since then, as documented in the BCEL newsletter. In 1988 and 1989 the Departments of Education and Labor awarded more than fifty small grants to public and private organizations for demonstration projects in workforce literacy. Unions have negotiated at least a half-dozen major collective bargaining agreements with corporations (including the three leading automakers) that require provision of basic skills service to their members. Employers have contracted with community colleges, vocational centers, and other literacy providers to carry out instruction, and several major publishers in the adult literacy field, as well as some newcomers, are preparing workforce literacy product lines.

Happily, these developments are converging with both theory and practice in the adult literacy field. Among the long-

standing concerns of the field have been how to motivate adults
to participate in programs, how to design the logistics of programs to attract learners to an instructional site on a regular
basis, how to ensure that the instruction makes a difference in
improving learners' lives, and how to find stable auspices to sponsor adult literacy programs.

In recent years many literacy leaders have come to conclude that the answer to all of these concerns is some form of
contextual instruction (Sticht, 1987; Hunter and Harman, 1985).
This concept, more fully discussed in Chapter 2, is the result
of a long evolution of learning theory and experimentation. To
oversimplify, it reduces to the notion that adults will be more
motivated to learn, and will learn more quickly, if they are learning for a clear purpose — to achieve a personal goal, perform
a task necessary in their everyday lives, or solve a problem that
is important to them. The logical extension of this idea is that
literacy instruction can be most effectively delivered if it is
presented as a way of achieving some individual purpose, if it
is delivered in the location where adults need to apply the skills
they will learn, and if the materials are customized to meet that
need.

The best known example of contextual instruction is the
system developed by Thomas Sticht and others for the U.S.
Army. Sticht and his colleagues (1973) analyzed the basic skills
soldiers needed to perform particular work tasks, such as maintaining a piece of equipment. They then developed materials,
such as word lists and math exercises, that were relevant to each
task. Each soldier's skill level was then assessed, and those soldiers found deficient in particular skills were given instruction
with the task-relevant materials while they were on the job.

The results were large and rapid learning gains. This
should come as no surprise. The Army's contextual approach
solved each of the problems that had been troubling the literacy field. It solved the problem of motivation, because the soldiers were learning skills that would presumably help them succeed in their jobs. It solved the problem adults have with the
logistics of participation, because it brought learning to the work
site. And it solved the problem of making a difference in learners'
lives, because the soldiers could see an immediate benefit from

the instruction — evidence they were performing their jobs better. Finally, the program solved the problem of auspices: The Army was willing to invest considerable time and money in a literacy program designed to improve soldiers' performance in ways it considered important.

Many leaders of the literacy field believe that it should be possible to develop analogous contextual learning approaches for other people with limited basic skills, and that contextual learning should become the norm in the field (Sticht, 1987; Hunter and Harman, 1985). This would be a major change from most current instructional approaches. Today most literacy instruction uses generic materials that have been designed to achieve goals exactly the opposite of those of contextual learning. That is, the materials developed by most educational publishers and most widely used in the field are designed to be applicable to almost anyone with limited skills, in almost any circumstances; and they are usually employed in stand-alone learning centers that have no close ties to other activities in which learners may be engaged. Although individual instructors often try to customize the materials, they are handicapped in the effort by a product that is designed for general-purpose applications.

Many leaders in the literacy field believe this generic approach to instruction is suboptimal. They believe that the problems of motivation, logistics, time, and relevance can be overcome only by more widespread use of contextual approaches. Otherwise, it will be far more difficult to meet the needs of 20 to 30 million adult learners in a timely and cost-effective way.

Whether or not these larger claims are true, the military experience, together with other evidence and theory, indicates that contextual learning approaches could easily be applied to the workplace environment and that large learning gains should be achievable. In short, workforce literacy should be an easy case for adult literacy instruction provided that four rules are observed:

- Instruction should take place at the workplace.
- It should be sanctioned and encouraged by the employer.
- It should make use of materials that are clearly relevant to the work or other employment issues (such as understanding

fringe benefits) that employees have at hand or are likely to face, and that employers care about.

- Both employees and employers should be able to reap tangible benefits from the instruction. For employees, the benefits might be doing their job more effectively, eventually gaining a promotion, or, in firms undergoing rapid technological change, being able to keep up with job demands and staying employed; for employers, the benefits might be increased productivity, higher profits, or a more satisfied workforce.

If these four conditions are met, large learning gains should be achievable through workforce literacy instruction. Both employees and employers will turn out winners; and at least one form of adult literacy instruction will find a major sponsor: employers interested in enhancing productivity.

The Reality. One might expect that the convergence of a heightened awareness of the job-skills gap, the new workforce literacy initiatives, and theoretical developments in the literacy field would be hastening the workforce literacy problem to a rapid solution. Unfortunately, this is not the case.

Most of the corporate leaders who have been outspoken about the skills gap have concentrated their energies on school reform, not adult literacy. The vast majority, in other words, seem to be overlooking the fact that at least three-quarters of all Americans who will be working in the year 2000 are *adults* today (Brizius and Foster, 1987).

The federal demonstration grants mentioned earlier have seeded some interesting experiments in learning software, collaborative efforts, and program design. But the grants have been small (on the order of a few hundred thousand dollars each) and limited to one or two years in duration. As a result, the projects have been on a small scale and of limited value beyond their immediate context. Because of inadequate information, it is difficult to assess the results of efforts by unions and educational institutions, but it is reasonable to surmise that most of those efforts carry similar limitations.

Moreover, both the size and the scope of the workforce literacy initiatives that have been launched are woefully limited.

Each of the programs identified by the AAACE survey covers at most only a few hundred employees. And in most cases the programs merely allow providers of conventional, generic basic skills instruction to set up shop on corporate premises. Only a few offer contextual learning systems, portable skills instruction, released time to attend classes, incentives for participation, or rewards for success. That is, few exemplify the four rules for successful workforce literacy programs presented above. Among this handful are the programs at Aetna, Motorola, and Polaroid. At Motorola, for instance, the executives believe that a corporate commitment to lifelong learning for *all* employees is essential to remaining competitive in today's global economy. They caution, however, that the commitment requires a top-to-bottom transformation of corporate culture and operations (Berger, 1989).

Thus, while Motorola and other leading-edge companies are pointing the way, few others are following. At most a few tens of thousands of workers nationwide are being served by workforce literacy efforts of any sort, and the numbers served by state-of-the-art standards are far smaller. Why the inertia? Conversations with corporate leaders elicit a series of reasons that not only answer this question but also offer guidance in mapping out a long-term solution.

1. *"Leave it to the public sector."* Employers tend to view education as a public sector responsibility, especially when numbers of 10 to 15 million adults are bandied about. Employers know that significant funds for adult literacy education exist in the public and voluntary sectors and wonder why they should have to contribute themselves. Another common allegation is that the lower tier of the workforce is highly mobile. Employers, particularly small firms, say they cannot make significant training investments in workers who are likely to take their newly learned skills to another employer or, worse yet, a competitor.

Yet at the same time, U.S. employers are spending about $30 billion annually in direct costs for employee training programs, according to recent estimates by the American Society of Training and Development (ASTD). Employers obviously are willing to spend large sums on upgrading the skills of their employees—if they believe that the employees are at a skill level where they can benefit from the training. In fact, the ASTD study shows that most training dollars go to managerial and technical employees; only a very small percentage goes to basic skills education (Carnevale and Gainer, 1989). Furthermore, other recent evidence suggests that the mobile worker theory may be a fallacy. Vaughan and Berryman (1989) indicate that workers trained by their employers tend to be less mobile than other workers.

As the skills gap continues to widen over the 1990s (see Johnston and Packer, 1987), employers will eventually be forced to take the issue more seriously and extend more training dollars down the occupational ladder. Until then, though, the opposite argument will continue to hold sway in many executive suites.

2. *"We don't have the problem."* Many employers in fact have not yet witnessed the skills gap firsthand, certainly not on a large scale. Some may acknowledge that it lies around the corner for them, but as many commentators have lamented (for example, Dertouzos, Lester, and Solow, 1989), American business suffers from toeing the line to profit margins in the short term. While they are prepared to bear the cost of upgrading their capital equipment, many employers are willing to accept low productivity from the lower ranks of their workforce.

3. *"We have alternatives."* And so they do. Outsourcing is one. Corporations may subcontract their production or support services to firms in other parts of the country not experiencing a labor shortage, or to overseas firms with labor shortages and low wages. This "hollowing" of the corporation can work well for individual firms. But the skills gap means that, without a major intervention to achieve workforce literacy over this decade, many employers will be hard-pressed to find other U.S. locations for their production. Moreover, carried too far, outsourcing would leave us with massive unemployment and a two-tiered society made up of the haves and have-nots — an unacceptable alternative to many Americans.

Another option pursued in recent years has been to invest heavily in technology. Technological innovation, from robotics to statistical process control, has in fact been a success in the manufacturing sector. It is among the factors making productivity gains there much larger than in the service sector. But while it has reduced the growth in demand for new entrants to the workforce, it has also increased the demand for workers with higher levels of basic skills.

4. *"Show us the product."* For those employers that have reached the limits of the benefits to be gained from these alternatives — those struggling to close their skills gap — the question is where they can find an effective training product: a literacy program or curriculum that can teach their potential job candidates or current employees the skills they need to function effectively in the workplace. In demanding "Show us the product that has taught or can teach these skills," employers looking to reduce the skills gap of their own firm can look neither to the publicly supported adult literacy system nor to most commercial vendors of instructional materials. Few publicly supported literacy programs can promise employers that learners who complete their programs will have achieved the skill levels required for employability. And vendors have not yet received adequate guidance on what the performance standards for adult literacy in general, let alone workforce literacy, should be. Vendors are loath to develop contextual materials until they can identify viable markets — a task that awaits stable and well-organized sponsorship of literacy programs.

Few employers view solving these problems of public and private providers to be part of their job. They are unlikely to make large investments in workforce literacy until they are offered a product that meets their needs far better than any that is now available. And finally, at least one other source of inertia remains.

5. *"Whose goals will be served?"* Employers that embark on a workforce literacy initiative may face some serious negotiations over the issue of goals. On the one hand, the employer may be unwilling to pay for training that is not necessarily of use on the current job. If so, the employer's goal will be job-specific training, possibly with supplemental basic skills training offered as required. On the other hand, this strategy is unlikely to prevent the skills obsolescence that was the lot of many workers during the 1980s. Representatives of organized

labor have been vocal in their distaste for the idea of limiting workforce literacy to job-specific skills training (see Sarmiento, 1989). Their view is that workforce literacy should give workers the broader skills they need to adapt to the changing workplace over the long term.

In nonunion settings the initiative for a workforce literacy program will likely rest with the employer. But even in this case, disagreement over goals may still surface between top management and the human resources department. In both union and nonunion settings, these differences of opinion may serve to delay literacy initiatives.

An Incremental Strategy for the Long Term

The inertia holding back the expansion and refinement of workforce literacy service is unlikely to be overcome by any one dramatic step on the part of employers, employees, unions, government, literacy providers, or any of the other interested parties. The workforce literacy problem is more likely to be solved by a series of modest, incremental steps involving all of these parties and others. Recent experience with workforce literacy points to a number of highly feasible steps that could be taken now and that, collectively, would add up to a realistic approach to closing the job-skills gap in the years to come.

Those steps logically fall under four main calls to action. First, employers should establish workforce literacy as a top-management priority. Second, all levels of government should take a stronger leadership role and fine-tune their current initiatives. Third, all parties should work to strengthen partnerships for delivering services. And fourth, all should focus on defining the relevant needs of employers and employees and tailor the design of services to those needs. No one of these elements has priority over the others. All four must be pursued simultaneously if the nation is to close the job-skills gap.

A Top-Management Priority. New-wave theories of management notwithstanding, most major U.S. corporations are still managed from the top. Major priorities are set by CEOs or those near to them. Unfortunately, as the Omega Group (1989) concluded in its recent survey of twenty-eight CEOs in the Philadelphia area, "While these executives agree that literacy exists as a serious problem in society, there is little awareness of the magnitude of the problem within their own organizations." On the other hand, surveys by ASTD and other groups show that corporate human resources directors are well aware of the bottom-line implications of the skills gap for their own firms (Carnevale and Gainer, 1989). A reasonable inference from this and other information is that there is a failure of corporate communication on this issue. Or there may be a difference of opinion between those CEOs who are primarily concerned with short-term profits and their human resource directors, who are more inclined to promote a long-term strategy of investing in workforce skills.

Whom do CEOs listen to about issues such as this? In part, they listen to other CEOs. Measured against any historical standard, it is remarkable how successful business leadership organizations have been in promoting the general cause of corporate investment in education over the last few years. Research sponsored and positions adopted by such groups as the Conference Board, the Committee on Economic Development, the Business Roundtable, the National Association of Manufacturers, the United States Chamber of Commerce, and others have led to an enormous increase in corporate commitments of time and dollars to elementary and secondary education.

None of these groups, however, has put workforce literacy high on its priority list, and rationales for failing to do so will not hold up much longer. Business leadership groups should explain the economic stake employers have in closing the skills gap and propose steps CEOs can take in terms that are relevant and credible to them. And as these organizations often do with other positions they promote, they should seek and obtain commitments from CEOs to place workforce literacy high on their priority list. If past experience is any guide, these modest steps stand a good chance of influencing employer priorities.

Corporate leaders also listen to other sources of influence in American society. The public awareness campaigns and media coverage touting the literacy story in general terms over the last few years have rarely focused on workforce literacy, and they should. Many newspapers, for example, sponsor community literacy programs (see American Newspaper Publishers, 1989). They could easily focus on workforce literacy as well, while at the same time addressing the needs of their own employees.

Employers often work with state and local government officials in developing strategies for economic development. As Chapter 9 points out, many states and at least some cities have made literacy a priority and command resources that could be used to seed corporate efforts. Public officials should raise the workforce literacy issue in the context of economic development negotiations and seek commitments from CEOs to work with the public sector in developing more substantial programs.

Finally, CEOs listen to their competition. They are encouraged by success stories, and they are reluctant to lag behind the accomplishments of their competitors. Until there are more success stories, human resources directors, public officials, and other concerned parties will have a hard time convincing CEOs to consider making a major commitment to workforce literacy instruction. Here government has an especially important role to play.

Government Leadership. Special intervention by government to spur the pace of change is both required and appropriate. In fact, the priorities of the federal government need only fine-tuning to embrace the workforce literacy issue; the precedent is there. First, the size and number of the workforce literacy demonstrations mentioned earlier should be increased, so that the experiments can yield evidence sufficient to motivate an employer response. Instead of merely refining instructional techniques or piloting small-scale projects, as the current efforts do, the federal government should subsidize the creation of large-scale success stories, with grants to encourage entire firms, groups of small businesses, or industry sectors (such as health care or banking in a particular region) to develop comprehensive workforce literacy programs.

To be effective on this scale, the grants should offer support for at least three to five years. And to produce results that are replicable outside the immediate context, the projects should be carefully designed to measure both inputs (the instructional approaches and costs incurred) and outputs (learner gains and bottom-line benefits in improved productivity). Participating employers should be required to put up earnest money, but the government should recognize the potential of large-scale demonstrations for the public interest and not skimp on funding levels. A proposal to devote $100 million to demonstations of this sort (H.R. 3132) was placed before Congress in 1989. This modest investment is well within federal means, and it is probably the most compelling way the federal government can signal to employers that workforce literacy is a national priority and encourage them to develop more robust programs of their own.

A second fairly simple measure the federal government should take is to extend the eligibility for literacy services offered under existing second-chance programs, such as the Family Support Act (FSA) and Job Training Partnership Act (JTPA), beyond the period during which participants in those programs are unemployed. As Chapters 1 and 10 explain, a number of federal human service programs now mandate that their participants receive literacy instruction to enhance their employability. But because employment is the major goal of those programs, most participants do not, and probably should not, spend much time in the programs — certainly not enough time to make much difference in their literacy skills. Once they become employed, federal support for their education ends.

This is a missed opportunity both for the learners involved and for federal policy. By definition, most people enrolled in second-chance programs face serious barriers to employment. When they become employed, most will be new entrants in low-level jobs — precisely the types of jobs for which employers are least likely to provide training (Vaughan and Berryman, 1989). Yet both public policy and the rhetoric of employers acknowledge that the future labor market success of these program participants will depend in large part on their workforce literacy skills. Because the federal government has started them down the road to improving those skills, it should capitalize on its investment by extending eligibility for educational services for at least two years after the participants have found a job. This rule change is entirely compatible with other provisions of human service programs, such as the FSA provision that extends child care subsidies for one year after participants accept employment and provisions in Title III of JTPA that serve employees at risk of losing their jobs.

One other step the federal government should take is to lead by example. The federal government is a large and diversified employer; its one million civilian employees perform almost every type of job that can be found in the economy at large. Like other employers, the federal government spends large sums on training, about $600 million in 1989 (pers. comm., Office of Personnel Management, 1989). But it has no basic skills program at all for its civilian workforce. The federal government could greatly enhance the state of the literacy field—and encourage interest in the private sector—by becoming a model sponsor of workforce literacy. The Office of Personnel Management should be directed to set aside some portion of its existing training budget for just this purpose and set standards that subsume the four rules for workforce literacy programs outlined earlier.

State and local governments can and should develop means of their own to promote the creation of success stories, extend service to marginal workers, and make government a model employer. As detailed in Chapter 9, some have already begun to do so. States seeking to attract business investment have been among the leaders, realizing that a leading consideration in corporate decisions about where to locate operations is the skill level of the local workforce. Governors have sought to lure companies to their states by promising to devote funds from the 8 percent educational set-aside under JTPA, as well as state resources, for joint ventures with business. This form of state entrepreneurialism is different from traditional "smokestack chasing" through the use of tax and zoning concessions. Under the latter strategy the national economy as a whole achieves no net gain. But when literacy instruction is part of the economic development strategy, the skills and productivity of the national workforce will increase. This win-win strategy implicitly realizes the large economic stake that both industry and the nation at large have in closing the job-skills gap. It could be abused (for example, if a state used all of its resources to subsidize training in one firm), but when applied responsibly it is a form of state priority setting that should be expanded.

Partnerships. Among the diverse workforce literacy initiatives now in progress, a common thread stands out: the idea of partnership between the public and private sectors. Almost all the projects reported in the AAACE study and other sources are partnerships that join companies or unions, or both, with public educational institutions (such as local school systems, vocational centers, or community colleges) or with not-for-profit providers (such as volunteer or community-based organizations). The highly regarded program of Motorola, for example, was jointly developed and is jointly managed by the company and a local community college. Although, in theory, employers might develop strong in-house training capacities for workforce literacy, and some have begun to do so, this has not been the dominant pattern.

Partnerships also take other forms. The federal demonstration grants for workforce literacy are a form of federal-corporate partnership. Other examples are small-business collaboratives, such as the Consortium for Worker Education in New York City, which joins the unions representing employees in twenty-three small companies (Packer, 1988); and joint corporate-union efforts, such as the auto industry example mentioned earlier.

Partnerships make good sense as a key ingredient in fledgling initiatives. In a field that is only beginning to find its feet, everyone involved understandably wants to share the risk with someone else. Moreover, at present there is too little evidence to refute employers' claims that workforce literacy instruction is at least in part a public responsibility — a social good without large net benefits to them. Under these circumstances, the only realistic path to greatly expanding literacy service is to include some element of public subsidy, and partnership is the form of subsidy that appears to work best.

Finally, for the near term at least, partnership seems to be the only feasible way of dealing with the skills gaps facing small employers. Even under the most optimistic scenarios, it is hard to imagine that employers with fewer than 100 employees could develop the in-house expertise to operate a workforce literacy program. They are more likely to contract for service with an educational agency, union, or community-based organization. In these forms of partnerships, the nonbusiness partner serves to aggregate the demand of the various employers into units large enough to support a service delivery system.

If partnerships are key in workforce literacy efforts, how can they be encouraged? The measures aimed at encouraging employers to adopt workforce literacy as a priority discussed earlier will help stimulate their interest. Other measures are required to stimulate the interest of their potential partners.

Unions and community colleges have been the most active partners to date. Unions probably need no further incentives to continue enlarging their role, beyond greater recognition by business, government, and others of the contributions they have made and can make in the future. Community colleges, on the other hand, probably do need help to expand their literacy service.

In some cases the role of community colleges in the literacy field is restricted only by the vision of their leaders. Some are highly entrepreneurial and accustomed to designing services for employers in their region and then marketing those services vigorously. Others, however, are more wedded to traditional academic goals. Although both approaches have their merits, state and local educational authorities should review the mandates of community colleges to determine whether the economic goals of the region warrant writing a responsibility for developing workforce literacy programs into their charters. North Carolina recently completed a planning exercise of this sort, which could serve as a model for other states (Commission on the Future, 1989).

At the same time, state and local authorities should try to eliminate procedural barriers to community college initiatives in the literacy field. For example, some state education systems discourage contracting with employers by directing that any proceeds from the contracts revert to general state revenues. And in many states the provision of literacy services by community colleges or vocational centers is either not reimbursable by the usual state funding formulas for education or reimbursable only a rate lower than that applied to other educational services.

Local literacy programs supported by the Adult Education Act (AEA) and other public sources are also potential partners for employers, and some play this role. Most, however, are too small to develop a full range of workforce services of their own, and many of their administrators are unaccustomed to marketing their programs to business. One possible source of help is the state or local education department that administers AEA funding. It could extend technical assistance to individual programs and divide labor among them, so that one or a few programs in a particular locality would specialize in workforce literacy. Another source is the federal government, which should maximize its investment in these programs by making workforce literacy a significant component of the expanded federal research, training, and technical assistance efforts proposed elsewhere in this book.

In at least some localities, community-based organizations (CBOs) and volunteer groups may be viable partners for workforce literacy efforts. SER Jobs for Progress is one CBO that has actually specialized in this type of service, and others, such as Push Literacy Action Now in Washington, D.C., are moving into the field. To encourage more CBO administrators to entertain this possibility, public support in the form of funding, training, and technical assistance should be available to all who can make effective use of it.

Finally, business and civic groups can play an activist role in engineering partnerships. The United Way of America recently adopted literacy as a major priority, but most of its energies have been directed at supporting efforts that are not specifically targeted to the workforce. In individual communities, both the United Way and other local leadership groups, such as the Chamber of Commerce and the Ad Council, could do much more to publicize the need for, and successes of, partnerships between their members and local literacy providers.

These proposals for building partnerships are, again, modest, incremental extensions of arrangements already under way. If the pace and scope of the arrangements grow, the momentum of workforce literacy efforts will certainly do the same. At some point the issue of allocating costs between the public or not-for-profit partners and the business partners will doubtless have to be resolved. But in the current, beginning stages of workforce literacy efforts, wide-open experimentation should be the rule, and many different financial arrangements should be tried. Only after more operational evidence is available can ultimate questions of cost allocations be addressed in an informed way.

The Product. Most workforce literacy efforts today take one of two forms: either tailor-made or one-size-fits-all. The first is exemplified by the specialized curricula developed by community colleges and others for companies, such as Motorola, that have taken the leadership role in this field. These programs were developed through a long process of consultation to meet specific corporate needs, and they may not be applicable to other companies. It is hard to imagine that workforce literacy service can expand very fast if each company has to tailor-make a program for its own special purposes. And it is probably flatly impossible for small businesses to develop tailor-made products. As a result, the future of the workforce literacy curriculum is bleak unless we can move beyond this cottage industry approach.

The other — and more prevalent — pattern is exemplified by employers that either buy a prepackaged learning system and make it available to their employees or invite a public or private literacy program to offer generic basic skills instruction at the workplace. Generic service of this sort is obviously not focused on the special needs of the employer or the employees, and it may not meet those needs very well. Moreover, it fails to take advantage of the opportunities for contextual learning that the workplace setting offers.

Literacy providers, employers, and other concerned parties have not yet come up with better systems for providing workforce literacy than the tailor-made and generic approaches. This is largely because they have directed too little attention to what should be one of the threshold questions for workforce literacy: What exactly is it that employees and employers need and want when it comes to workforce literacy instruction?

One answer to this question is the job audit, a laborious process of assessing what reading, writing, math, and other skills each job classification (or in some cases, each job or even each employee) in a particular workplace requires and evaluating the skills of the present or potential job holders. The gap between the two assessments can then be used as the basis for deciding what curriculum to offer (U.S. Department of Labor and U.S. Department of Education, 1988).

Although job audits may be a step in the right direction, they have several serious shortcomings. To begin with, they can end up being simply a combination of tailor-made and generic services in disguise. Skill needs may be assessed in a "tailor-made" way, but instruction is often only whatever generic service the organization conducting the audit can easily supply. In addition, job audits are very expensive and time-consuming. Finally, as Sarmiento (1989) has pointed out, they may result in teaching no more than job-specific skills, rather than preparing employees with portable skills that will allow them to adapt to the changing workplace, advance in their careers, or participate more fully in the broader community.

Workforce literacy needs a middle-range approach: a means for developing curricula that are both *generic* enough to be applicable to a given cluster of workplaces (for economies of scale and cost-effectiveness) and *customized* enough to take advantage of contextual learning opportunities (for rapid learning and more immediate benefits to employees and employers). In fact, several middle-range approaches are on the drawing board. Arnold Packer (1988) has proposed categorizing the 1,200 job definitions in the *Dictionary of Occupational Titles* into ten broad occupational skill clusters, such as health and dependent care, construction and maintenance, and financial services. Packer believes that the range of workforce literacy skills required for each cluster can be defined, and assessment tools as well as contextual instructional materials can be developed for each one. If this proves to be possible and attractive to both employers and employees, it would result in a discrete number of workforce literacy curricula that could be easily and economically put in place.

A variation on Packer's idea is under development by a partnership of Simon & Schuster publishers and the American Banking Institute, the educational arm of the American Bankers Association ("Banking and Basic Skills," 1989). The aim is to develop an industrywide workforce literacy curriculum for entry-level employees, such as tellers and clerks. The textile and graphic arts industries are working on similar projects for their workers ("Corporate Literacy Action," 1989). If the learning systems eventually developed are more generic than task-specific instruction, and if they meet with acceptance by the members of the industry associations, they will be important steps toward the type of middle-range product that is required.

Another intriguing beginning is the interest on the part of both unions and the Department of Labor in determining whether contextual curricula for workforce literacy can be developed for apprenticeship programs and whether the apprenticeship model can be applied to more occupations than it now is. Learning theory supports the notion that learning by doing is a model that can usefully be generalized beyond the occupations that have traditionally employed the apprenticeship approach to job training, and that teaching basic skills in context can readily be adapted to that model (Resnick, 1987).

Finally, some proponents of workforce literacy advocate dividing the field by the types of skills that may be needed, rather than by the types of occupations or industries in which the skills will be employed (Carnevale, Gainer, and Meltzer, 1989). Realistically, a middle-range approach will probably have to be a combination of both.

In themselves, however, assessment tools and curricula will not guarantee skills gains. Sooner or later the issue of evaluation will arise. How can employers quickly determine whether employees in workforce literacy programs have acquired the skills they need to function well at the workplace and in their particular job? How can employees chart their own progress? Credentialling is the usual answer to these questions in our society and economy. As of now, the only widely accepted credentials aside from the high school diploma and higher education degrees are the General Educational Development (GED) certificate and its equivalents and the licenses granted by apprenticeship programs and the professions. In their present form, however, none of these credentials necessarily captures the workforce literacy skills of concern to employer and employee.

For middle-range workforce literacy products to garner wide acceptance, some form of certification that accurately reflects achievement of workforce skills will have to be developed. Leaders of the educational testing field, such as the Educational Testing Service and the GED Testing Service, are beginning to explore this possibility. Industry associations and unions, in combination with recognized educational testing agencies, may prove to be the most appropriate certifying bodies. Addressing this issue should be high on the leadership agenda of these and other organizations, because it is crucial to system accountability. The sooner they act the better, though, because the issue will be highly contested and will take some time to resolve. Prominent in the debates should be the concern to ensure that credentials are used for inclusion rather than exclusion.

Red Herrings. Any incremental strategy causes a certain level of frustration: Some of those carrying out the strategy will inevitably be tempted to grope for a quicker fix. But workforce literacy efforts are so critical to national economic health that all concerned parties should beware of red herrings that could divert attention from the efforts themselves. The largest red herring afflicting the workforce literacy field today is the idea that employers can narrow the skills gap by concentrating their energies on school reform alone. But an equally seductive red herring is the idea of a job-training tax credit.

The Labor Department's Commission on Workforce Quality and Labor Market Efficiency (1989) has proposed such a credit for the federal income tax code, claiming that it would serve as an incentive for employers to embrace a longer term perspective on their human resources and invest more in basic skills as well as other forms of training. The report draws an analogy to the research and development credit now in the tax code, which allegedly has encouraged companies to make more long-range, high-risk investments in R&D than they otherwise would have made.

On the surface, this is an appealing proposal. It is simple, requires minimal intervention by government, and appears to marshal market forces for long-range social and economic goals. But under more careful scrutiny the tax credit appears not only damaging and unnecessary but also unlikely to have the desired effect. A training tax credit is certainly bad policy at a time when the nation is struggling to overcome a massive federal budget deficit. If widely used, the credit could set back deficit reduction efforts by many billions of dollars; if not widely used, it would not accomplish much. In any event, like other tax credits, it would be an unpredictable drain on federal revenues of the sort that the 1986 Tax Reform Act attempted to minimize and that Congress is unlikely to welcome.

At the same time, the credit is probably unnecessary because the tax code already subsidizes training expenses by allowing employers to deduct them fully in the year in which they are incurred, instead of requiring that they be amortized over the period during which their benefits are realized, as most investments are. Moreover, as Vaughan and Berryman (1989) point out, there is no evidence that employers underinvest in most forms of training, although there is evidence that they underinvest in basic skills. Since employers are least likely to train workers with low skill levels, a general training credit would likely result in either no increase in training at all or an artificial increase in training for higher level employees.

Finally, and most important, there is no indication that cost per se is the primary barrier to corporate investment in workforce literacy instruction. The sources of inertia discussed earlier, a shortage of strong partners to deliver the instruction, the lack of success stories, and an inadequate definition of the product are much more serious barriers. Thus, even if a training tax credit were targeted entirely to workforce literacy skills, there is next to no evidence to suggest that it would work.

Nonetheless, our understanding of workforce literacy is so limited that tax credits should not be ruled entirely out of bounds. The State of Mississippi adopted a limited literacy tax credit in 1989, and this form of state experimentation is a good way to evaluate the tax credit idea, as well as to learn more about other aspects of establishing workforce literacy service. We simply do not know enough to render a final judgment, and the issue of tax credits is far too important to wholly reject. As with many other aspects of the larger adult literacy problem, the greatest need is to learn more.

Near-Term Recommendations

Eliminating the job-skills gap must be one of our nation's primary economic and social goals. Carrying out the incremental strategy proposed here will require that all the parties involved give the problem higher priority, accelerate their efforts, and take the logical next steps beyond their current endeavors.

The most crucial first step is for government and business leaders, employer associations, unions, and civic groups to raise a forceful and informed call to action. The message should be that school reform, second-chance programs, and basic skills instruction alone will not solve the problem. The solution must include adult, working Americans and instruction in the work-force skills needed for the jobs of today and tomorrow.

The federal government should move quickly to promote success stories though large-scale demonstrations and to model workforce literacy programs for civilian government employees. It should make these investments in the larger context of its other efforts to strengthen the literacy field as a whole. Extended eligibility for the second-chance programs is another step that should be taken without delay. And meanwhile, more states and localities must make workforce literacy an integral part of both their education and economic development agendas.

It is on the shoulders of employers, employees, and their unions, however, that workforce literacy will be carried. As consumers, these parties set the demand for the educational product, and they are the ones that must be satisfied by the goals, means, and ends of the instruction. Employers must be willing to commit resources to lifelong learning for their employees and be prepared to invest in the purchase or development of contextual, portable skills learning systems that can meet the long-term needs for better basic skills in the workforce that they and their employees share. And they must give employees the released time they need to take advantage of the instruction. At the same time employers and unions must keep a sharp eye out for potential partnerships with both public and private providers, so that the development of workforce literacy products can proceed efficiently and cost-effectively.

Much of the burden of meeting employers' and employees' needs rests with the public literacy providers and private vendors of instructional materials. Both groups should devote more energy to realizing the opportunity and promise posed by workforce literacy and to defining, developing, and marketing vigorously services to reach the neglected half of the adult literacy population.

Acknowledgment

We wish to express our gratitude to Arnold H. Packer, who guided us toward many of the ideas and much of the information in this chapter.

References

Adler, P. S. "New Technology Is New Skills." *California Management Review,* 1986, *29* (2), 9–28.

American Newspaper Publishers Association Foundation. *Showcase of Newspaper Adult Literacy Projects.* Washington, D.C.: American Newspaper Publishers Association Foundation, 1989.

"Banking and Basic Skills." *Adult Literacy* (Business Council for Effective Literacy newsletter), October 1989, *21,* 1, 4–6.

Berger, J. "Companies Step In Where Schools Fail." *New York Times,* September 26, 1989.

Brizius, J. A., and Foster, S. E. *Enhancing Adult Literacy: A Policy Guide.* Washington, D.C.: Council of State Policy and Planning Agencies, 1987.

Business Week. "Human Capital: The Decline of America's Work Force," special issue, September 19, 1988.

Carnevale, A. P., and Gainer, L. J. *The Learning Enterprise.* Alexandria, Va.: American Society for Training and Development, 1989.

Carnevale, A. P., Gainer, L. J., and Meltzer, A. S. *Workplace Basics: The Skills Employers Want.* Alexandria, Va.: American Society for Training and Development, 1989.

Commission on the Future of the North Carolina Community College System. *Gaining the Competitive Edge: The Challenge to North Carolina's Community Colleges.* Research Triangle Park, N.C.: MDC, Inc., 1989.

Commission on Workforce Quality and Labor Market Efficiency. *Investing in People: A Strategy to Address America's Workforce Crisis.* Washington, D.C.: U.S. Government Printing Office, 1989.

"Corporate Literacy Action." *Adult Literacy* (Business Council for Effective Literacy newsletter), October 1989, *21,* 9–12.

Dertouzos, M. L., Lester, R. K., and Solow, R. M. *Made in America: Regaining the Productive Edge.* Cambridge, Mass.: MIT Press, 1989.

Finney, M. I. "The ASPA Labor Shortage Survey." *ASPA Personnel Administrator,* February 1989, *3,* 6–12.

Fiske, E. B. "Impending U.S. Jobs 'Disaster': Work Force Unqualified to Work." *New York Times,* September 25, 1989.

Hirschorn, L. *Beyond Mechanization.* Cambridge, Mass.: MIT Press, 1989.

Hunter, C. St. J., and Harman, D. *Adult Literacy in the United States.* New York: McGraw-Hill, 1985.

Johnston, W. B., and Packer, A. H. *Workforce 2000: Work and Workers for the Twenty-first Century.* Indianapolis, Ind.: Hudson Institute, 1987.

Mark, J. L. (Ed.) *Let ABE Do It: Basic Education in the Workplace.* Washington, D.C.: American Association for Adult and Continuing Education, 1987.

Omega Group, Inc. "Literacy in the Workplace: The Executive Perspective," monograph. Bryn Mawr, Pa.: Omega Group, Inc., 1989.

Packer, A. H. "Retooling the American Workforce: The Role of Technology in Improving Adult Literacy in the 1990's," discussion paper. Washington, D.C.: Southport Institute, 1988.

Resnick, L. "Learning In School and Out." *Educational Researcher,* December 1987, *16,* 13–20.

Sarmiento, T. "Involve Workers before Investing in Them: A Case Against Literacy Audits." *WorkAmerica,* September-October 1989.

Sticht, T. G. *Functional Context Education: Workshop Resources Notebook.* San Diego, Calif.: Applied Behavioral and Cognitive Sciences, Inc., 1987.

Sticht, T. G., Caylor, J. S., Kern, R. P., and Fox, L. C. *HumRRo's Literacy Research for the U.S. Army: Progress and Prospects.* Alexandria, Va.: HumRRo, 1973.

U.S. Department of Labor and U.S. Department of Education. *The Bottom Line: Basic Skills in the Workplace.* Washington, D.C.: U.S. Government Printing Office, 1988.

U.S. Department of Labor, U.S. Department of Education, and U.S. Department of Commerce. *Building a Quality Workforce.* Washington, D.C.: U.S. Government Printing Office, 1988.

Vaughan, R. J., and Berryman, S. E. *Employer-Sponsored Training: Current Status, Future Possibilities.* New York: Institute for Education and the Economy, Teachers College, Columbia University, 1989.

8

William B. Bliss

Meeting the Demand for ESL Instruction: A Response to Demographics

On the evening of May 5, 1988, fire swept through four floors of the First Interstate Bank tower in Los Angeles. Inside were forty or more janitors cleaning offices. Many of them spoke little or no English, and many could not shout warnings or instructions to one another because they spoke different languages. One, a Mexican immigrant, could not understand the spoken fire alarm and wound up running toward the fire rather than away. Fortunately, firefighters found him, administered oxygen, and carried him to safety. There was one fatality, but given the density of the smoke and the confusion of communications, it is a miracle that more lives were not lost.

It is a tragic, real-life parable, played out in this nation's modern-day Ellis Island, the metropolis of Los Angeles. A workforce providing essential office-cleaning services that would seem not to require any measure of language ability was imperiled as much by limited proficiency in English as it was by flames and smoke.

Limited English proficiency is usually defined as a limited ability to listen, speak, read, and write in English. It is further defined as a limited ability to meet basic survival needs and satisfy routine social demands using the language. Today the population of adults with limited English proficiency is playing an increasingly important role in the economic, social, and political life of the United States because of compelling demo-

171

graphic trends. But many members of that population are hampered in carrying out that role because of the particular difficulties nonnative speakers face and the inadequate national response to their problems.

Indeed, as a nation we lack a firm resolve—and a clear public policy—to provide all adults with limited English proficiency the opportunity to learn the language. Confusing contradictions abound. At a time when population trends translate into severe labor shortages, immigration reform has removed a few million undocumented workers from the labor force. And at a time when rising nativist sentiment accuses immigrants of not wanting to learn English and enter the mainstream of American life, waiting lists grow longer for English classes that are overenrolled and underfunded.

The alarm is now being heard, and it is sounding the loudest from business and industry, as the private sector faces a shrinking labor pool and must adjust to a burgeoning minority labor force. But like the janitor in the office tower, we stand confused about what the alarm is saying, and in what direction we should run.

What the Alarm Is Saying

The field of English as a Second Language (ESL) instruction stands in obvious contrast to the adult basic education (ABE) field in the needs and demographics of its students. (*ABE* refers to basic skills instruction that is not usually directed toward students with limited English.) But ESL differs from adult basic education in less obvious ways as well—most importantly in the problems it faces. Unlike the situation described in the previous chapters of this book, many ESL educators have reached a relatively well-developed understanding of, and agreement on, what works and what does not in teaching their subject. Largely through an infusion of support for instructional programs from the U.S. Departments of State and Health and Human Services, the ESL field has benefited from extensive research, curriculum innovation, and methodological advances (in assessment, teaching, and performance standards) since the tremendous inflow of Southeast Asian refugees began in 1975.

Thus, although the ESL field needs improvement in some of the same areas as those identified in the previous chapters — such as more and better research, more full-time teachers, and more training of teachers — basic issues of pedagogy are *not* its most salient problems. In simplest terms the alarm being sounded in ESL is one of supply and demand. Leaders in the public and private sectors looking for ways to ensure sufficient numbers of workers cannot ignore the population of nonnative speakers, but they must understand both sides of the problem. On the demand side, the population needing ESL instruction is large, diverse, and growing each year. Its members have some common needs and some special ones — both of which professionals in the field (but not policymakers) have clearly defined. On the supply side, not only are the public funds available for ESL instruction inadequate, but also they flow through a variety of federal departments with different goals and objectives that do not necessarily line up with the diversity of needs among nonnative speakers.

A Compelling Portrait of the Demand. Various census bureau reports estimate that between 4 million and 6.5 million residents in the United States do not speak English well or do not speak the language at all. These numbers, however, underestimate the total potential demand for ESL instruction because they do not account for the continuing flow of newcomers into the country and they underreport the number of undocumented aliens.

The 1980s are likely to set a record as the decade with the greatest number of immigrants to the United States, exceeding the total of 8.7 million who arrived in the first decade of this century. In recent years up to 1 million newcomers have arrived annually. These include refugees and undocumented entrants, as well as immigrants. The immigrants have come mainly from Asia, Mexico, Central and South America, and the Caribbean; the refugees, mainly from Southeast Asia and Eastern Europe; and the undocumented entrants, from Mexico and Central and South America. Once the amnesty provisions of the Immigration Reform and Control Act of 1986 are fully implemented, an estimated 2.5 million undocumented residents who had entered by the cutoff date of 1982 will have applied for permanent resident status; they will then be able to call for the immigration of their relatives to reunify their families on U.S. soil.

Beyond immigration, the numbers of these nationalities are growing because of their preference for large families. Combining these two factors leads to a compelling portrait of the demographic change under way in this country. In 1980, 7.9 percent of the U.S. population was of Hispanic or Asian origins; by the year 2000, it will be 12.3 percent; and by the year 2030, 18.1 percent (Bouvier, 1986).

The growing language-minority populations are providing a youthful infusion into a U.S. population that is otherwise aging rapidly because of the dropping fertility rates of the past two decades. A major study conducted by the Hudson Institute for the U.S. Department of Labor dramatically portrays the impact of these population trends on the nation's economy. In 1986, 21 percent of the 115 million jobs in the labor force were held by minorities, including black Americans. Between the years 1986 and 2000, fully 57 percent of the 21 million new jobs that will be created will go to this segment of the population, which is growing most significantly through increases in the nation's Hispanic and Asian populations (Johnston and Packer, 1987).

By the turn of the century, nonnative speakers will make up more than 10 percent of the U.S. labor force, and 25 percent or more of those workers are likely to require instruction to improve their English. We will depend on those workers not only to fill job openings and keep the economy going but also to help bear the burden of supporting a social security system and other assistance for the baby boomers in their retirement years.

Most immigrants arrive in their twenties or thirties, a perfect age to jump right into the labor force and take the jobs that are going begging. But new immigrants are only one segment of the language-minority labor pool. The other segment consists of children who have been raised here, schooled here, and perhaps were even born here, but who have somehow still emerged from our public school systems as young adults with limited English proficiency. The language barriers of the *new* immigrants thus are not the only cause for alarm; another is the lack of proficiency among those who have reached adulthood *here,* just as though they themselves were only recent arrivals.

While the economy will require nonnative speakers to overcome labor shortages, it will also demand ever-increasing levels of communication and critical thinking skills, as the service sector continues to outpace the manufacturing sector and as the workplace becomes more sophisticated through innovations in technology and management. As noted in Chapter 7, jobs in general are now requiring higher levels of language proficiency, the performance of more complex tasks, and more extensive communication with co-workers and supervisors, customers and suppliers, than they did in the past. If we are to depend on nonnative speakers to fill a large percentage of those positions, we must see to it that both new immigrants and established residents can acquire the language skills they need to handle those job requirements.

A Dismal Picture of the Supply. Although the available data do not permit a summary estimate of the total numbers served in ESL programs or of the dollars spent, the waiting lists for ESL instruction in many parts of the country serve as testimony to a serious problem of supply that cannot keep up with the demand. Los Angeles has from 20,000 to 40,000 students on waiting lists for ESL at any given time. New York City has thousands on waiting lists that are not even complete, because the programs do not have the human or technical resources to maintain the lists. These statistics likely reveal only the tip of the iceberg, however, since the very existence of the lists discourages many from coming forward to apply. Because news of ESL course offerings travels mainly by word of mouth, so too does the news that courses are filled and it may be futile even to bother applying.

Just as there are insufficient classroom seats for ESL students, there are insufficient funds to offer instruction that is intensive enough to make a difference. The community of ESL teachers, as well as staff at the U.S. Departments of State and Health and Human Services, know with some certainty what it takes to achieve progress in language learning. As described in more detail below, the State Department's training program in overseas refugee centers provides 500 hours of intensive instruction to move students one full level higher in their English language ability. At their peak several years ago, the stateside refugee training programs were providing students with daily instruction for a year or longer to achieve a similar goal.

This degree of highly effective, intensive instruction is now available to only an extremely small segment of the nation's newcomers each year, namely, those who are accorded refugee status. This status is essentially a political designation based on foreign policy considerations. Émigrés escaping from certain countries under communist control are much more likely than others to receive refugee status. The reality, however, is that this distinction blurs once newcomers have arrived on U.S. soil and are sought after by business and industry, whose concern is simply whether or not the new arrival has the requisite language and job skills to be able to fill a position in the workforce. In a sense, then, the tying of instructional services to these political classifications hurts the economy and the nation as much as, if not more than, it harms the new arrival.

A Question of Diverse Needs. Beyond the number of ESL openings and the intensity of instruction lies a more complex question of supply: Does ESL instruction meet the needs of the language-minority population? As noted earlier, nonnative speakers have many needs in common—namely, acquiring proficiency in speaking, comprehending, reading, and writing the English language and in workplace communication. Because ESL pedagogy prescribes the same methods and approaches for the effective instruction of all students, teachers can meet these common needs even in a classroom filled with persons of diverse language backgrounds.

ESL programs face a serious problem, however, in addressing the social, psychological, and survival needs of nonnative speakers. Moreover, nonnative speakers exhibit wide diversity in these other needs — a diversity that cuts across simplistic classifications of the population by countries or languages of origin.

One important distinction is between long-time residents and immigrants. Most new arrivals to this country face myriad issues of practical survival: obtaining housing, food, and clothing; figuring out how to make use of the transportation system, the bank, the supermarket; and enrolling their children in school, among other things. Another distinction is between legally sanctioned immigrants and undocumented entrants. For the latter the greatest challenge is their illegal status, which prevents them from gaining access to essential services, to the protection of the law, and increasingly, under immigration reform, to regular employment. Social service agencies are reporting dramatic increases in requests for food and shelter by those newcomers who have lost their jobs because of the new immigration policies.

A third group with special needs is refugees. Psychological distress is particularly acute among these newcomers. Many fled open hostilities in their towns or villages; many have suffered — in some cases, witnessed — the loss of family members and friends, whether at the hands of the Khmer Rouge in Cambodia or the death squads in El Salvador. For many their escape was marked by extortion, beatings, or rape. And many of these same refugees, and others, arrive here bereft of the support of family, community, and their own culture's practices for dealing with stress; and they may be unfamiliar with, or suspicious of, Euro-American forms of counseling.

A fourth and crucial distinction is between those nonnative speakers who are literate in their own native language and those who are not. For the latter the challenge is not only to learn to speak the new language but also to make the connection between sounds and meaning and printed matter for the very first time. And a last distinction is between those newcomers and residents raised in an urban, industrialized region and those from rural, agricultural villages. The latter, often refugees or undocumented aliens, may have greater difficulty than other immigrants in understanding American mores and expectations, especially in the workplace.

For almost any new immigrant the immediate need is to sustain self and family through employment. Although employers often praise the industriousness and motivation of their language-minority employees, they are often perplexed when these same employees fail to call in sick, resist supervision by a woman or younger person, or ask probing questions about one's salary or the price of one's car or house. In a survey of employers of Southeast Asian refugees, for example, the commonest problem the respondents reported was the refugees' inability to understand instructions and procedures, which would often lead to costly mistakes or injuries — obviously a communication problem. But another common problem was an inability or unwillingness among some refugees to discuss and resolve sensitive issues, such as their dissatisfaction with the salary or a personality conflict. In these cases the employee reportedly would rather resign than confront the issue. Many employers also stated that the refugees seemed uncommunicative, unfriendly, and standoffish, unable or unwilling to engage in small talk (Latkiewicz and Anderson, 1984). These kinds of problems may be traced to particular cultural differences, but they may also be part and parcel of post-trauma stress, among refugees, or of unfamiliarity with urban, industrial work settings, among immigrants of rural origins.

The dismal picture of the supply of ESL instruction exacerbates the problems ESL programs face in meeting these diverse needs of nonnative speakers. If the programs are struggling to meet the demand for English instruction per se, and to offer the intensity of instruction required to impart language skills, they can hardly be expected to help meet these other, equally critical needs. The ESL teacher is often the immigrant's only or most trusted point of reference in the native population, yet most ESL teachers work only part-time, a few hours a week, often in makeshift classrooms. For that reason we can hardly expect that the teacher will have the resources or the contacts even to refer the student to another appropriate agency for help.

Leaders concerned to find the means to enable more members of the language-minority population to participate fully in American life therefore need to bear in mind three fundamental problems—two very simple, and one more complex. First, the demand for ESL instruction is large and growing. Second, the supply of instruction is woefully inadequate to meet that demand. And finally, although nonnative speakers share the same need to learn English, they differ in important ways that cut across nationalities and foreign language groupings. For example, it is assuredly important for policymakers and program planners to recognize that the U.S. population of Asian origin is not monolithic; it comprises Chinese, Taiwanese, Koreans, Cambodians, Laotians, Vietnamese, and several other nationalities. Likewise the rubric "Hispanic" stands for Spanish speakers from Mexico, Puerto Rico, Chile, Nicaragua, Cuba, and so on. But the distinctions among nationalities are probably not as important as the distinctions separating, for example, rural refugees from urban entrepreneurs. Before we examine an appropriate national response to the problems delineated here, however, it is also important to understand the basic outlines of ESL offerings today and the considerable progress that has been made to date.

Where the Alarm Is Ringing

The growing demand for ESL instruction has, indeed, already had some effect. In fact, it has resulted in a redirecting of federal funds away from ABE and General Educational Development (GED) programs toward ESL programs. In just the one year from fiscal year 1984–85 to FY 1985–86, ESL enrollments in programs funded under the Adult Education Act (AEA) jumped from 853,000 to 1,267,000—an increase of 49 percent. During that same year, enrollments in ABE programs decreased from 1,293,000 to 948,000, a drop of 27 percent. Over the preceding eight years (from 1977–78 to 1985–86), ESL enrollments showed a 219 percent increase, while ABE enrollments showed a mere 14 percent increase. As a result, by 1985–86 ESL represented almost 42 percent of all enrollments under Adult Education Act funding (U.S. Department of Education, 1987a).

Where are these many students being served? The majority of ESL instruction offered to adults in the United States takes place in adult education programs operated by local public school districts and community colleges. Many ESL programs supplement federal and state funds with county and local government funds. These programs usually emphasize general, "all purpose" English speaking, grammar, and vocabulary, with a smattering of "survival English" topics, such as shopping, health care, and banking.

Refugee-assistance programs — again, representing only a small percentage of ESL enrollments — offer a more comprehensive range of instructional and support services to those relatively few new arrivals who have official refugee status, such as most Southeast Asians and many Eastern Europeans. The Office of Refugee Resettlement of the U.S. Department of Health and Human Services funds these programs, which in fiscal year 1989–90 offered English language instruction to about 37,000 refugees (Staff of the Office of Refugee Resettlement, pers. comm., February 27, 1990). The instruction is offered by a variety of community service agencies, including church-affiliated social service agencies, other community agencies, and refugee self-help organizations known as mutual assistance associations. The Office of Refugee Resettlement requires that programs operating with its funds follow a competency-based ESL curriculum that is built upon performance objectives for tangible life skills. Some schools offer vocation-specific language training for particular jobs or clusters of similar jobs. In many institutions the array of extrainstructional support services includes job counseling, training, and placement assistance, and, in some, personal counseling, child care, and health and nutrition services.

Community-based organizations (CBOs), operating in diverse community settings with limited, patchwork funding, play a special role in reaching out to the hardest-to-reach students and providing them with language instruction and other services. A CBO's funding sources might include churches, the United Way, and foundation, corporate, and private donations. Most states do not provide AEA funding to these organizations. Since they are, by definition, organizations of, by, for, and within the communities to be served, CBOs often manage to enroll those students least likely to be served by the larger institutions outside the ethnic community. A fundamental strength of ESL programs operated by many CBOs is that the program managers view language education as only part of a larger matrix of social services the learner needs. Within the same institution the learner and members of his or her family may be able to benefit from job counseling, family counseling, health screening, treatment for substance abuse, and other services.

Vocational education programs are supported by funding that is separate from the adult education and refugee education programs, but the instruction is often delivered by those institutions already described, especially the local school systems and community colleges. Traditionally, adults with limited English proficiency are seldom eligible to enroll in these programs. Modest efforts, such as the national Bilingual Vocational Training projects, demonstrate the success of program models that combine job-specific ESL training with actual vocational training. These programs exist in few places, however; only ten or so are funded each year. The Job Training Partnership Act (JTPA) programs have, to date, not been a very effective venue for ESL instruction, since JTPA requirements for program performance have tended to prevent the enrollment of applicants with the lowest skill levels.

The U.S. Department of State, on the other hand, operates intensive English, cultural, and work-orientation programs for U.S.-bound Southeast Asian refugees at centers in Thailand and the Philippines. The department also offers short orientation programs for Eastern European refugees at sites in Austria, Italy, and Germany, and for refugees from countries in Southern Africa at a training site in Botswana. These programs are designed to take advantage of the time refugees spend in processing centers while their documentation is reviewed for their eventual admittance to the United States. The program for Southeast Asians is a particularly effective model of intensive instruction and also demonstrates the ability of the U.S. government to fund a program that works. Students participate in at least 500 hours of instruction over a twenty-week period. They learn English through a competency-based curriculum that emphasizes the survival skills they will need upon arrival here. They also receive a daily diet of cultural information about life in the United States, to prepare them for a more successful adjustment and to make their expectations of what they will find here as realistic as possible.

A third instructional component is designed to impart the communication skills students will need for successful employment.

Volunteer organizations represent another sector that has traditionally devoted significant attention and resources to providing ESL instruction. Laubach Literacy Action reports having served over 35,000 in ESL instruction during its 1987–1988 fiscal year, or roughly 35 percent of its total enrollment (P. Waite, Laubach Literacy Action, pers. comm., November 10, 1988). In its 1988–1989 fiscal year, Literacy Volunteers of America reportedly served about 11,000 nonnative speakers, or about 29 percent of its total enrollment (J. Crouch, Literacy Volunteer of America, pers. comm., February 27, 1990). An increasing number of volunteer programs at colleges offer ESL instruction; CBOs also frequently use volunteers, not only because of funding limitations but also to fulfill their mission of helping the mainstream population from which the volunteers are drawn become more attuned to the needs of the nonnative speakers served by the institution.

In business and industry in-house ESL instruction is no longer a rarity, but neither is it common. Course offerings range from basic English for entry-level employees to more advanced English for employees who are engaged in further job training or are in line for promotion. Here the instructors are usually teachers from the local school system or community college. In a few cases, such as at various hotel and manufacturing settings in Orlando, Florida, the classes are paid for with AEA funds and a teacher is assigned to teach the class at the work site. In other cases the company purchases the instructional services from a school or college or may privately contract with one or more teachers to deliver the instruction. In-house programs are usually offered an hour a day for two or more days per week. Labor unions are also emerging as new venues for ESL instruction, with programs now under way in New York and Houston, among other cities that have large numbers of nonnative speakers in the labor pool.

Some correctional institutions offer modest forms of ESL instruction, with funding from the AEA or with tutors from a local volunteer organization. The instruction is very limited, however, and it is common for the ESL students to be combined with the ABE students during class time. Programs for migrants could be, but in general are not, sites for ESL instruction.

Significantly, the first states to implement welfare reform — California, with its Greater Avenues for Independence (GAIN) program, and Massachusetts, with its Employment Training (ET) program — have started to reach larger numbers of nonnative speakers, with ESL as a specified instructional activity for registrants with limited English proficiency. The California program has an especially sophisticated design, including competency-based instructional plans to assure that the instruction will further the goal of helping welfare recipients gain jobs. These kinds of programs should become more widely available over the 1990s as the states fulfill their obligations to institute similar programs under the Family Support Act of 1988.

Answering the Alarm

ESL instruction should be a high priority for our nation, not only for economic reasons, to match nonnative speakers' need for good, stable employment to our rising labor demand, but also for social and humanitarian reasons. Newcomers to the United States are highly motivated to adjust to their new culture and economy — after all, they chose to come here. Although the federal government has promoted their entry through immigration policy, it has not yet resolved, through education policy and that same immigration policy, to provide the means by which all nonnative speakers can begin to participate fully in the nation's life.

The answer to the alarm therefore must begin with a coherent public policy toward newcomers once they are here and with greater funding to meet the ever-growing demand for ESL instruction. Only then will it be possible to address the more specific programmatic issues still facing our otherwise relatively well-developed ESL system.

Linking Federal Funds to the Size and Nature of the Demand. As a first step toward addressing the mismatch between the demand for and supply of ESL instruction, the federal government should separate the ESL program from the other AEA programs, namely, ABE and GED. What is needed is a new funding formula for ESL that allocates monies to the states based on the size of their population of adults with limited English proficiency. This new ESL program would continue to be based in the U.S. Department of Education, with funds flowing, as they do now, through state education departments. But the program should be designed along the lines of the more intensive services that have been delivered for more than a decade through refugee education programs, under the auspices of the State Department and the Department of Health and Human Services.

As noted earlier, the ESL profession knows what works, and what it takes to move an ESL student from point X to point Y on a continuum of language learning. Thus, in addition to funding more intensive and longer periods of instruction, federal support for ESL programs should specify firm requirements or guidelines regarding the appropriate curriculum emphasis at given levels of instruction, so that the funds go to performance-based courses emphasizing survival English, workplace communication, or, at higher levels, more academic English. And as the Family Support Act does for the welfare population, federal regulations should encourage ESL programs — perhaps through incentive grants — to integrate or coordinate their services with those of child care providers, CBOs, and job-training and placement agencies, such as JTPA agencies and state employment offices.

This more serious effort to provide basic survival English and workplace-oriented language instruction to nonnative speakers would require an average of 600 hours per student. Based on data from the Office of Refugee Resettlement, the likely cost of this instruction would be about $1,500 per student (Reder and others, 1984). This cost is close to the education allocation to each applicant for legalization under the immigration law's State Legalization Impact Assistance Grants, which requires a cap of $500 per year, or $2,000 total over the four years of the program, for any individual applicant.

By these estimates a national effort to provide intensive English language instruction to 1 million newcomers per year would require funding of $1.5 billion, or 7.5 times the 1988 authorization of $200 million for *all* federal adult education programs. Because a funding increase of this magnitude is unlikely, a more realistic proposal would be to expand our ESL capacity to meet at least one-third of the need.

Under this proposal ESL, as a program separated from ABE and GED, would need to be funded at a level of $200 million. Those other two progams should also be fully funded at their 1988 authorized level of $200 million. This total allocation of $400 million would be in line with the split — about fifty-fifty in recent years — between ESL and ABE-GED programming, while the separation between the programs would address the problem of ESL expansion's diverting limited resources from the ABE-GED effort.

In addition, over the fiscal years 1989–90 and 1990–91 an additional $300 million or more per year is likely to have been committed to ESL programming for applicants for legalization through the State Legalization Impact Assistance Grants, a billion-dollar-a-year program providing public health, public assistance, and education services. The nation's capacity to deliver ESL instruction to adults eligible under the provisions of the law thus may virtually be doubling over this two-year period. When this special legalization programming concludes in 1991, there should be a federal maintenance of effort to apply the nation's expanded ESL capacity to the continuing flow of newcomers who require English instruction as well as to those existing residents who remain limited in English proficiency. Beginning in 1991–92, therefore, Congress should begin appropriating funds for ESL totaling $500 million per year. Again, this funding would meet only one-third of the ESL demand, but it is an initial step in the right direction.

The English Literacy Grants Program under the AEA should also be funded at its full authorization level. This program serves as a critical supplement to the core ESL effort under the AEA through grants to states for English literacy programs, many of which serve significant numbers of ESL students. A key feature of this program is that at least half the funding goes to CBOs for instructional services. The law also provides needed funds for improvements in methodology and curricula.

Finally, it is imperative to ensure that other publicly financed instructional programs are open to ESL students. Bilingual vocational education programming should be expanded and vigorously funded; workforce literacy funding should be expanded and should target ESL populations; performance criteria in the JTPA system must be revised to allow entry by ESL students; and states must design their Job Opportunities and Basic Skills Training (JOBS) programs under the Family Support Act to encourage local outreach to nonnative speakers in the welfare population.

Reconciling Immigration Policy with Reality. International problems and U.S. immigration policy determine the size of the demand for ESL instruction. Immigration policy affects different groups of nonnative speakers differently. The landmark Immigration Reform and Control Act, for example, is a very generous program for those eligible to benefit from it — namely, those undocumented aliens who were in residence here prior to January 1, 1982. They have been granted temporary resident status and will have the opportunity to gain permanent resident status upon demonstrating that they have developed a knowledge of English and U.S. history and government or upon submitting a certificate from a school stating that they are studying toward this goal. As mentioned earlier, significant funding in the form of State Legalization Impact Assistance Grants is available for the provision of instruction to these students. Instructional programs have a way to go to deliver the required courses — which are in any case unlikely to lead to full English proficiency for all students — but they will likely do as well as they did in responding quickly and effectively to the initial waves of tens of thousands of Southeast Asian refugees over fifteen years ago.

While the energies of these programs are now focused on gearing up to instruct these beneficiaries of the immigration law, a more critical issue is beginning to emerge: What about the estimated 3 million or more residual aliens who are not eligible for amnesty? The law's architects and the staff of the Immigration and Naturalization Service (INS) had assumed that these individuals would be compelled to leave the country. The law, after all, for the first time provides for stiff penalties for employers who hire undocumented aliens. All indications are, however, that few are actually leaving, and according to many migration service organizations, the influx of new undocumented entrants may be back up to the usual levels after a temporary chilling effect following implementation of the law. The premise that the remaining undocumented aliens would pack up and go home was faulty on two scores: It failed to account for both the "push factor" of economic hardship or instability in the native country that drives people across our borders and the "pull factor" of a labor market in the United States that still desperately needs new workers.

This problem is particularly acute among Salvadorans, of whom an estimated 500,000 to 900,000 are undocumented residents of the United States (Arocha, 1988, p. A12). It is further estimated that up to 20 percent of the entire population of El Salvador resides either in the United States or in refugee camps in Honduras or El Salvador (Crittenden, 1988). Half of those who are here arrived after the 1982 cutoff date for amnesty eligibility. Many have lost their jobs but are making ends meet through day labor, domestic work, or the setting up of household repair or landscaping services, in some cases working with false documentation. A resurgence of sweatshops in the garment and restaurant industries indicates that many small businesses are taking advantage of the vulnerability of this labor force. For the ESL program or the individual instructor, the problem is hitting home as former students seek out the school or social agency for shelter, food, and medical assistance.

Ironically, the demographic trends cited earlier make a strong case for dramatic increases in immigration over the next ten to fifteen years. But what we have instead is a potentially dangerous mismatch between the nation's demographic, economic imperatives and its current immigration policy. One solution would be to reinstate the amnesty process and move the cutoff for eligibility from 1982 to 1986, the year amnesty was announced. This would serve to legalize a large number of the remaining undocumented residents in the country and make them immediately employable again. But such a solution does not address the larger problem: The United States has no broad, systematic immigration policy that seeks to match the flow of newcomers with the nation's labor demand. This should be an important task for both the executive branch and Congress over the 1990s.

Removing Barriers to Participation. Beyond the most obvious barrier to participation in ESL instruction — no room for more students in the classroom — inflexible scheduling is probably the next most serious one. Many ESL programs restrict their hours because classroom space is limited or instructors are available only at certain times, or both. In both cases this usually means classes take place at night, when many potential ESL students cannot attend. Those who work in the building maintenance, hotel, and food service industries, for example, are very likely to work an evening shift. And for many women, evening instruction is out of the question because of fears for personal safety, child care responsibilities, or the fact that the native culture frowns upon women being out in the evening without a spouse or escort.

Hand in hand with evening instruction is the lack of adequate transportation to classes. ESL training tends to be offered in schools or community colleges, not necessarily in the neighborhoods where nonnative speakers are concentrated. Buses may still run at 7 P.M. for the trip to school, but they may not at 10 P.M. for the return home.

Moreover, for many potential students a formal school building may be unfamiliar or even threatening. The undocumented students may fear that INS agents will be on school grounds. An ESL program director has recounted the evening she invited a local police officer to visit the classes to talk about burglary prevention. The police car was parked in the school's lot, and at the start of classes hardly any students were to be found in the building. They were all circling the perimeter of the school grounds. The program director sheepishly asked the officer to move his car a block or so around the corner, and by the time he returned, so had the students.

To overcome barriers to participation, ESL funding must promote a pluralistic system for delivering instruction. Although much of the funding can continue to flow to the traditional service providers—the local school districts and the community colleges—a good share should also go to CBOs, which, as noted earlier, have the most experience serving the hardest-to-reach and often do so in their immediate neighborhoods. One model for service delivery, in which traditional providers set up satellite classes in neighborhood centers, should indeed be employed, but it should not replace the direct granting of funds to CBOs to operate their own programs. The latter model offers the additional advantage of allowing the CBOs now serving the potential ESL population to expand their capacity and thereby extend their other support services, such as counseling and child care, to a larger part of their population.

Along with pluralism is a need for greater communication and coordination among local educational agencies, so that services are not duplicated but rather mutually enhanced. One possible model, worthy of federal seeding through demonstration programs, is a form of triage. One service provider, perhaps a CBO, would offer the lower levels of instruction right in the neighborhoods and along with the requisite support services. Another service provider, perhaps a school system or community college, would offer the upper level of ESL instruction and serve as the students' gateway to further educational opportunities, offered at a job-training center or in a college setting.

Finally, all institutions, especially the large, traditional ones, need to offer a much wider selection of course schedules so that all potential students who wish to enroll can do so.

Creating a Full-Time, Well-Trained Teaching Force. The average ESL teacher is a woman who works part-time an average of twice a week for a total of only three hours a week (U.S. Department of Education, 1987b). Many ESL teachers are moonlighting from their daytime jobs as public schoolteachers, often in the same building. Given their part-time status, ESL teachers seldom have the time or the incentive to upgrade their professional skills in this field. And turnover in these teaching positions is high. The most dedicated teachers who wish to devote a career to ESL instruction (and these are often the most competent as well) often have to piece together two, three, or more part-time jobs in order to earn a living. These teachers have no classroom they can call their own, let alone a place to put their books, visuals, and other teaching materials. When one offers you a ride, you can expect to be sitting atop a classroom set of textbooks and next to a box filled with empty grocery cans, boxes, and other *realia* that are the tools of the trade. They are modern-day wandering minstrels, and what they might lack in professional resources they will often try to compensate for with energy, enthusiasm, and compassion for their students.

Those who aspire to the few full-time positions available often find that they must move into administration and leave the classroom if they want the stability of a full-time salary and a job guarantee that goes past a given term's assignment. There are few opportunities anywhere to grow professionally and in terms of salary, without forsaking the classroom and the students.

In addition, there are large numbers of volunteers working within the ABE-ESL system itself. Too often they must jump right in and cover classes, without much opportunity to observe a seasoned teacher in action.

In the process of redesigning course schedules to provide instruction at various times of day, ESL programs can also create the context for developing full-time teaching positions. A full-time instructor receiving a salary and benefits might cover four or five hours of class time each day and devote the remaining work time to developing the curriculum, training volunteers or new instructors, or registering or assessing new students.

A new position should be created and built right into the funding formula for ESL: that of *lead teacher,* or supervising teacher. This full-time adult education professional would work with instructors on preparing lesson plans, developing instructional materials, training in methods and approaches, and observing classes. Ideally, there should be one lead teacher for every ten instructors. If a site has fewer than ten instructors, the lead teacher could serve at an additional site. In this manner an educational system that remains predicated on the use of part-time instructors would institutionalize the capacity to support those instructors and improve their performance as they work.

In particular, the part-time workforce in ESL has little or no background in teaching the subject; in fact, many part-timers have no previous teaching experience at all. Ironically, it is sometimes easier to train a nonteacher to work with adult ESL students than it is to "deprogram" an experienced K–12 teacher who has strong convictions about how to teach, for instance, junior high school language arts or third-grade reading. The problem in relying on inexperienced ESL teachers is that few programs offer extensive preservice training or in-service training, and if they do, the programs rarely have the funds to pay teachers to attend.

Existing teacher training programs in colleges and universities are heavily oriented toward teachers who will be working with foreign students in academic institutions in the United States and overseas. Coursework emphasizes linguistic theory and teaching techniques; indeed, attention to adult learning theory, adult development, learning styles, needs assessment, syllabus design, program supervision, training, and evaluation is virtually nonexistent.

Federal funding for ESL programming should allow for at least twenty-five hours of preservice training stipends for all new teachers and volunteers and up to ten hours of in-service training stipends annually for all other teachers on an ongoing basis. Training sessions should be planned along with and made available to other local institutions delivering ESL instructional services, especially CBOs, which tend to be out of the loop for this type of staff development activity. Additionally, programs should be required to accrue funds for tuition rebates for instructors who attend graduate-level courses in adult education topics related to their teaching responsibilities.

Investing in Research and Development. Existing research and development activities occur in scattershot fashion through the Section 310 funding mechanism of the AEA. There is little or no coordination among the activities within a state, and next to none among states. The results of the research conducted are not disseminated, and few studies are designed to be replicable. While our Soviet counterparts undertake solid basic and applied research in language learning through the centralized Academy of Pedagogical Sciences and leading language-instruction institutes in Moscow and Leningrad, we here trickle out dribs and drabs for little projects: a video here, a curriculum guide there.

A few exceptions to this rule are notable—but they did not come about through Department of Education funding. It is the overseas refugee training program of the Department of State that has done the seminal work on competency-based materials for adult ESL instruction and on workplace ESL curricula. And it is the Office of Refugee Resettlement at the Department of Health and Human Services that has overseen the specification of consistent levels of ESL student performance, as well as content standards for each of those levels. The specification spells out actual performance objectives for each of several levels of instruction and serves as a common yardstick by which English proficiency can be described and assessed and for which English classes and materials can be designed. This valuable work now sits on the shelf, the project over, implemented in the relatively small number of refugee training sites, and for the most part not adopted in the larger ESL service delivery system (U.S. Department of Health and Human Services, 1985). Only the competency-based project in California has built upon this work by successfully incorporating many of its features into the state's comprehensive assessment system.

As is true of the literacy field in general, and as described in Chapter 5, a vigorous federal role in ESL research and development would most appropriately be housed within a national center looking at all aspects of adult learning. Specific research and development activities should include the following:

- dissemination of consistent professional standards and descriptors for adult language competence, to replace the archaic elementary and secondary school grade-level designations
- development of descriptors of workplace communication ability and of quantifiable measures to assess this ability
- research on how such variables as motivation, circumstances of immigration, type of occupation, and intensity and dura-

tion of instruction affect rates of learning and language skills retention

- research on curricula appropriate to populations with particular needs and particular learning goals
- protocols for integrating ESL and literacy instruction, for students illiterate in both English and their native language
- research on the effectiveness of alternative approaches to instruction, such as phonics versus whole-word approaches to teaching English literacy
- development of a competency-based academic skills curriculum that emphasizes critical thinking skills and other higher order skills, while at the same time advancing communicative competence and other language skills

Fostering Better Attitudes Toward Immigrants. The rapid growth of the nation's language-minority populations in the 1980s and on into the 1990s has critical implications for the civic life of the nation. Immigrants and their children have chosen the monumental upheaval of uprooting themselves from a homeland, often leaving many family members behind, to build a new life for themselves in this country. Their motivation to identify with American ideals and participate in American civic life is often as high as their determination to succeed economically. But that motivation may be undermined if the newcomers are greeted with hostility and resentment.

At other times in U.S. history, especially during the largest waves of immigration, those who have established themselves as "natives" have voiced crescendos of anxiety that the very fabric of American culture and polity was in danger of being torn apart. The current manifestation of this nativist sentiment rails against bilingual education and other services that provide a measure of support to language-minority groups. This is not only an unfortunate way to treat these minority populations, but it also demonstrates a general lack of public appreciation for the crucial role these groups are playing in securing the current and future economic well-being of the country, as well as in revitalizing the nation's cultural diversity.

The administration and the Congress, states and local

leaders — all must establish a new tone of acceptance, appreciation, and welcome for these newcomers. Our leaders' rhetoric
must help us look at today's immigrants and see our parents,
grandparents, or whichever generation we have to thank for ven-
turing to this land to make a new life. Perhaps the establishment
of a national Immigration Day would promote an annual nationwide celebration of our ethnic richness. On this day all groups
would have an opportunity to rekindle the legacy of their origins
and their immigration, and communities might hold weekend
international festivals of music, arts, and food. The day might
also include a national event, comparable to the Kennedy Center
Honors, to recognize current immigrants' unique contributions
to science, the arts, public affairs, and other spheres. It might
be the occasion as well for an additional Fourth of July–style
naturalization event, in which historic sites within each community would be the scenes of special morning naturalization
ceremonies.

Near-Term Recommendations

Among the various proposals offered in this chapter, those
most crucial to accomplish as next steps in answering the alarm
of ESL demand versus supply are:

1. The federal ESL effort should be funded separately
from ABE and GED programs, through a formula based on
the size of each state's population with limited English proficiency. To meet only one-third of the existing demand, ESL
should be funded at a level of $200 million under the AEA.

2. When the special ESL programming for legalization
concludes, there should be a maintenance of this federal effort
in order to apply the nation's expanded ESL capacity to the continuing flow of newcomers. Total federal funding for ESL as
of fiscal year 1991–92 should be $500 million to maintain this
level of activity.

3. Immigration policy must be revised to increase the
population of legal immigrants necessary to stem our labor shortages. Moving the existing cutoff date for amnesty eligibility from
1982 to 1986 would legalize a significant number of the remain-

ing undocumented aliens in the country and make them available for regular employment.

4. Funding regulations should foster a pluralistic system for delivering ESL instruction nationwide, including not only local school districts and community colleges, but also CBOs and other smaller institutions.

5. Classes should be scheduled at a variety of times during the day and be offered in students' own neighborhoods.

6. ESL programs must develop more full-time teaching positions, as well as the new position of lead teacher, or supervising teacher, at a ratio of one lead teacher for every ten instructors. The lead teacher would train, support, supervise, and evaluate the instructional staff.

7. Federal funding should allow for a minimum of twenty-five hours of preservice training stipends and a minimum of ten hours of in-service training stipends annually. The training should be offered to all service providers in the area, especially CBOs.

8. A national center concerned with basic and applied research in adult learning should have a vigorous program of research and development in the ESL field.

9. National, state, and community leaders must set a tone of acceptance, appreciation, and welcome for the immigrant population. An annual holiday should be established to recognize the importance of immigration to the history and vitality of the nation.

10. A last recommendation, not mentioned earlier, is to reexamine fully our primary and secondary school offerings for language-minority youths—but that is the subject of another chapter, if not book.

Immigrants are here to stay, and immigration is likely to expand over the next decade at least. If the economic bottom line points to the inevitability of an increasingly diverse minority labor force, the civic and social bottom line requires that these minorities be accorded the full respect and opportunity for civic participation that they deserve. The sincerity and strength of our welcome to these newcomers in the months and years ahead will be a telling sign of this nation's confidence in itself and of its adherence to the fundamental values upon which it was founded.

Acknowledgments

The author wishes to thank the following for serving as professional advisors in the preparation of this chapter: Joe Castro, Church St. John Vianney Hispanic Ministries, Houston, Texas; Mary Carol Combs, National Immigration, Refugee and Citizenship Forum, Washington, D.C.; Jodi Crandall, Center for Applied Linguistics, Washington, D.C.; Patricia de Jesus, Palo Alto College, San Antonio, Texas; Jamie Draper, Joint National Committee for Languages, Washington, D.C.; Charles Kamasaki, National Council of La Raza, Washington, D.C.; Nick Kremer, El Camino Community College, Torrance, California; Jeanne Lopez-Valadez, Northwest Educational Cooperative, Des Plaines, Illinois; David Spener, Spanish Educational Development Center, Washington, D.C.; Pat Tirone, Riverside Adult Learning Center, New York, New York; Marielena A. Villamil, Miami-Dade Community College, Miami, Florida.

References

Arocha, Z. "Study Pegs Salvadorans in U.S. at 1 Million." *Washington Post,* Sept. 23, 1988, p. A12.

Bouvier, L. F. *New Immigrants/New Minorities.* Washington, D.C.: Trend Analysis Program, American Council of Life Insurance, 1986.

Crittenden, A. "El Salvador, U.S.A." *New York Times,* October 3, 1988.

Johnston, W. B., and Packer, A. H. *Workforce 2000: Work and Workers for the Twenty-first Century.* Indianapolis, Ind.: Hudson Institute, 1987.

Latkiewicz, J., and Anderson, C. "Industries' Reactions to the Indochinese as Employees." *Migration Today,* 1984, *11* (2/3), 14–20.

Reder, S., and others. *A Study of English Language Training for Refugees in the United States.* Washington, D.C.: Office of Refugee Resettlement, U.S. Department of Health and Human Services, 1984.

U.S. Department of Education, Office of Vocational and Adult Education. *National Data Update*. Washington, D.C.: Office of Vocational and Adult Education, U.S. Department of Education, 1987a.

U.S. Department of Education, Office of Vocational and Adult Education. *Teaching English to Adults with Limited English Proficiency*. Washington, D.C.: Office of Vocational and Adult Education, U.S. Department of Education, 1987b.

U.S. Department of Health and Human Services, Office of Refugee Resettlement. *Mainstream English Language Training (MELT) Project*. Washington, D.C.: Office of Refugee Resettlement, U.S. Department of Health and Human Services, 1985.

9

📖 Jack A. Brizius

What States Can Do About the Literacy Problem

Adult literacy is crucial to America's future because skilled people are needed in a competitive world economy. The goals, shape, and content of a new system for improving adult literacy in America will be developed and implemented by the states. There are several reasons why states should take the primary responsibility for enhancing adult literacy. First, states have traditionally been the builders of education systems in America. Second, states can develop targeted approaches that differ as needs differ. Third, states now manage many of the efforts to ameliorate social conditions that require literacy as a precondition for improvement. Fourth, state governments have substantial experience in working with employers — an important resource since much of the effort to improve literacy will have to be made in the workplace. Finally, states can create the institutional base and find the resources to build a new system of literacy improvement in America. Building a new system will entail strengthening the professional cadre of persons whose expertise is teaching basic skills. States set standards and promote professional education through state regulatory agencies and higher education institutions.

States now spend more than the federal government on basic skills instruction, and signs are that major new state initiatives will increase this amount. High federal deficits mean that federal resources will be constrained for the foreseeable future. Local governments are unable to contribute large amounts to deal with a problem that spills over local boundaries.

Thinking About the State Role

State governments have much to do in order to build a new system of literacy improvement. Here are only a few tasks that must be accomplished quickly:

- *Strategic planning.* Strategic planning and policy development must take place, and efforts at the state and local level must be coordinated for maximum effectiveness.
- *Motivation.* Millions of adults need to be motivated to invest considerable time and effort in upgrading their skills.
- *Program effectiveness.* Thousands of existing programs will have to be improved and made more effective in delivering literacy services.
- *Program expansion.* New types of literacy enhancement programs must be created, ones that are more effective and accountable.
- *Professionalism.* Literacy providers will have to be trained, and a professional cadre of adult basic skills educators will have to be expanded and strengthened.
- *Technology.* The current system of literacy provision will have to adopt new technologies and approaches to delivering services to widely divergent populations of adults who need basic skills.
- *Evaluation.* Programs will have to be evaluated and made more cost-effective. Performance measurement and performance-based funding of programs must be developed.
- *New resources.* Given the size and extent of the literacy problem, substantial new resources must be allocated to delivery systems for imparting basic skills. These resources will have to be targeted to certain groups of adults.

Literacy and State Policy: Where Are the States Today?

If states are to carry the burden of the national effort to improve the basic skills of adults, state officials will have to take dramatic steps to change the way adult education systems currently operate. Some states are well on their way to making fundamental changes in priorities and operating procedures for adult literacy. Others have far to go.

The interest of governors and legislators in adult literacy grew rapidly during the 1980s. By 1989, more than forty governors had created literacy programs or coalitions in some way connected with the governor's office. Many of these efforts have involved not only state officials but also representatives of businesses, volunteer organizations, school systems, and other institutions concerned with the issue of adult literacy. Most of these groups have combined advocacy, study of the current system, and outreach to adults.

In most states, literacy policy has focused on accomplishing other priorities: economic competitiveness, educational reform, alleviating labor shortages, correctional rehabilitation, or welfare reform, for example. A sampling of activities in a variety of states illustrates the diversity of approaches being taken by state policymakers in addressing the issue of literacy.

Arkansas. In Arkansas, Governor Bill Clinton's approach has been to focus on upgrading the skills of the state's large low-income population. To address the issue of basic skills, Governor Clinton appointed a blue-ribbon Commission on Adult Literacy. In August 1988 the commission reported to the governor, proposing the AAPLE plan, the Arkansas Action Plan for Literacy Enhancement (Arkansas Governor's Commission on Adult Literacy, 1988). The plan formulated the following goals:

- By 1992–93, increase from approximately 29,000 to 100,000 the number of adult learners enrolled in pursuing at least one higher functional level of literacy.
- Develop achievement objectives for those enrolled in literacy improvement programs and implement a tracking mechanism to measure achievement.
- Quadruple the involvement of the private sector through donations of money, human resources, facilities, and a significant increase in workforce literacy programs.
- Maximize the effectiveness of the public sector delivery and develop a strong coordination of public and private activities in the statewide literacy effort.

Within the context of these four goals, the commission proposed a specific set of target groups for special attention. The Arkansas policymakers are placing emphasis on a strategy of reducing welfare dependency through literacy. The number of public assistance recipients receiving literacy services is to increase tenfold, while the number of employed persons who receive literacy services is to double. An especially interesting target group for the AAPLE plan is adult offenders who are not sent to prison but are under correctional or court supervision. The plan envisions a nearly tenfold increase in services to this group of adults.

The Arkansas strategy involving public assistance recipients, recipients of unemployment insurance, and adults in the criminal justice system uses both negative and positive incentives. According to the recommendations of the commission, by July 1, 1989, all recipients of welfare and unemployment benefits and those subject to parole, probation, or alternative sentences were to have undergone a screening process to assess their levels of basic skills. By 1991, all recipients judged to be "at risk" of welfare dependency because of low skills would be required to enroll in a literacy training program. Support services, such as counseling, child care, and transportation, would be made available to those seeking additional skills.

The plan calls for a quadrupling of private sector resources through an annual statewide "Literacy Support Drive" as well as through continuing contributions from businesses, especially contributions for classroom space at the work site and time off for employees to seek literacy instruction. Noting that only 17 percent of Arkansas businesses responding to a survey indicated a willingness to allocate funds to literacy in the workplace, the plan calls for state incentives, possibly including tax incentives, for businesses to participate in literacy programs.

In response to the governor's commission report, Governor Clinton has moved to implement several aspects of the plan. The governor's fiscal year (FY) 1989–90 budget called for about $8 million in additional funds for adult education, targeted to welfare dependent populations and workforce literacy efforts. Other structural reforms include changes within the state department of education to upgrade the status of literacy efforts and a continuing advisory role for the commission.

Unfortunately, the failure of the governor's broader tax and fiscal reform package in 1989 meant that many of the reforms proposed by the commission and the governor had to be delayed. Some of the structural changes are being implemented, but major program expansions have had to be deferred because of the lack of resources.

California. California's adult basic skills programs are the most extensive in the nation. About 80 percent of the adult basic skills funds spent in California are devoted to English as a Second Language (ESL) programs, primarily because the recent influx of immigrants has overwhelmed the existing delivery system. California has also mandated that most welfare recipients seek additional basic skills instruction, and adult literacy services have been expanded for participants in the GAIN (Greater Avenues for Independence) program of welfare reform. Early results from the GAIN program show that for about 30 percent of welfare recipients, participation in mandatory basic skills programs has had a positive effect on skill levels (Riccio and others, 1989).

California's superintendent of public instruction has recently released a long-term plan to design a system of "Adult Education for the 21st Century." If this plan is implemented, California will increase funding for basic skills instruction, invest in new technology and share that technology with other programs, establish an extensive network of community-based information and referral centers for adult education, and improve access to adult basic skills instruction through the establishment of an "Educard" — a single credit card for adult education and job-training services. In addition, the plan envisions implementing performance standards throughout the adult education system in California, making the curriculum more contextual and extending the reach of the state's planning and coordination mechanisms to help develop a systematic approach to adult basic skills instruction. Released in June 1989, the report has gained a favorable reaction in the legislature. The department of education is working on implementing legislation and budgets.

Massachusetts. In Massachusetts, state efforts have taken advantage of the state's tight labor market to focus on upgrading the skills of the existing labor force and welfare recipients. Governor Michael Dukakis originally envisioned the creation of a Massachusetts Literacy Corps, a volunteer effort organized by the state to tutor adults in literacy skills. After a year of planning and implementation, the original idea blossomed into the Massachusetts Literacy Campaign (MLC), a multiyear effort to coordinate state programs to improve literacy as well as strengthen the voluntary effort.

MLC has prepared a plan for literacy enhancement that involves expanding several current programs to include literacy services as well as improving volunteer outreach activities and public awareness. A large student recruitment campaign through the media has begun. Working through the Massachusetts Jobs Council, a coordinating body established in 1988 by the legislature, MLC plans new literacy services to be offered in the workplace, through community groups, and through the adult education programs of the state. A special feature of the campaign is to work with mature industries through the Industrial Services Program, a state initiative to help industries that might otherwise not remain competitive and therefore might have to lay off workers. MLC has also worked with labor unions to support workforce literacy efforts. In addition to these activities on behalf of currently employed people, MLC has secured agreements with administrators of job-training programs to sponsor literacy instruction for welfare recipients as a prelude to entry into the state's welfare reform program.

Given its severe labor shortage and a state budget crisis, Massachusetts has chosen not to argue for large infusions of new resources for literacy enhancement, but rather to divert resources to literacy from existing programs for job training, welfare, education, and employment services. Since many of the people once served by job-training programs now have jobs, job-training funds have been liberated to provide services to people whose basic skills are so deficient that they cannot even be trained for work. Similarly, funds once used to serve dislocated workers now are being used to improve workers' literacy in order to prevent dislocation.

Severe budget constraints have slowed the implementation of MLC's plans, but where new funding is not required, the administration is putting a new system of literacy provision in place. After the current budget crisis subsides, Massachusetts should be in a good position to move forward on its plan.

Michigan. Michigan is second only to California in the amount of state funds allocated to improving adult literacy through adult education programs. In 1988 the state appropriated over $81 million to expand adult education programs (Chynoweth, 1989). This commitment resulted from a two-year gubernatorial effort spearheaded by the Michigan Adult Literacy Task Force. This task force grew out of recommendations in the Michigan Strategic Plan, a set of initiatives designed to revitalize the Michigan economy under the leadership of Governor James Blanchard. In the strategic economic plan, the state opted for an economic development strategy that emphasized the future of "smart manufacturing"—manufacturing enterprises that are smaller and more competitive and use higher technology than the traditional "Rust Belt" industries. A corollary to helping develop smart manufacturing was that workers had to be better trained to compete. Michigan's policymakers had examined their labor force and discovered that many current workers had progressed through tenth grade or so and had very basic skills, but that they needed extra help to be able to communicate more effectively, solve problems, and work in teams.

In his January 1988 "state of the state" message, Governor Blanchard unveiled his Countdown 2000 initiative, including eight major steps involving literacy. These included adopting a new definition of *workforce literacy* to encompass language skills, quantitative skills, problem-solving skills, attitudinal skills, and job-seeking or self-advancement skills. In addition, the governor announced his intentions to implement a "Michigan Opportunity Card," a credit card to help make literacy and job-training services available to more people in Michigan. As a result, the emphasis in Michigan is on workforce literacy efforts aimed at higher level skills. Additional funds were appropriated through the adult education system for literacy, and most of the money seems to be flowing to the community college system.

Minnesota. Minnesota Governor Rudy Perpich appointed a Task Force on Adult Literacy in 1984 to assess the state's literacy problem and make recommendations. The task force proposed a five-year campaign to increase the number of adults served by literacy programs and "ultimately to achieve the highest level of literacy in the nation." In 1985 the governor created the Minnesota Adult Reading Campaign, a coalition of literacy providers, advocates, and community leaders. In 1986 the missions of the campaign were revised and the organization was renamed the Minnesota Adult Literacy Campaign (MALC).

MALC prepared a "Five-Year Plan to Address Functional Illiteracy in Minnesota." The plan estimated that over 600,000 Minnesotans lacked adequate literacy skills and that only about 32,000 were receiving literacy services (MALC, 1988). The plan enunciated the following goals:

- Establish adult literacy as a priority in the state of Minnesota.
- Expand the capacity, quality, and effectiveness of literacy programs to provide educational services to adult learners.
- Develop opportunities for all segments of the Minnesota community to participate in the campaign and the literacy effort in the state.
- Increase funding for existing literacy programs.
- Improve the accessibility of literacy programs to potential participants.
- Develop a long-term strategy, including plans to reach 200,000 adult learners per year with literacy services by 1991.
- Encourage innovation in the delivery of adult literacy services through the present provider system and, as needed, through the development and funding of new programs.

Since 1986, MALC has worked not only with the provider community but also with program administrators and other state officials to increase the awareness of the literacy issue, recruit students, increase legislative appropriations for literacy services, and coordinate programs. In addition, the literacy campaign in Minnesota has designed a new workforce literacy initiative and has taken steps to help local literacy providers evaluate and assess the effectiveness of their programs.

MALC has operated general outreach programs in the media and a specialized learner recruitment program and has coordinated services in a variety of state and local agencies. Significantly, MALC has helped build a coalition of support for new resources for adult literacy provision. Legislative appropriations for adult basic skills instruction increased from $1.8 million in FY 1987 to $4.2 million in FY 1989. New state funding amounting to $200,000 was obtained to assist nonprofit organizations in providing literacy services, and other state funds were appropriated for a television-based general educational development (GED) preparation program.

Virginia. In the late 1980s Virginia Governor Gerald Baliles took a twofold approach to the development of adult literacy services. After two years of planning, his administration proposed the creation of a freestanding Office of Adult Literacy in state government to coordinate the expansion of literacy services. Under the plan, twelve local service districts have been created, coordinated by boards combining private sector interests and state agencies with responsibilities for literacy services. Together with the office of literacy, these services boards will coordinate the provision of expanded literacy services based on local needs and state priorities. A crucial part of Virginia's effort is the commitment of the state education department to coordinate programs to comport with the local service district priorities.

The state also helped create a private Virginia Literacy Foundation to support efforts by voluntary groups and to help create public-private cooperative programs. An important feature of the foundation is that it will provide support services rather than fund programs directly. To that end, $3 million has been raised to endow the foundation, which will give start-up grants to local groups and sponsor in-service and preservice training for literacy instructors and administrators. The foundation also has begun to attract substantial private funding, including corporate gifts. Working with the private sector, the foundation's officials hope to be able to engender increasing interest in workplace literacy and other private sector initiatives over the next few years.

Virginia hopes to double its literacy services within the next two years. State efforts will be targeted to unemployed adults and heads of households in single-parent families. In 1989 the legislature appropriated over $4 million in new funds for literacy programs over the next biennium, a significant increase from prior years. Literacy advocates believe that state appropriations can be increased further during the next budget cycle.

What Needs to Be Done

States will have to build an effective system of literacy improvement without the institutional trappings that have accompanied the evolution of other large service systems. Unlike the elementary and secondary education system or the higher education system, there will be no large buildings dedicated to adult literacy, no marching bands, no football teams. There will be trained professionals, but at least at first, few credentials will be required for teaching. Students will be free to come and go, so the system will have to motivate them and hold their attention. The system will be diverse, distributed in hundreds of neighborhoods and provided through the facilities and staffs of a variety of existing and new programs. The new system will combine both public sector provision of services and private incentives. The system will be a mixture both because the services needed are diverse and because the nation cannot afford to build a freestanding system of adult education.

To build this system, state policymakers will have to answer a number of crucial questions creatively and with dispatch:

1. How should the institutional leadership and organization necessary for a sustained effort for adult literacy improvement be identified and developed?
2. How can states best target resources to particular groups of adults who need to improve their basic skills?
3. How can states improve the quality of existing programs and retention rates, the speed of learning, and the portability of basic skills?

4. How should states provide incentives for student or employers to participate successfully in activities to develop basic skills? What other mechanisms, besides increasing the supply of services, might be used to address the problem?
5. How can productivity and performance measurement be injected into a system of shared service provision?
6. How can the states encourage literacy providers to employ new technologies and to apply research and development to techniques of imparting basic skills to adults?
7. How should states create a more professional corps of teachers and administrators of adult literacy programs?
8. How can more resources be generated at the state and local levels to address the problem?

Leadership and the Institutional Base. To date, most of the policy development for improving basic skills in the states has been carried out by task forces, commissions, coalitions, or small staffs in the governors' offices. In the short run, it is appropriate for governors to keep development of adult literacy policy and coordination of services closely associated with the governor's office. In the longer run, however, state leadership must be institutionalized for a sustained effort to be mounted.

Candidates for assuming major responsibility for adult literacy include the economic development system, the community college system, the system of elementary and secondary education, or new entities created for the purpose of pursuing the basic skills agenda.

Economic development agencies could take on the job of preparing adults for better jobs by improving basic skills. These agencies were once devoted primarily to attracting outside industries, managing tourism promotions, and sometimes assisting small businesses. Today, however, economic development agencies are becoming much more involved with upgrading the skills of the labor force. State officials have recognized the important linkage among education, job training, and the ability of firms to compete in an international marketplace.

A second candidate for taking on the long-term responsibility for managing basic skills instruction is the community college system. Community colleges are the sites for many adult basic skills classes right now, and many community colleges have gone into the business of customized job training. Community colleges in many states have a long tradition of dealing with the remedial education needs of adults. In states such as North Carolina, for example, the political and public entrepreneurial spirit of the community college system has led to a substantial involvement in the issue of adult literacy. Community colleges tend, however, to go their own way and are very resistant to gubernatorial or legislative direction. Like other institutions of higher learning, their goals have traditionally involved educating young people in higher level skills, especially technical skills.

A third option for governors and legislators seeking a long-term institutional home for adult literacy programs is the system now responsible for most publicly funded adult literacy programs — the elementary and secondary education system. Several reasons exist for removing the nucleus of state basic skills efforts from current adult education governance systems in the states. First, it is unlikely that leaders in the elementary and secondary education system will ever be able to make adult basic skills the highest, or even a very high, priority. State education leaders will continue to view improving elementary and secondary schools as their top priority for many years to come. In addition, most state education officials are not part of the governor's executive span of control. This independence arguably has some benefit for elementary and secondary education, but for adult literacy efforts the lack of coordination with job-training, welfare, social services, and other executive branch programs could be fatal. Finally, the tradition of adult education programs is to provide stand-alone classroom-based instruction — an inappropriate strategy for the workforce.

To say that elementary and secondary educational institutions should not hold primary responsibility for implementing adult literacy policy, however, is not to suggest that adult literacy programs be divorced from the public schools. The public schools can contribute facilities, operate family literacy programs, share technologies, and provide many other assets to the literacy effort. In turn, literacy policymakers can learn from reforms in the elementary and secondary system.

A fourth option in seeking a long-term institutional base for literacy is to create new departments or institutional entities. Basic skills advocates argue that the magnitude of the literacy problem precludes tacking the responsibility for literacy efforts onto the priorities of other major systems. New organizational entities could be created by combining the functions of adult education and job training into freestanding systems dedicated primarily to upgrading the skills of the labor force. In Kentucky, for example, the governor proposed just such a new Department of Adult Learning, but the legislature has yet to approve that proposal.

Targeting Resources. Over the years, state policymakers working on literacy have come to realize that they must target resources carefully and effectively. Rudimentary calculations show that to provide basic skills to all adults who do not have a high school diploma, for example, would require building a new system roughly as large as the current public higher education system. Given budget constraints at the state level, it is most unlikely that governors and legislatures will undertake the fiscal commitment to building such a system.

Governors may target resources not only to specific population groups, such as welfare mothers, but also to people with specific skill levels. Depending on the social and economic circumstances of states, the mix of targeted groups and skill levels may be quite different. Targeting may also be driven by the goals pursued through programs other than literacy. In Massachusetts, for example, adult literacy and job-training policymakers have decided that a major target group for literacy services is currently employed people who may be displaced if their employers cannot remain competitive. In Mississippi, on the other hand, the issue of literacy relates not so much to retaining jobs as to creating them. Levels of literacy are low for so many people in Mississippi that policymakers are targeting unemployed people with very low skills. Mississippi policymakers realize that targeting resources to low-skilled people may be only a near-term strategy, since job requirements may be increasing faster than the pool of people qualified for even higher level jobs.

Improving the Quality of Instruction. Judged by retention rates, speed of learning, and the few evaluations available of program outcomes, many adult basic skills programs have very limited success. Practitioners in the field attribute this lack of success to insufficient resources, ill-defined program goals, use of inappropriate instructional materials and techniques, the lack of a professional teaching corps, and low student motivation. Whatever the causes of low program quality, states will have to improve the operations and outcomes of adult basic skills programs if the necessary new funds are to be well spent. Here are a few steps that state officials can take to improve program quality.

First, adult basic skills programs should be related directly to the context in which the adult is seeking to learn new skills. State officials should avoid putting resources into "one size fits all" classroom-based programs for all target groups. Increasing the contextual basis of adult literacy instruction should help increase the retention rate for adults.

Second, programs should be aimed at teaching portable skills. By *portable skills,* we mean basic skills that are related to job or life experiences but that can be carried over into new situations. These types of skills would include such abilities as reading and using transportation schedules, interpreting documents, or making job-related calculations.

Third, adult literacy programs must improve retention rates. Current retention rates are abysmally low. Most adults who do take the effort to upgrade basic skills spend very little time before growing discouraged and dropping out. Up to 30 percent of those enrolled in adult educational programs drop out before having received twelve hours of instruction (Brizius and Foster, 1987). This "revolving door" problem must be solved by the states. Support services — such as help with child care arrangements or transportation or dealing with sick family members — can make a difference in the ability of adults to complete literacy instruction.

Fourth, because much remains to be learned about the most effective ways to teach adults, every program should have built in a system of performance measurement and an evaluation capacity. Programs must be able to track individual progress and programwide performance.

Incentives and the Marketplace. Possibly the most important, and least explored, challenge for the states is motivating both employees and employers to participate in the quest for improved basic skills. Without incentives, it is not clear that millions of adults will come forward seeking new skills, nor is it inevitable that employers will invest in basic skills training.

Large businesses and highly organized industries have recognized that their competitive positions depend on increasing the skills of their workers. Smaller businesses — those that are likely to fuel the future economy — have not yet recognized the link between literacy and their bottom lines. If they have, they do not have the resources to provide literacy programs, or even to allow workers time off to improve basic skills. With the exception of recent immigrants, adults needing basic skills have not been flooding to literacy programs, despite the Project Literacy U.S. initiative and other media efforts across the country.

States tend to start programs where the need for motivation is not an issue. Requirements for prisoners to take literacy classes, for example, have been made in part because the state can identify a captive audience. Welfare recipients can be required to attend basic skills classes as a condition of receiving the welfare grant.

Motivating employed adults will be especially difficult. Single parents not on welfare have little time to attend adult literacy classes. Child care will pose difficulty, as will transportation. Support services will have to be improved if large numbers of adults, especially employed people, are to spend more time and energy improving their basic skills. While workforce literacy and other basic skills programs at the job site will help make these activities more convenient, simply placing traditional literacy programs at work sites will not be enough.

States will have to offer financial incentives to adults and employers to induce them to participate in literacy improvement efforts. Not all of what needs to be done can be accomplished through expanding existing programs or creating new programs. Regulation, tax policies, vouchers, or other forms of grant funds may also be needed to motivate private sector involvement in addressing literacy issues.

States should also experiment with vouchers and stipends for adults in target groups to motivate them to spend their time and energies on improving their skills. These demonstrations could help determine if direct financial incentives can help improve recruitment and retention rates in basic skills programs. States should also link on-the-job training programs within current Job Training Partnership Act (JTPA) programs to completion of basic skills programs, in effect guaranteeing jobs to unemployed adults as a reward for successful completion of literacy enhancement programs.

Small business assistance programs should be expanded to help small, struggling businesses improve their workers' skills. Small businesses may respond to tax breaks or changes in the regulatory environment tied to assisting their employees in improving their skills. Since many small businesses depend on large businesses for markets, it may also be possible to tie small businesses into the workforce literacy programs offered or supported by large businesses.

Even without organizing major demonstrations or experiments, states and local governments could move rapidly to offer incentives to, and provide literacy programs for, their own workforces. Employees of state and local governments amount to over 10 percent of the labor force today. Providing even a small portion of those workers with access to basic skills enhancement and incentives to take part in improvement programs would be a major contribution of state and local governments.

Productivity and Performance. The current system of adult literacy and basic skills service is operated by a wide variety of service providers. Deliverers of basic skills instruction include volunteer groups, community colleges, community-based organizations, school districts, businesses, job-training organizations, and many others.

If providers were all of one type or if there were known relationships between inputs (teaching hours or hours in front of a computer) and outputs (skill level increases or the ability to solve new kinds of problems), the state could specify standards for program eligibility and be fairly certain that providing a given level of resources would produce a given level of achievement. Despite many efforts to define these relationships, they are largely unknown throughout the field of education.

At present, most funds for basic skills instruction are distributed according to enrollments or the costs of programs and specific classes, without much investigation of what students are actually learning or exactly who those students are. As states invest more money in adult literacy, however, they will have to develop measurement systems and performance-contracting systems if they are to track the progress of service delivery and pay providers for performance. State leaders and the public want to know not only how many welfare recipients are enrolled in literacy programs, for example, but also how much their skill levels increase and whether improved basic skills lead to employment.

Literacy and Technology. Adults do not learn the same way children learn. Some adults with limited basic skills had bad experiences in traditional classrooms. If they are motivated to learn new skills, it is usually because they see a direct link between acquiring those skills and achieving specific goals: getting a job or a better job, reading to their children, participating in community activities, or keeping up with public events. Teaching techniques and materials that are oriented toward adult concerns are more useful to adults than techniques and learning resources that present knowledge and skills the way the traditional school system presents them.

A variety of new technologies, based on the computer and video techniques, hold promise in speeding the learning of adults (see Chapter 6). New teaching techniques related to imparting portable skills are being developed. New curricula for adults are also being developed in response to the national concern over literacy. These new approaches are not just hardware and software, they are whole learning systems.

States should develop mechanisms to evaluate promising new techniques and technologies and to make sure that the appropriate techniques are infused into the programs operating within the states. States should create staff positions to evaluate new techniques for adult learners and training curricula for literacy providers. These staff members could also offer assistance to local service providers, including private businesses, to implement these new techniques. These staff functions need not be located in a single institution, although some states have found that creating centers to handle evaluation and technical assistance has been useful.

In addition, states should create new financing mechanisms for acquiring technology for adult literacy improvement. States should explore the uses of medium-term financing for learning systems, including bonds. States should determine the feasibility of group purchase of learning systems financed by short-term or medium-term financial instruments or by general fund appropriations. New financing mechanisms should also encourage sharing of technologies among programs, particularly the sharing of learning systems with relatively expensive initial investments that must be amortized quickly.

Professionalization. Unlike other education systems, the current adult literacy system is staffed primarily by part-time teachers and administrators, many of whom have primary employment responsibilities elsewhere. For existing adult literacy staff, there is little incentive and virtually no support to learn the most effective techniques of imparting basic skills. Consequently, staff frequently use inappropriate materials and provide instruction in ways that are inappropriate to the needs of the adults they are serving.

Professionalization is closely tied to the need to evaluate and disseminate the best practices in the field. To provide professional development opportunities for adult literacy teachers and administrators, states will have to mandate in-service and preservice training of teachers. They also must disseminate curricula for adult literacy providers and offer a mechanism through which adult literacy teachers can receive more compensation if they achieve a more professional status.

At the same time, states must recognize that the field of adult literacy is not static. No one system of pedagogy or technique of teaching is appropriate for all types of literacy instruction. As a result, states must be careful not to allow professionalization to rigidify the field, as it has in other areas of professional endeavor. Training programs should be practice-based.

Resources. Like the federal government, states have historically underinvested in the delivery system for adult literacy service, yet in recent years states have begun to devote substantially more resources to adult basic skills instruction than in the past. In 1987, for example, states spent about $260 million to provide adult basic skills instruction at grade levels 0–8. Total state and local spending through the adult education programs monitored by the U.S. Department of Education amounted to about $318 million. (This figure should be considered somewhat low, because many state and local programs do not report spending on adult education to the federal government unless they are required to do so in order to maintain federal matching amounts. In a perverse twist, federal maintenance-of-effort regulations cause states to underreport current spending in case an actual cutback occurs in the next year.)

While the total amounts allocated to adult basic skills instruction by the states seem substantial, the amount per student is very low. In 1987 state and federal funds spent on adult basic skills instruction (grade levels 0–8) amounted to only $143 per student. Part of the reason that this figure is so low, of course, is that students do not stay in programs very long. Enrollment figures are somewhat misleading, since students attending adult basic skills classes are counted as enrollees whether they stay one week or one year. Another reason why the spending per learner is low, however, is because adult basic skills programs pay instructors very little, provide little support to students, and generally operate on a shoestring. By contrast, total annual spending on elementary and secondary education amounts to roughly $4,000 per pupil.

State spending on adult basic skills instruction varies dramatically by state. Well over half of all state spending on adult basic skills instruction occurs in just two states—California and Michigan. Although some states have made substantial commitments to adult basic skills, most do not allocate significant resources to the literacy problem of America.

Patterns of state support relate to the individual political and economic situations in the states. In North Carolina, for example, the governor and legislature have focused attention on the problem and new resources have been allocated. Virginia has just doubled its appropriation for literacy services. In Arkansas new resources are expected in 1990. In Mississippi the governor will have to fight for new resources for adult literacy as part of his educational reform package in 1990. California and Texas are starting to respond to the influx of immigrants and their need to learn English and other skills. New York has recently appropriated over $50 million in additional funds for adult basic skills instruction and will probably add more resources next year.

To meet the challenge of improving basic skills, states will have to spend more. States will have to increase both total spending and spending per adult learner to provide quality programs that have an impact on the problem. Not only must states spend more per learner and overall to support basic skills improvement, but also they will have to spend in different ways. Several ways that spending can be increased and improved at the same time are presented here as options:

First, states can make the acquisition of basic skills by adults an entitlement. In this way, states would be committing themselves to substantial expenditures over many years.

Second, states can appropriate more funds to a central literacy coordinating agency. While funds for adult basic skills can be drawn from a variety of state and federal sources, states should consider placing incremental funds in the hands of people at a central level who can use incentives to coordinate the efforts of various state agencies.

Third, states can use their tax systems and other mechanisms to provide an incentive for the private sector to spend more on basic skills enhancement.

Finally, regardless of the mechanism for directing new resources to the problem, states should specify performance standards for local providers of services.

Near-Term Recommendations

To build the state role in basic skills improvement, state officials need to resolve ten hard questions about the future of literacy efforts in their states. These questions may serve as a checklist for concerned citizens, literacy providers, and state policymakers alike. They focus on the immediate issue: how to strengthen the literacy effort.

1. Have you defined literacy in terms of a continuum of skills, and have you defined the issue as it relates to other state goals and priorities? It is important that state policymakers, literacy providers, and citizens alike understand that literacy is not an on-off condition, nor is literacy just reading. The issue is how to improve basic skills of all types to meet both state goals and the goals of individual learners.

2. Have you developed a methodology for estimating the size and characteristics of the populations requiring upgraded literacy skills to meet other state goals? You cannot target your resources well until you understand which populations need what kind of help. Estimating the size and characteristics of various populations that need improved basic skills requires hard work in order to develop more sophisticated measures of the need than are now available.

3. Have you targeted particular groups of individuals whose skills must be upgraded in order to achieve state goals? Targeting resources will be the only way to address the literacy problem in the short term without spreading efforts so thin that no measurable effect will be achieved. Targeting involves making difficult decisions about who receives what services, but it must be done.

4. Have you identified the full range of tools available to reach the targeted population(s), and have you developed mechanisms for attracting and retaining program participants? Offering more money to existing service providers is not the solution to the basic skills problem. If states limit themselves to this approach, they will never have enough time or money to solve the problem. States need to use incentives for the private

sector and find better ways to motivate adults and employers to participate.

5. Have you adopted a set of standards for quality programs? Unless many current programs are upgraded and new programs live up to high standards, basic skills improvement efforts will fail. They will fail because not enough people will stay long enough to gain skills and because governors and legislatures will not appropriate more money to run programs without high standards of performance.

6. Have you developed a strategy for the long term to strengthen the literacy profession? The literacy effort will not be sustained unless a profession dedicated to upgrading the basic skills of adults is augmented. At the same time, however, the profession should not be characterized by restrictive credentials and others barriers to entry.

7. Have you identified a long-term institutional base for literacy enhancement, and have you clarified the relationship of the stakeholders to the literacy initiative? You do not have to know exactly where the long-term institutional home for literacy improvement is going to be, but it would be a good idea to encourage your state officials to address this question. Staffs coordinating responses to important issues such as adult literacy are often placed in the governor's office or another central location. But these issues have short "half lives" at the top of the agenda. Eventually, the continuing function of providing basic skills instruction to adults must be the job of full-time people in a line agency. Start looking for the most appropriate home now.

8. Have you identified the full range of funding alternatives? Some new federal funds are being made available through welfare reform and job-training laws in 1990. Other funds can be reallocated as the labor shortage warrants more emphasis on basic skills instruction. Ultimately, however, most of the cost of providing basic skills instruction for adults will have to be borne with state funds. You should be studying state budgets now, looking for ways to allocate more money to literacy efforts.

9. Have you tied literacy programs and activities to performance and made provisions for continuing assessment of ef-

fectiveness? Money will not be forthcoming if literacy programs are not firmly tied to performance and if provisions are not made for evaluation. On the other hand, if the new adult literacy system is built with performance measurement as a standard feature, governors and legislatures will feel very comfortable about allocating new funds to this enterprise.

10. Have you developed plans for national advocacy for increased federal support for state and local literacy efforts? Although the primary responsibility for building an expanded system of basic skills instruction for adults will rest with the states, the federal government needs to help with research, technical assistance, and financial support. We should all be working to make sure that the federal government does its share to support the states in the massive undertaking of enhancing adult literacy.

References

Arkansas Governor's Commission on Adult Literacy. "Arkansas Action Plan for Literacy Enhancement." Little Rock: Arkansas Governor's Commission on Adult Literacy, Summer 1988.

Brizius, J., and Foster, S. "Enhancing Adult Literacy: A Policy Guide." Washington, D.C.: The Council of State Policy and Planning Agencies, 1987.

Chynoweth, J. "Enhancing Literacy for Jobs and Productivity." Washington, D.C.: The Council of State Policy and Planning Agencies, May 1989.

Minnesota Adult Literacy Campaign. "Minnesota Adult Literacy Campaign." St. Paul: Minnesota Adult Literacy Campaign, 1988.

Riccio, J., and others. "GAIN: Early Implementation Experiences and Lessons." New York: Manpower Demonstration Research Corporation, April 1989.

10

📖 Forrest P. Chisman

The Federal Role in Developing an Effective Adult Literacy System

By itself, the federal government cannot solve the adult literacy problem in America. Most of the "hands on" responsibility for delivering literacy service rests, and will continue to rest, with states, cities, local programs, employers, unions, voluntary groups, and others. But the federal government must play a critically important role. It must create the conditions within which these other agencies can find a solution to the problem of adult literacy. It must play a leadership role.

Federal leadership is required because of the enormous social and economic stakes involved. The problem of adult literacy poses a severe threat to the well-being of the nation as a whole, and only government at the national level can lead a nationwide attack on a problem of this scale. In a more immediate sense, federal leadership is required because the federal government has already linked the success of a large part of the nation's human service agenda to the literacy field. Unless a more robust system of literacy service is developed, recent federal initiatives in the fields of welfare, training, and immigration, among others, simply will not work.

The Emerging Federal Agenda

Until the late 1980s federal policy in the adult literacy field was fairly straightforward. The only substantial federal commitment was a program of grants in aid to the states which operated under the authority of the Adult Education Act (AEA) and was managed by the U.S. Department of Education. Slightly less than half of the service provided under this program in recent years has been instruction in English as a Second Language (ESL)—usually very basic courses in survival English. The balance has been split between instruction in elementary reading and writing (usually called adult basic education, or ABE) and preparation for high school equivalency certificates (adult secondary education, or ASE). While high school equivalency courses are structured around passing a particular test, instruction in ESL and ABE is fairly open-ended. Students progress as far as their interest in upgrading their skills takes them.

The Adult Education Act focuses exclusively on the goal of improving adult literacy. It does not specify how much participants in ABE or ESL programs should learn or what the purpose of learning should be. In effect, the act treats learning as an end in itself, and any learning gain can be considered adequate within its guidelines.

Congress has supported the Adult Education Act, under various names, for more than twenty years but has never shown much enthusiasm for it. Until recently, appropriations were under $100 million (the fiscal year 1990 appropriation was $185 million), rarely keeping up with inflation and never providing a level of service that would meet more than a small percentage of the estimated national need.

Then, in 1988, through a series of circumstances too complicated to relate here, Congress discovered adult literacy. But what it discovered was not only, or even primarily, the Adult Education Act. What Congress thought it discovered was that adult literacy instruction could be a solution to a wide range of problems in other federal programs with which it had been struggling for some time.

To oversimplify, starting in 1988, it became faddish to attach adult literacy mandates, or their equivalents, to measures aimed at reforming programs that are far larger and, in the eyes of Congress, far more significant than the Adult Education Act had ever been. The result was a stream of legislation that treated adult literacy not as an end in itself, but as a means to some other goal.

The Legislation. The most celebrated of these enactments was the Family Support Act: an effort by a Democratic Congress to respond to conservative criticisms of the Aid to Families with Dependent Children (AFDC) program, which had become a political football during the Reagan years. The keystone of the Family Support Act is the newly created Job Opportunities and Basic Skills Training (JOBS) Program, a set of measures aimed at enhancing the employability of welfare recipients and placing them in employment. JOBS will eventually provide over $1 billion per year to states for these purposes. One of the key elements of the program is provisions that require states to increase employability by providing educational services, including literacy instruction, to welfare recipients who require them.

Because the basic skill levels of welfare recipients are usually very low, JOBS can achieve its professed goals only if the state and local welfare officials charged with implementing it find some way of providing a large part of their caseload with basic literacy services that will significantly increase employability and actual job placements. The resources potentially available for this purpose are very large—certainly a significant portion of the $1 billion funding for JOBS. This is a far higher level of support than the Adult Education Act, or any other public or private adult literacy program, has ever received. The program is managed not by the U.S. Department of Education but by the U.S. Department of Health and Human Services.

A second development in 1988 was the adoption of final regulations to implement the Immigration Reform and Control Act of 1986. The act establishes a process for normalizing the status of over 3 million illegal aliens. As part of this process, it provides $1 billion per year in State Legalization Impact Assistance Grant (SLIAG) funds to support social and educational services aimed at better integrating illegal aliens who meet certain qualifications into American social and economic life. Because a large portion of the people eligible for service under the SLIAG program have limited English proficiency, the Immigration Reform and Control Act allows states to spend up to $500 per year for each individual to provide ESL and other educational services. Moreover, several provisions of the act effectively mandate ESL service. For example, everyone participating in the normalization process must eventually pass an English-language naturalization test.

The end result of these requirements is a pool of approximately $300 million available for ESL service from a program managed by the Department of Health and Human Services. Although the Immigration Reform and Control Act was passed in late 1986, the process of developing final regulations that would interpret Congressional intent was so protracted and politically charged that national policy — with regard to the educational provisions at least — was not established until 1988.

The third important development in 1988 was the reauthorization of the Adult Education Act itself. In the process of reauthorization, Congress not only increased the authority for the state grant program to $200 million (although it initially appropriated only $132 million), but also grafted onto the act new programs for experimentation and service in workforce literacy and English literacy, initially authorized at $30 million and $25 million, respectively. In effect, Congress injected more specific goals for literacy service into the act: literacy should be a means of improving employment skills and the social integration of people with limited English proficiency, not just an end in itself.

In 1989, Congress followed up on its newfound interest in literacy by making proposals for improving both the Carl D. Perkins Vocational Education Act and the Job Training Partnership Act (JTPA). The vocational education proposals took the form of a requirement that programs for both adults and youth operated under the act's almost $1 billion state grant program must ensure that their participants have a mastery of "core academics." In context, this means a commitment of vocational programs to ensure that all students will attain a level of both basic and applied skills that is sufficient to help them find and keep jobs in their areas of specialization. The 1989 proposals for JTPA reform mandated that all participants in the $1 billion adult portion of JTPA must receive basic skills instruction to increase employability if they require it.

The Result. The net result of these two years of legislative history and regulatory action was a complete transformation of the federal role in adult literacy. From a small program in the Department of Education, literacy became a key element of major programs in the Departments of Health and Human Services and Labor, as well as the focus of new Education Department responsibilities. The federal funding stream for literacy, which consisted primarily of an appropriation on the order of $100 million for the Adult Education Act in 1987, swelled to almost $1 billion by the end of 1989, and proposals for even more funding were on the table.

Most important, the literacy system was given new jobs to do. In the 1988–89 enactments, Congress asked literacy providers to deliver services that would increase employability and integrate the population with limited English into mainstream American life. This is a major departure from the Adult Education Act, which places responsibility for setting goals with individual programs or learners. The 1988–89 legislation charged the literacy system with attaining major social and economic goals and for these purposes asked it to provide services that would change the lives of program participants in specified ways.

The literacy system was also saddled with very heavy political burdens. In each of the 1988–89 enactments a Democratic Congress turned to adult literacy as one means of defusing fundamental criticisms of the programs involved: the criticism that AFDC led to "welfare dependency," that legalization of aliens would overburden social services, that vocational education was a "dummy" program teaching outmoded skills, and that JTPA was just a disguised job-placement subsidy to employers.

Most of these criticisms were hurled by conservatives, although some had a broader base of support. During 1988–89, adult literacy played an important role in interparty competition at the national level, because congressional Democrats assumed that provisions for literacy service could give a new lease on life to interventionist social programs that were under fire. In doing so, they tied the fortunes of a good deal of the federal human service agenda to the effectiveness of the literacy system in performing the new jobs assigned to it.

Dream or Nightmare? By rights, leaders of the adult literacy field should have been jubilant about these developments,
and many were. Not only did Congress greatly increase the
federal funds available for literacy service, it also implicitly
adopted a reform agenda that had been maturing in the literacy field for several years (see Chapters 2 and 4).

Throughout the 1980s, and even before, many literacy
leaders had been arguing that learning occurs best in context,
when it is directed toward specific economic or social goals, and
when it is associated with other social support systems aimed
at advancing those goals. In each of its 1988–89 actions, Congress adopted these notions, if only by the back-door route of
placing literacy in the service of the social and economic goals
of a number of large social programs and by setting it in the
context of their other activities.

Moreover, for some years before the 1988–89 enactments,
many literacy experts had been arguing that basic literacy instruction should go beyond elementary, or even advanced, reading and writing. They believed it should also embrace mathematics, communication, and problem-solving skills. They also
argued that instruction should be more individualized, to accommodate the learning styles, motivations, and social situations of learners. The requirements for adult literacy service that
Congress created in 1988–89 can only be satisfied by a broad-
gauged notion of literacy that takes account of individual differences. The skills needed to improve employability and social
integration are inevitably of this sort.

In short, literacy leaders received what should have been
a dream mandate from Congress in 1988–89. There was only
one problem: practically no one was equipped to carry out that
mandate.

The typical literacy program in 1988 or 1989 did not improve employability and social integration by providing a wide
array of basic skills training individualized to meet particular
needs. The typical literacy program taught basic reading and
writing, survival English, and academic material required to
pass a high school equivalency test. Nobody could say for sure
what relationship this sort of instruction had to the larger goals

expressed by both Congress and literacy reformers. And very few programs had much expertise in the more ambitious agenda for instruction. They knew how to do what they had been doing.

Moreover, even if the literacy field had known exactly what to do to fulfill its new mandate (and at least some leaders claimed that they did), meeting the increased responsibility called for a highly skilled teaching force many times the existing size and administrative structures able to accommodate a vastly increased number of students. Neither was readily available in 1988 or 1989.

It is not much of an exaggeration to say that all but a few members of Congress assumed that literacy instruction is a well-defined, readily created commodity, like housing. They assumed that they could simply buy more literacy instruction and give it to people in need, just as they subsidize the construction of low-income housing for the poor. A closer analogy to the requirements for literacy that emerged from Congress in 1988 and 1989 would be a mandate to cure cancer.

This is not to say that the congressional requirements were a mistake. But the 1988–89 legislation raised an enormous number of very difficult issues for the literacy field, and those issues must be resolved before the goals of that legislation can be met.

Questions

An easy way to understand the extent and difficulty of the problems created by the 1988–89 legislation is to review the issues that it raised for each of the participants in the literacy enterprise.

Learners. Any learner involved in one of the literacy programs established by the 1988–89 legislation might rightly ask, "What exactly am I expected to learn, and how do I know if I've learned it?" Only the most rudimentary curricula for increasing employability through basic skills training now exist. In fact, we have only a very limited understanding of how to assess needs for basic skills other than reading, writing, and math, and experts differ about how best to assess even those skills. We know very little about how to tailor curricula to workforce needs or how to measure progress or certify achievement, except by high school equivalency exams. We have more experience in teaching survival English to people with limited proficiency in the language, but not much experience in guiding them, or other learners, to large gains in basic skills competency.

The next question a learner might ask is "Where do I go to get the service?" The new congressional mandates have spread authority for providing various types of literacy services across education, labor, and social welfare agencies at the state and local levels. Will learners receive essentially the same service delivered by different agencies in the same locality, or will there be some division of labor? Will the model of the free-standing literacy program be maintained, or will the greater emphasis on employability and learning in context lead to more instruction either on the job or in other settings?

A final, good question for a learner to ask is "What's in it for me?" Are the new programs pledged to deliver decent jobs and a greater ability to deal with the problems of everyday life? Or are they just cosmetic exercises to harass the needy with more classes and requirements that have uncertain results? Congress certainly has not guaranteed that learners will benefit. To ensure that participants will take the new literacy programs seriously, both public policy and service delivery systems must be designed to create a reasonable possibility that "real world" benefits will result from those programs.

Teachers. Many of the questions teachers might ask are variants of the student's initial query about curriculum, except they take the form of "Exactly what am I supposed to teach, and how do I know if it's working?" But teachers should have other concerns as well. Where will they receive the training to take on the new responsibilities? Will the pay be adequate? Will the new demands on the system lead to a need for full-time teachers, and will this career ladder be stable over the long run?

Teachers should also be concerned with how they will be expected to interact with other professionals, such as social workers and members of the business community. Who will set the goals and evaluate the instruction — the teacher and the education system or someone else? In fact, teachers might be concerned that the new congressional mandates will deprofessionalize the field. Since nobody really knows how to achieve the goals set forth by Congress, volunteer groups and community-based organizations (CBOs), on the one hand, and proprietary schools, on the other, may stand as good a chance as today's semiprofessional adult literacy teaching force in public programs in winning control of the system by winning the new government contracts.

Program Administrators. Administrators of existing literacy programs should share all of the perplexities of both teachers and learners and have some concerns of their own. They are being asked to go beyond current practice and models of both instruction and program design into uncharted territory. Like teachers, program administrators should wonder whether the new regime of service delivery will continue to be based on existing literacy programs, largely controlled by state and local education systems, or whether they will become just one player among many. If so, administrators may wonder who will set the rules and how the competition will take place so that their programs have a reasonable chance of winning. If, on the other hand, today's programs are to retain a dominant role, to whom will they be accountable?

But beyond these questions of responsibility and mission, program administrators may well wonder where the resources to reconfigure their efforts will come from. Congress has authorized enormous sums for enhanced service, but it has not authorized very much at all for teacher training, capital expenditures, or other new administrative burdens. Yet without covering these costs, program administrators will find it impossible to meet the goals that Congress has set.

States. State-level administrators should have, on a much larger scale, all of the same concerns as program administrators. But state governments as a whole will have additional problems.

Most of the new federal mandates are embodied in programs that are grants-in-aid to the states. States therefore are held accountable for seeing that they succeed. But is there any real accountability for the literacy provisions in these programs? Most of the legislation specifies both inputs and outputs in very general terms. If the federal government is in earnest about the need for more literacy service to meet the goals of human service programs, what standards will it apply? How can a state know if it is doing a good job?

States should also be concerned about whether they will have the discretion to do the job well. Overall, the new literacy mandates seem to call for a comprehensive upgrading of literacy service. Will states be able to reconfigure existing systems and build new ones across the board, or will they be hamstrung by federal mandates running directly to their various education, welfare, and economic development agencies?

And what about the dozen or more states that have tried to create comprehensive and well-coordinated literacy planning and service delivery systems by stitching together bits and pieces of federal and state resources? Will they be allowed to blend the new federal mandates and money into these initiatives, or must they start again from scratch?

Federal Officials. The major question that cabinet officers, and those who represent them in the literacy field, should be asking is "Who's in charge?" A few years ago it was fairly clear that the Department of Education was responsible for adult literacy, by virtue of its authority to administer the Adult Education Act. As a result of the 1988–89 legislation, the Education Department is only one of several roughly equal shareholders in the literacy enterprise. At least as many program dollars are now flowing through the Labor Department and the Department of Health and Human Services as through the Education Department. Yet, broadly speaking, each department is being asked to do similar things: to improve employability and social integration for the underprivileged. These overlapping mandates immediately raise the question whether there should be a lead agency, or a coordinating body of some sort.

The other major question that federal officials should be asking has to do with accountability. They are charged with executing the laws. How will they know in this new and complex literacy environment whether states, cities, program administrators, and others are actually doing a good job? What measures should they use, and how can they facilitate success?

Employers. Corporate America is obviously intended to be one of the ultimate beneficiaries of the new federal literacy initiatives that are aimed at increasing employability. Moreover, none of those initiatives will work unless employers are willing to hire the people who have participated in basic skills programs. In all likelihood, this means that employers must have at least some influence over the form those programs will take. How will employers know whether people who have participated in these programs are, in fact, ready for jobs? Should the learners be certified in some way, and if so, how? What form should the employers' influence take? Will the instruction provided and the expectations created be in line with corporate realities? These are only the initial questions that employers should be asking.

Vendors. In a free enterprise nation, it is reasonable to suppose that any task as ambitious as training the millions of people eligible for the new literacy service authorized by Congress in 1988–89 will call upon the ingenuity of the private sector. For example, the designers of computer-based instructional systems and companies that specialize in training doubtless have a contribution to make. But this contribution will be forthcoming only if the federal government creates a large enough market for these and other vendors to develop their wares. It is unclear in at least some of the existing legislation whether any of the new dollars can be invested in instructional technology and whether contracts with private instructional companies are allowed. As a result, it is unclear whether a substantial new market has been created or not.

The Voluntary Sector. Volunteer groups and CBOs have long played an important role in adult literacy. Although they provide only about 10 percent to 20 percent of the service nationwide, some volunteer groups and CBOs have been innovators in providing individualized, contextual instruction and in linking literacy instruction to other types of social services. Since no one has very much expertise in fulfilling the new congressional mandates, volunteers and CBOs should be wondering whether and how they will have an opportunity to participate in this process.

Their concerns are particularly pertinent because the same Congress that created large new streams of funds for literacy in the context of other programs also passed a number of bills offering support and encouragement for volunteer and CBO literacy efforts. For example, it created a Literacy Corps in the VISTA program and authorized a Student Literacy Corps. It is therefore reasonable to surmise that Congress intended that volunteers and CBOs should have some role to play in implementing the 1988–89 mandates for literacy service. But what exactly will that role be? Will they be expected to develop a separate stream of service parallel to the major public efforts, or will they become partners in those efforts? Will they be on a more or less equal footing with public programs in competing for new federal resources, or will public providers enjoy a monopoly?

The Research Community. Although only a fairly small number of researchers specialize in adult literacy, they should be asked to play a very important role in implementing the 1988–89 legislation. Because the services called for in that legislation are at or beyond the boundaries of the present state of the art, major advances in research to assist both practitioners and policymakers are clearly required. All of the federal human service programs have at least some research budget, but no special provisions for research in adult literacy were made in the 1988–89 enactments, and no provisions were included to facilitate the dissemination of either new findings or the best existing knowledge. As a result, researchers should be wondering whether they will be able to make a significant contribution at the time when their expertise is needed most.

Answers

This listing of questions and concerns is by no means exhaustive. It merely demonstrates the point that the 1988–89 legislation and regulations opened up almost every important issue that could possibly arise for the literacy field. Those measures revealed that the nation's system for providing adult literacy service is seriously inadequate in a great many ways. Federal policymakers assumed that the literacy system was capable of helping large numbers of learners make extensive gains in all the basic skills and achieve real-world benefits from literacy instruction. They were wrong. And until we develop a system that is capable of achieving those goals, the new federal mandates for literacy service will sow confusion throughout the literacy field, jeopardizing the future of a large part of the nation's human service agenda. Moreover, until we develop such a system, there is no way that the United States can come to grips with the problems of 20 to 30 million Americans who have limited basic skills.

The federal government has a large stake in assuring that the 1988–89 legislation achieves its goals; and finding ways to overcome the enormous economic and social problems posed by limited literacy is inevitably a federal concern. Building a more effective literacy system will require the active involvement of leaders in all the public and private agencies concerned with adult literacy, but the federal government must play a leadership role. Federal programs already provide the lion's share of the funding and structure a large part of the adult literacy effort in the United States. Moreover, the 1988–89 legislation has greatly expanded the scope of federal influence. As a result, it is virtually impossible to build a more effective literacy system unless the federal government develops policies to redirect its existing programs toward the new legislative goals. Conversely, because federal influence is already so great, the federal government is uniquely equipped to develop and implement a comprehensive approach to upgrading the literacy field. Only the federal government can identify the missing elements in the overall system of service delivery and help fill those gaps in a systematic way — building a truly effective system for delivering adult literacy services from the presently fragmented efforts. Finally, because its responsibilities are nationwide in scope, the federal government is in a far better position than other public or private agencies to provide common user services to the literacy field—services that everyone involved with adult literacy needs and that can be most effectively provided by one or only a few sources.

Because the adult literacy field is decentralized and pluralistic in the extreme, the federal government cannot solve each and every problem of each and every literacy provider. Nor should it attempt to do so. Elements of pluralism must be part of any solution to the literacy problem in America. But the federal government can and must use its nationwide influence and its substantial resources to create the conditions within which the literacy problem can be solved by states, localities, and the great variety of nongovernmental institutions concerned with adult literacy. Only government at the national level can perform a leadership role of this sort.

The basic dimensions of the leadership role that the federal government must assume were mapped out by a number of study groups operating in 1988–89 (Adult Literacy Taskforce, 1988; Chisman, 1989; Mendel, 1989; Working Group on Adult Literacy, 1988). All of those groups concluded that there is a pressing need for new federal initiatives, and collectively their recommendations point to four top priorities for action: (1) building greater expertise in the literacy field; (2) improving the quality of professionals and providing them with the tools they need to do the job; (3) improving coordination among programs and agencies; and (4) filling the gaps in service left by the recent legislation.

Expertise. The federal agenda for literacy embodied in the 1988–89 legislation cannot possibly succeed, and the nation cannot possibly come to grips with the adult literacy problem in an effective way, unless there is a crash program to create a solid understanding of how to develop a much more extensive array of literacy services than we now have. And that understanding must be developed in a systematic way. This requires, among other things, clearly defining the goals of the services that must be provided, as well as creating assessment tools, curricula, teaching materials, and models for program design, staff training, and accountability. It also involves disseminating this information in a form that will be useful to everyone involved in providing literacy service.

A federal investment in basic and applied research and experimentation strategically targeted toward this agenda is required. The major locus of such an effort should be one or more national centers of excellence created to serve the literacy field. Because the number of experts qualified to perform this type of work is now quite small, and because energies should be focused on the most pressing issues facing the field, the creation of a single national center is the most appropriate first step.

Much of the success of such an institution will inevitably depend upon its governance structure. Unless it clearly reflects the pluralism of the literacy field, it is unlikely to develop an agenda that has relevance across the board, and its findings are unlikely to have much impact on the field as a whole. It should not be, or even appear to be, the captive of any one federal department or of any one level of government. It should not exclusively represent the interest of public literacy providers. Rather, to effectively serve the needs of the field as a whole, it should be an independent organization, federally supported, under the governance of a board representing all the stakeholders in the literacy enterprise.

The major functions of a national center should be research, information dissemination, technical assistance, and assessment of national progress toward literacy goals (see Chapter 5). But an equally important function would be symbolic. A national center would create a highly visible home, and a sense of institutional identity, for everyone concerned in any way with adult literacy.

It is, however, unrealistic to expect that any single institution could meet the national need to upgrade expertise in the literacy field. For example, a single national center could never give ongoing assistance in staff development to the myriad of local programs or help develop state-specific strategies for coordinating efforts supported by different funding streams, sharing resources, or enforcing accountability. State or regional centers, or both, will also be required to perform these particularistic tasks and to establish a two-way flow of communication with a national center that is essential to assess its effectiveness, refine its agenda, and filter up new insights from the grass roots.

In short, a pluralistic literacy system requires a pluralistic system for developing expertise: a national focal point under the governance of all the major stakeholders in the literacy enterprise, and a dispersed set of correspondent institutions that will reflect the diversity of the field. The federal government should be prepared to invest in both.

Upgrading the Field. One of the major shortcomings of the recent spate of literacy legislation was that it greatly increased the funds for service delivery available to the literacy field without increasing very much the funds available for investment in upgrading the field. In particular, funds were not earmarked for staff training and investment in instructional technology or other materials.

These oversights are the functional equivalent of asking a corporation to expand its operations without allowing it a capital budget to acquire more plant and equipment or train more workers. It cannot be assumed that most of the existing staff in literacy programs have the expertise required to provide the extensive, contextual instruction required by the new congressional mandates. Also, a large increase in staff will be required to expand literacy service. Moreover, in many cases, not just literacy staff but also teachers and administrators in vocational education, JTPA, and other programs will have to develop new skills. As a result, a large investment in staff training must be made if the new congressional mandates are to succeed. Since Congress did not provide for this in the 1988–89 legislation, it should develop a substantial program of staff training grants.

In crafting this program, Congress should adopt measures

that will help to integrate, rather than balkanize, the literacy field. It would be wasteful to make separate provisions for staff training in each federal program. To achieve economies of scale in training and help foster cooperative efforts, the staff of any federally funded literacy program should be eligible to participate in training supported by federal training grants.

The other major investment literacy programs must make is an investment in capital equipment, ranging from the most basic instructional materials, such as books and classroom space, to sophisticated learning technology. Although it is probably safe to assume that local programs will be able to use some of the new federal program dollars to purchase basic materials — of which there is often now a shortage — the threshold cost of most instructional technology is probably too high for individual programs to bear. As Packer and Campbell explain (Chapter 6), learning technology can probably help to achieve large economies of scale in the literacy field. But there are "chicken and egg" problems in putting technology to work for literacy: Vendors are reluctant to make large investments in developing better learning systems or to bring down their price because the market for them is too small; and the market does not expand because providers believe the existing products are not optimal and the price is too high.

To achieve the economies of scale potentially available from learning technology, overcome the resource problems that most individual programs face, and cultivate the market, the federal government should develop a system of technology investment grants for the literacy field. Like the training grants, they should not be tied to any one program. Rather, they should encourage the joint use of technology by all federally supported programs. Joint-use requirements would promote the most efficient use of technology and help to integrate the field. They would also encourage literacy providers to better define their needs and specify common requirements that can guide vendors in developing more effective systems.

Coordination. The question "Who's in charge?" has always haunted the literacy field. Even in the days when the public system was centered on programs supported by the Adult Education Act, leaders of the literacy field were concerned that the proliferation of volunteer and community-based efforts as well as other small, public programs would lead to wasteful duplication of effort at the level of service delivery. Today at least three federal departments and many more programs at all levels of government have an equal claim to being "in charge" of at least some aspect of literacy service, and the concern about duplication of effort is greater than ever.

Many people who have been involved with Adult Education Act programs would like to see this problem resolved by a declaration that federal, state, and local education departments will manage the entire system. After all, those departments have most of the existing expertise and established resources, and literacy instruction is, by definition, an educational service.

In the near term, however, this solution is unlikely to work. The net result of the 1988–89 legislation was that Congress made literacy an aspect of other human service programs and other national goals, not just an educational service. And if that meant anything at all, it meant that the people responsible for guiding those other programs should call the shots on literacy, insofar as it affects their work.

In this environment, it is not realistic to believe that concerns about duplication of effort can be resolved by centralizing authority for adult literacy service. A more realistic goal is coordination among the various federal, state, and local authorities responsible for literacy. And coordination is required. Although the new congressional mandates create programs that differ somewhat in their aims, all are charged with providing essentially the same type of literacy service, and cooperative efforts will help them carry out their missions more efficiently.

For example, sharing of staff and materials where they are in short supply would benefit all programs charged with delivering literacy service. Moreover, sharing would help to promote the development of a full-time teaching force and create a critical mass of resources for investment in technology. Adopting common standards, definitions, and testing instruments would facilitate sharing of staff and materials as well as other forms of coordination.

Another form of sharing is making full use of the expertise that already exists in the literacy field. In many cases it would probably be more efficient for human service programs that have limited experience with adult literacy to contract for service with more experienced programs, such as those supported by the Adult Education Act, than to develop their own instructional systems.

Finally, because the goal of literacy programs is, or should be, to help students achieve large learning gains that will translate into real-world benefits, there should be some division of labor among them. It should be possible for students with very limited skills to progress from elementary adult education classes to more job-related training in vocational education or JTPA programs. "One-stop shopping" for literacy instruction and related social services, such as child care and job placement, is a model that state and local providers should explore.

To bring about these and other types of cooperative efforts, coordination must begin at the top. The federal departments responsible for literacy must be brought together in a coordinating body to identify the barriers to collaborative action and to remove them. Removing barriers should involve both fairly simple measures, such as developing common standards and definitions, as well as more complex measures, such as creating operational guidelines that would require programs to coordinate their efforts.

But a federal coordinating body should not just focus on maximizing the efficiency with which today's public programs achieve their goals. It should also perform a critically important task that no other agency can perform. It should decide what measures are needed to improve the effectiveness of the nation's literacy system as a whole. A federal coordinating body for adult literacy should set measurable nationwide goals for upgrading basic skills and for improving the system by which literacy service is provided. And it should monitor progress toward those goals, refine the guidelines of federal programs in light of any barriers to progress it discovers, and, as appro-

priate, ask Congress to adopt new legislation to fill any gaps
in literacy service it discovers.

It is unlikely that a federal coordination and policy development structure of this sort will meet all expectations. It will
have to balance the realities of a robust, pluralistic system with
the aspirations for greater coordination and accountability. In
the end, neither set of goals can, or should, be completely served,
and attempts to find the proper balance will inevitably encounter
friction and disappointments. But a federal coordinating body
will at least provide a high-level forum in which tensions in the
field can be aired and, hopefully, channeled in constructive directions. Furthermore, having such a body in place would at least
allow the federal government to identify and respond to the major system breakdowns that so often drive the evolution of public
policy.

One thing that a federal coordinating body cannot be expected to do, however, is coordinate efforts at the grass-roots
level. In a highly pluralistic system, any one way to deliver
literacy service is unlikely to be right for every locality. Each
will have different strengths to build on, weaknesses to overcome, and needs to serve. And even if this were not true, the
experience of other human service programs indicates that it
is virtually impossible to micro-manage thousands of local efforts
from Washington.

Accordingly, the federal government must delegate a large
part of the responsibility for coordinating literacy services at the
grass-roots level. For the variety of reasons set forth by Brizius
(Chapter 9), states are the logical middlemen to assume this
responsibility. A number of states have already begun literacy
initiatives aimed at building better coordinated and more effective service delivery systems. The federal government should
support those initiatives and encourage other states to follow suit.

To accomplish this, federal policy will have to combine
mandates to the states with measures to empower them. As a
first step, state governments should be required to develop
statewide plans to upgrade the quality of literacy service and
improve the basic skills of their citizens. And those plans should
establish measurable goals and systems for tracking progress.

But, as Haigler and Brizius point out (Chapters 3 and 9), mandates of this sort will be effective only if federal policy designates someone within state government to carry them out. Because states, like the federal government, are confronted with the fact that new federal legislation places literacy responsibility with several different state agencies, it is unrealistic to select any one of those agencies to perform planning and coordination functions. The best approach would be to place responsibility for those functions with state governors and to allow them to sort out how the responsibility should be exercised in their respective states.

This combination of federal mandates and state discretion is a realistic way to improve coordination among service providers, and it would also help to overcome one of the major barriers to effective action at the state level. As Brizius points out (Chapter 9), although many states have developed promising literacy initiatives, very few of those initiatives have found a stable institutional home. Because initiatives in most states have resulted from the personal interest of governors or first ladies, or both, they may not survive the present incumbents. Federal mandates for state planning and coordination would force states to institutionalize programs for upgrading the overall quality of their literacy service, and state discretion would allow each state to accomplish this in a way that meets its individual needs.

Filling Gaps. Taken as a whole, the 1988–89 federal mandates for literacy service came very close to expanding the nation's response to the adult literacy problem across the board. Each of the measures adopted during those years is targeted at a specific group of people—for example, welfare recipients, in the case of the Family Support Act—but collectively, the groups make up a large part of the population with limited basic skills in the United States. But the 1988–89 legislation still left several major gaps in the nation's system of providing literacy service, and the federal government would be remiss in not closing those gaps, at the same time it attempts to improve the service delivery system.

The first gap is a provision in federal legislation that will eventually result in a reduction of support for ESL service. Since 1988, additional funds for ESL over and above those provided in the Adult Education Act have become available under the Immigration Reform and Control Act. But authorization for educational services under that act is due to expire in 1991, and this will result in a major reduction of service.

Because of the pressing need for ESL instruction and the other considerations reviewed by Bliss (Chapter 8), Congress should ensure that funds are authorized to maintain at least the present level of service beyond 1991. At the same time Congress should place authority for this new funding under the Adult Education Act, rather than the Immigration Reform and Control Act. The latter provides ESL service only to newly legalized aliens who fall under the provisions of the law. While this group certainly merits assistance, it makes up at most one-third of the population with limited English proficiency in the United States. Congress should ensure that any extension of funding supports instruction for the *entire* population in need of ESL service.

The second gap left by the 1988–89 legislation is that many of the measures adopted during those years are unclear about how extensive the literacy and other educational services newly mandated by Congress should be. For example, the Family Support Act requires that educational services be provided to increase the employability of welfare recipients under the provisions of the JOBS program; and a large portion of the $1 billion funding for the act is potentially available for these purposes. But the act also requires that 20 percent of the AFDC caseload must participate in the JOBS program in the out-years. As a result, although the total amount available for educational services is very large, the act provides at most only a few hundred dollars for each participant. The evidence available from states that have attempted to increase the employability of welfare recipients indicates that this amount will not be sufficient to do the job (Riccio and others, 1989). But it is unclear whether states may increase the level of instruction available by targeting Family Support Act funds to a limited portion of participants in the JOBS program, or whether they must spread the funds out more or less evenly across everyone who is eligible to receive service.

The provisions for educational service contained in the JTPA amendments proposed in 1989 give rise to a similar concern. Because the goal of these measures is to place participants in jobs as quickly as possible, most participants will not spend enough time in the programs to attain very large learning gains. Nevertheless, it is unclear whether the funds provided by JTPA can be used to help participants continue to upgrade their skills after they have become employed.

Finally, in the reauthorization of the Vocational Education Act and the JTPA amendments, the amount of resources that may be devoted to "core academics" is not specified, nor is the degree of proficiency that students should attain spelled out very explicitly. This leaves open the possibility that vocational education and JTPA programs will be able to pass muster with only token efforts.

All of these concerns reduce to one central question: Was Congress really in earnest when it wrote literacy into a wide range of human services programs? The theory advanced here is that Congress never addressed that question. But if the professed goals of the legislation are to be achieved, and the authorized funding well spent, the federal government must be in earnest. Either through the process of writing regulations to implement that legislation, or by amending the legislation itself, the federal government should allow states to target some JOBS participants for intensive service; specify that participants in ESL programs may continue service beyond the legalization process; clarify the level of proficiency expected to result from vocational education and JTPA programs; and allow for continuity of service after employment in both JTPA and JOBS.

The final gap in the federal policy structure for literacy left by the 1988–89 legislation is that there is no significant attention devoted to workforce literacy — particularly service to individuals who are employed. This is a glaring omission. By the best estimates, about half of all adults with limited basic skills are employed. They are the working poor or near-poor. If we

want to address the economic problems created by inadequate
literacy, ensuring that this group receives assistance should be
a top priority.

Yet people who are employed are ineligible for almost
every form of federal literacy assistance. They qualify for the
Adult Education Act state grant program, and some assistance
is also offered by the small workforce literacy demonstration program in the Adult Education Act and by experimental programs
that operate under Title IV of JTPA. But in total, at most a
few tens of millions of dollars are spent on serving this half of
the population with limited basic skills.

In 1989, Congress considered significantly increasing
assistance to the employed under the authority of the Adult
Education Act, JTPA, or both. Hopefully, Congress will act
on this proposal. And if it does, it should do so in a way that
will make employers full partners in workforce literacy efforts.
One aspect of national leadership in literacy must be to demonstrate to employers that it is worth their while to invest large
resources of their own in upgrading the American workforce.
Until this case is made, it seems unlikely that the nation will
make much progress on the neglected half of the adult literacy
problem.

Near-Term Recommendations

In the interparty competition of the late 1980s, Congress
wrote literacy mandates into a wide range of human service programs as a way of defusing conservative criticisms of the performance of those programs. This created a large flow of new
service dollars and real-world mandates that marked the beginning of a more substantial federal attack on the national literacy problem.

But Congress will be hoist with its own petard unless it
finishes the job that it began. The programs to which literacy
was attached can succeed only if and when the federal government assumes a leadership role in building a larger and more
robust system of literacy service in the nation. This will require
new measures to enhance and disseminate expertise, invest in

staff training and technology, promote coordinated efforts, and fill in some gaping holes left by the recent legislative blitz.

Measures to achieve all of these goals were placed before Congress in the latter half of 1989, by Congressman Thomas C. Sawyer, in the House, and Senator Paul Simon, in the Senate. The price tag was about $500 million — a modest amount to promote the effectiveness of federal programs funded at the level of many billions of dollars and to prepare the nation for a comprehensive assault on the problem of adult literacy.

The legislation adopted in 1988 and 1989 left room for doubt about whether Congress was really serious about literacy. The Sawyer and Simon proposals would create the conditions within which the literacy problem can be solved in the United States. The Congressional response to those proposals should resolve doubt about whether the federal government is prepared to take adult literacy seriously, one way or another.

References

Adult Literacy Taskforce (State of Michigan). *Countdown 2000: Michigan's Action Plan for a Competitive Workforce.* Lansing, Mich.: Adult Literacy Taskforce, 1988.

Chisman, F. P. *Jump Start: The Federal Role in Adult Literacy.* Washington, D.C.: The Southport Institute, 1989.

Mendel, R. A. *Workforce Literacy in the South: A Report of the Sunbelt Institute.* Washington, D.C.: The Sunbelt Institute, 1989.

Riccio, J., and others. *GAIN: Early Implementation Experiences and Lessons.* New York: Manpower Demonstration Research Corporation, 1989.

Working Group on Adult Literacy. Unpublished Position Paper on Federal Policy, August 1988.

11

📖 Forrest P. Chisman

Solving the Literacy Problem in the 1990s: The Leadership Agenda

The preceding chapters map the dimensions of the literacy problem in America and the nation's current response to it. And they set forth proposals for building a more effective system of service delivery that would meet the needs of the 20 to 30 million Americans with limited basic skills. Individually and collectively, earlier chapters make the case that upgrading the literacy system is the necessary first step in responding to the problems that limited literacy creates both for the people who struggle with it and for the nation as a whole.

The Near-Term Agenda

It is critically important for both literacy leaders and everyone else concerned with this problem to focus their energies on taking the immediate next steps that the preceding chapters suggest. The adult literacy problem is far too serious for hand-wringing paralysis or daydreaming about easy solutions. The endemic weakness of the nation's response to this problem is clear, and the solutions are both fairly obvious and eminently feasible. There is no good reason why we should not begin to adopt them at once. While many have talked about the importance of literacy in recent years (literacy leaders, public officials, leaders of business and labor, the media, and others), few have moved to take action commensurate with the magnitude of the issue. The time for talk and deliberation has passed; the time for action is now. In particular, as the preceding chapters show, the United States must take the following steps in the next year or two:

- We must create one or more centers in the adult literacy field that would support a program of basic and applied research targeted on the highest priority issues, develop more adequate assessment and instructional tools, provide technical assistance to improve the state of practice in the field, and track progress toward national goals.
- We must provide more funds at the federal, state, and local levels for investment in teacher training and instructional technology, while at the same time developing better standards for teacher preparation and practice and a better understanding of the appropriate use of technology.
- We must develop management and planning systems at the federal, state, and local levels that would promote better coordination among literacy providers as well as establish responsibility for upgrading the service system and improving the level of basic skills.
- We must fill the gaps in the present service delivery system by devoting more attention and resources to the literacy needs of people who are employed and expanding the present level of service for people with limited English proficiency.

A Larger Vision

Although this immediate agenda is both clear and compelling, it addresses only first steps. And it is almost certain to leave a great many people dissatisfied unless literacy leaders articulate some larger vision of where those steps should lead. What would a better developed system for providing adult literacy service actually look like, and what would it accomplish? Ideally, this larger vision should be generated by literacy leaders themselves. Unfortunately, most leaders now have their hands full with more immediate concerns. Nonetheless, the scattered innovative programs run by literacy leaders with a larger vision offer reassurance that improvements are feasible.

To provoke more thinking about the long term, the balance of this chapter will be devoted to discussing four key questions about the future of the field: (1) What should be the long-term goals of the adult literacy system in America? (2) What will it cost to achieve those goals, and who should pay the cost? (3) What changes must take place in the way we think about and provide literacy service if we are to achieve our long-term goals? (4) What changes in the governance of the literacy system eventually will be required to fully implement the adult literacy agenda in the United States?

No one has wholly satisfactory answers to these questions at the present time, and any proposed answers are certain to be controversial. There has been far too little deliberation about the larger issues of the adult literacy field, and attempts to come to grips with questions about the long-term future are always frustrated by a shortage of adequate information about both the current state of affairs and the implications of new ideas. But it is important at least to begin the debate about long-term issues. Without a vision of its future, any field of endeavor is at a great disadvantage both in making its case to the larger society and in setting its own priorities. Someone must make a first attempt, at the risk of receiving brickbats from all sides. The following answers to long-term questions about the adult literacy field are offered as precisely such a first attempt, in the hope that they will encourage literacy leaders to develop better answers of their own in the years to come.

Long-Term Goals

Most people who are concerned with the literacy problem in America do not want only to *begin* to solve it; they want to solve it entirely. It is unlikely that vague promises of progress on the margins of the problem will be enough to bring about the changes in the literacy system that are required. Today both public leaders and ordinary citizens are demanding more accountability for educational spending of all sorts. The least that this means is spelling out the goals that investments in education should achieve and holding the educational system responsible for achieving them over some realistic period of time. This is a reasonable demand, and literacy leaders will have to formulate a meaningful response to it if they are to attract the support required for even the modest measures proposed in the preceding chapters.

What would constitute a solution to the adult literacy problem in America? What should be the nation's goals for the next ten years? More realistically, what should be our goals for solving the problem before the demographic deadline imposed by the retirement of the baby boom generation starting in 2010?

Many literacy leaders would argue that the notion of overall national goals for adult literacy is meaningless, because all literacy goals should be relative to the needs of individuals. Others would argue that the field is not yet well enough developed to set long-term goals. We do not now have enough information about the nature of the problem or good enough tools for setting benchmarks. Although these objections have some merit, they are likely to be regarded by the larger society as evasions. Moreover, they need not stop us from doing the best we can with the information we have, with the explicit understanding that any goals set now are subject to eventual refinement and that any outcomes projected must be understood in the context of a service system that accommodates individual differences. The purpose of long-term goals is only to characterize where the nation should be heading in general terms, not to specify the progress of literacy service in detail. The United States sets goals for many highly individualized services, such as medicine and welfare, even if it does not always achieve them. If national goal setting is possible for those service systems, it surely must be possible for adult literacy as well.

What, then, should be our long-term goals for solving the adult literacy problem in America? One reasonable national goal would be to assure that everyone has at least the threshold skills required to function in any imaginable future society and economy and that service systems are available to help people keep up with economic and social change. In other words, when we

think of solving the literacy problem we should think of a continual process of upgrading basic skills, rather than some final
fix. In this sense, solving the literacy problem is simply one aspect
of the "lifelong learning" concept that has been much discussed
in recent years (Grant Foundation Commission, 1988; Wirtz,
1975). Solving the literacy problem would mean lifelong learning of the most basic skills — reading, writing, mathematics, verbal communication, and problem solving.

Saying that the nation's goals for adult literacy should be
to help people who lack threshold skills to attain them and to
institute a system for continual upgrading of basic skills is probably a safe generality. But even within the limits of insufficient
knowledge about adult literacy and our inadequate measurement tools, it is possible to be somewhat more specific about
the first of these goals, attaining threshold skills.

Any imaginable society and economy of the late twentieth and early twenty-first centuries will offer few opportunities
for three types of people: (1) people who are completely illiterate
(who cannot read, write, or calculate at all); (2) people who cannot read, write, and speak the English language (the ESL population); (3) people whose reading, writing, mathematics, communication, and problem-solving skills are at only the most
rudimentary level by any measure. These three classes of people are well below the threshold at which continual skill upgrading is a relevant concept. They need to achieve large gains
in basic skills before the incremental fine-tuning provided by
lifelong learning will be of much benefit to them. Literacy leaders
hold differing views about whether those large gains should be
focused on the immediate functional needs of individuals or
whether they should be more generic. But by either measure,
20 to 30 million adults need to achieve a threshold of basic skills
ability. To put this in different words, 20 to 30 million adults
have not achieved "functional literacy," as discussed in Chapter
1, or "portable skills," as discussed in Chapter 4.

Helping people to achieve threshold literacy skills would
certainly be within the capabilities of the literacy system if it
was reinforced by the measures suggested in the preceding chapters, although we must allow for a few qualifications. Providing
threshold skills includes three subgoals.

1. We must eliminate illiteracy entirely as soon as possible. At present, we only partly understand how to teach even rudimentary basic skills very well to people with severe learning disabilities. Moreover, we do not know how many people fall into this category or how much it would cost to overcome their problems. As a result, there are no good grounds for deciding whether eliminating illiteracy is an achievable goal in all cases. But, in the absence of any compelling evidence to the contrary, it is reasonable to assume that the goal should be achievable for the bulk of the 1 to 2 million people who are completely illiterate.

2. We must promptly eliminate the problem of limited English proficiency among people who now live in the United States, and we must offer ESL service to all immigrants or native-born adults who need that service. As Bliss points out (see Chapter 8), the ESL field has developed what appear to be sound measures of English proficiency and sound techniques for achieving it. We must ensure that limited proficiency in English is no longer more than a temporary barrier to opportunity for anyone in America.

3. We must upgrade at least the reading, writing, and mathematics skills of people who function at only the most rudimentary level to some reasonable baseline of competence, and we should strive to improve their verbal communication and problem-solving skills as well. Baseline competency can be measured by a number of tests, such as the National Assessment of Educational Progress (NAEP) scale developed by the Educational Testing Service, the Comprehensive Adult Student Assessment System (CASAS) developed for the California State Department of Education, and various other measures of functional competency or grade-level achievement (Brizius and Foster, 1987). The educational provisions of employability plans required by the recent federal welfare reform and Job Training Partnership Act (JTPA) legislation may provide another useful measure of competency. While none of these measures is entirely satisfactory, they all show that at least 10 percent to 20 percent of adult Americans function well below the level required to meet everyday social demands or to hold jobs that provide a decent wage and a reasonable opportunity for retention and advancement.

Developing better and more sophisticated measures of basic skills competence should certainly be a high priority. But the lack of better measures should not stop us from setting the best goals we can now and working to achieve them. Most people concerned with literacy would agree that the nation will have solved a large part of its literacy problem if the skills of the least able 20 percent of adults are improved to the level of basic functional competence, as indicated by any reputable measure now available.

Beyond these threshold goals, solving the adult literacy problem will require providing all adults with service that would allow them to upgrade their skills on a continuing basis to meet social and economic demands. However, we cannot force people to be competent. As a result, all of the goals mentioned here should carry the qualification that they apply only to people who wish to upgrade their skills, given an opportunity to do so that takes account of their individual needs and differences.

What It Would Cost and Who Might Pay

The Cost. How realistic are these national goals for adult literacy? In part, the answer depends on whether we have a service system that can teach threshold skills and provide lifelong learning. The preceding chapters argue that we can develop such a system. In part, too, the answer depends on how much it would cost to solve the literacy problem in America and whether we can afford it. Because we do not yet have a truly effective adult literacy system or even entirely satisfactory information about the population with limited basic skills, cost calculations are very difficult to make. However, rough approximations are possible — and necessary. Unless advocates for literacy can indicate at least the order of magnitude of the resources required to solve the problem, their demands for more resources will sound like pleas to fill a bottomless pit.

There are many ways to estimate the cost of solving the literacy problem. The following approximation, like any such attempt, is based on too few data and too much supposition, but it has the virtue of simplicity. Literacy leaders who are dissatisfied with it should regard it as a challenge to do better.

Assume that 2 million Americans are totally illiterate — the highest range of recent estimates (Brizius and Foster, 1987). We know that, with today's teaching techniques, the cost of bringing illiterates to the rudimentary level of beginning reading and writing is fairly small — current programs spend about $500 per year on nonreaders, and those who remain in the programs usually achieve rudimentary reading and writing skills, and sometimes basic skills in mathematics, in a year's time. If these assumptions are correct, the total cost of eliminating illiteracy would be about $1 billion (2 million people multiplied by $500 each) — leaving aside the cost of helping the learning disabled and assuming that we can develop a literacy system that will reach all of the people who are totally illiterate.

Bliss indicates that about 6 million people require ESL service, and that the average cost of helping an individual to achieve full English proficiency is about $1,500 (see Chapter 8). That means that solving the ESL problem would require a total expenditure of $9 billion, plus an additional $2 billion per year to meet the needs of new entrants into the country who need ESL service, assuming that current immigration trends continue.

But eliminating illiteracy and solving the ESL problem would not greatly reduce the numbers of people whose skills are below threshold level. Illiterates and some portion of the ESL population would simply take one small step along the literacy continuum; they would not achieve a high enough level of skills to function effectively on the job or in everyday life. How many people would require skill improvement to a threshold level? To be on the pessimistic side, we can assume that the total population in need of literacy service is 30 million adults and that a good ESL system would reduce the number to 28 million. Today, the most expensive basic skills training programs cost about $2,000 per year. Helping people with very low basic skills is usually more difficult and expensive than helping people who are further along the skills continuum, but for convenience we can use $2,000 per year as a reasonable, but probably high, estimate of what the average cost of serving each learner would be in a very good program. Few people, however, would claim that even the best programs today produce satisfactory results for most learners in only one year.

A rough-and-ready way to approximate the cost of an adequate system would be to use Sticht's findings about the more successful existing programs (Sticht, 1988). Unfortunately, his findings are expressed in grade-level gains, but they will serve the purposes of this rough approximation. Sticht finds that the more successful programs achieve learning gains of 1.5 grade levels per year on average. Most studies indicate that, in grade-level terms, the population in need of basic literacy service is heavily concentrated between the fourth-grade level and the ninth- or tenth-grade level (Mikulecky, 1989; National Advisory Council on Adult Literacy, 1986). This means that the median learner would be at about the seventh-grade level and the average learning gain required would be about three grade levels (some learners would have to achieve less, others more). If the best programs can lead to gains of 1.5 grade levels per year, and they cost about $2,000 per year, then on average the cost of upgrading skills to a threshold level would be $4,000, or two years of service, if we could make all programs as good as the best. This would require a total expenditure of $112 billion ($4,000 multiplied by 28 million learners), plus an additional $4 billion per year to meet the needs of the 2 million people who are added to the limited literacy pool each year.

If we add up all of these rough calculations for eliminating illiteracy, providing ESL service, and building threshold skills, the cost of meeting the threshold literacy problem would be $122 billion, plus an incremental $6 billion per year to keep pace with the growth in the adult literacy problem. This is a large number, but it is far less than we now spend on either elementary and secondary education or higher education each year. Moreover, it is obviously impossible to solve the literacy problem in America in one or a few years. If we wish to solve the problem by the demographic deadline of 2010, the total cost spread over 20 years would be $122 billion to provide assistance to the population of adults who presently need literacy service, plus a total of additional $120 billion in yearly increments, or about $12 billion per year. This estimate is admittedly rough and ready, but it is close to the range suggested by David Harman and others (Harman, 1985).

The Resources. When the new federal programs described in Chapter 10 come on line in 1990, the federal government will be spending about $1.5 billion per year on basic skills for adults. If the proposals for federal action to improve the literacy system, contained in the preceding chapters, were adopted, total federal spending would be about $2 billion per year. States, localities, business, and voluntary groups provide at most $1 billion per year in cash or in kind. As a result, solving the threshold literacy problem would probably require a fourfold increase in the present national effort.

Where might these resources come from? One way to answer that question is to propose that each of the three major contributors to the present literacy effort should assume equal burdens of $4 billion per year. This would require the federal government to double its 1990 level of effort. It would require states and localities to earmark for adult literacy slightly more than 2 percent of the approximately $180 billion they spend each year on elementary and secondary education, and it would require corporations to devote to literacy about 13 percent of the $30 billion per year they now spend on employee training.

Of course, the cost to employers for workforce literacy programs might be higher than the $4,000 per capita instructional cost projected here, because of the costs of lost time on the job. But it is probable that employers will either recover those costs over the long term through increased productivity or they will not make the investment in literacy training. In fact, this is probably true of any business expenditure for basic skills, and it is arguable that the net cost of any business contribution to solving the literacy problem should be accounted as zero, thereby reducing the total social cost to $8 billion per year, if the division of responsibility proposed above was accepted.

But theorizing about exactly how costs should be allocated in a well-developed system for providing adult literacy is probably not worth the effort at the present time, because the available evidence is far too limited. The calculations set forth above have a more modest goal: to show that while solving the threshold literacy problem in the United States would be a very expensive undertaking, it would not be expensive beyond the realm of reason. The nation certainly makes investments on this order to achieve many other important social and economic goals. But in all likelihood the United States will not and should not make such an investment in the adult literacy field until a service system is developed that is capable of meeting national goals. That is, until the measures discussed in the preceding chapters are adopted, a solution to the adult literacy problem is impossible. If they are adopted, it is entirely possible that we could find the resources required to solve the problem. In fact, if we developed a service system capable of making rapid strides to improve adult literacy instruction, the costs just discussed might turn out to be gross overestimates.

None of this, of course, accounts for the cost of continual functional upgrading. We know so little about the types of service that would be required to meet this goal or their cost that only the wildest speculation is possible. A near-term investment in pilot programs that would develop models of lifelong learning systems for basic skills and establish their cost is the only expenditure that can safely be recommended or projected at this time. But even if the total cost of a lifelong learning system for basic skills were as great as the cost of achieving threshold literacy goals, a national investment in such a system would almost surely be worthwhile. If the nation had a system of basic skills instruction that could provide large gains in employability and social adaptation through lifelong learning, we could probably offset a large part of our $20 billion welfare bill and increase national productivity to the point where the benefits would far outweigh any likely cost of operating the system.

Changing the Paradigm

Finding the resources to solve the adult literacy problem in America may be difficult, but it is not the major difficulty that must be overcome. We know how to raise and spend money if we have the will to do so. Literacy leaders can and must spearhead the effort to develop a more effective literacy system, as described in preceding chapters. A more serious difficulty than gaining resources is changing the way literacy leaders and others who are concerned with the problem think about the provision of adult literacy services—changing our paradigm of what adult literacy service should be. Both research and theory within the literacy field and the demands of the political and economic systems indicate that the paradigm for literacy service must change in two major ways: (1) we must build greater accountability for achieving learning gains into the system of service delivery, and (2) we must foster a greater diversity of service delivery modes.

Accountability. Today, literacy service in America is almost entirely input-driven. Resources are allocated on the basis of the number of learners to be served, the numbers of hours of service, the cost of materials, or other input measures, and the success of programs is evaluated, if at all, in terms of whether these input measures have been met. This accountant's mentality pays little or no attention to what should be the major basis for allocating resources and measuring success: how much learners achieve, and in particular, whether their achievements make a difference in their employment prospects or in their everyday lives.

There is practically no accountability for performance in the adult literacy system today. This is also generally the case throughout the broad field of education. As a result, practically no incentives exist to improve efforts or to target them on the primary goals of the literacy enterprise. The nation relies almost entirely on the professional standards of individual literacy providers to ensure quality in the literacy system. And ironically the allocation of resources and evaluation of success in terms of input measures mean that literacy leaders who try to do a good job are often handicapped by standards of performance that take little or no account of their success.

This must change. The nation is unlikely to invest large new resources in a system that is not designed to reward success and penalize failure. In fact, whether new resources are forthcoming or not, the nation should demand greater accountability for the funds now devoted to this field. The new paradigm for service should be a system in which all programs assess the

needs of learners to achieve literacy gains that will make a significant difference in their employment prospects and everyday lives,
and in which instruction is directed toward achieving those gains.
In such a system, programs should be rewarded according to
how successful they are in helping learners to achieve real-world
goals. The end result should be a system that directs most resources to the most effective providers of literacy service. Moreover, if achieving learning gains is the paramount objective of
literacy service, there should be no discrimination among providers. Any public or private provider should be free to compete for literacy dollars.

The lack of adequate measurement tools and well-developed service systems makes it impossible to adopt this new
paradigm fully at the present time. But the measures proposed
in the preceding chapters should overcome these barriers very
soon. In addition, at least some of the recent federal legislation discussed in Chapter 10 takes a first step toward building a service delivery system for literacy in which accountability for outcomes is required. Both the Family Support Act
and the Job Training Partnership Act amendments demand
individualized employability plans and call for literacy service
to support the goals set in those plans. Neither program specifies who should provide literacy service. All that is missing
from these programs is a system of rewards for providers that
achieve the learning goals required and penalties for those that
do not.

Literacy leaders are dedicated to the needs of learners.
To fulfill their aspirations, they should commit themselves to
developing more accountable systems of service delivery at the
local, state, and national levels. For those who are now administering programs supported by funding streams that take
account only of inputs, this involves a willingness to accept some
risk. They will have to learn to compete with other providers
and market their wares to other public programs, employers,
and unions that demand accountability in terms of outcomes.
They will have to use the natural advantage that years of experience affords them to ensure that their programs are the most

efficient providers. They must continually strive for excellence, but inevitably some will fail.

Literacy leaders should insist that satisfactory measures of accountability are developed and that output-based systems are phased in gradually, so that problems can be assessed and solved along the way. But because of their dedication to learners, they should be among the prime movers of efforts to build a more accountable and efficient system of service delivery.

Service Delivery Modes. Today the paradigm for delivering adult literacy service is the freestanding literacy center or program. Public awareness campaigns urge people to call or come to the literacy center to improve their skills. Literacy is seen as a specialized product, provided in a separate location for a special purpose, rather than as part of mainstream social and economic life.

The freestanding literacy center will doubtless always have an important role. Today it meets the needs of millions of people, and it will probably always be the best way to provide service to some portion of the population in need. But both considerations of efficiency and the recent research on contextual learning indicate that we cannot solve the literacy problem until we broaden this paradigm. Presenting literacy as a more or less isolated service is analogous to merchandising in the days when shoppers went to one store for vegetables, another for meat, and still another for canned goods. Literacy service can be delivered efficiently and effectively only if it is one product in a supermarket of social services. It is inconceivable that we will be able to meet the needs of 20 to 30 million adults with limited basic skills, many of whom have pressing obligations at home and at work, by vastly increasing the number of freestanding literacy centers. The only conceivable way to meet the demand is to place more emphasis on bringing literacy instruction to the people, rather than asking them to seek out a specialized location where they can find help. Fortunately, in many states, there are some experimental adult literacy programs that have demonstrated that this can be successfully accomplished.

The recent federal policy changes discussed in Chapter 10 have begun a trend in this direction. Literacy is now provided in conjunction with an array of welfare and job-training services. Moreover, as discussed in Chapters 5 and 7, a few leading corporations as well as the armed services have begun to make literacy improvement a regular part of the job. Finally, organized labor is committed to improving literacy in the workplace, and unions have met with increasing success in promoting this goal through the collective bargaining process. In recent years they have negotiated contracts with the three major automakers, several of the larger steel producers, and a number of other companies that include provisions for offering basic skills instruction to employees.

But these developments will not necessarily change the paradigm. For example, if welfare agencies, job-training programs, and corporations integrate literacy into their organizational lives merely by sending people down the street to the literacy center to receive the same service they received before, little will have been gained. We must learn to deliver literacy service in environments where people are performing other important tasks, and we must learn to provide it in conjunction with those tasks — whether the tasks are training for employment, parenting, or performing a job. We must develop truly contextual learning systems and make those the norm.

We are a long way from that goal now. The techniques of contextual learning have not been fully developed. Moreover, implementing those techniques will require profound institutional change. Both public programs and employers will have to build systems for literacy improvement into many facets of their operations. They will have to allocate time for literacy instruction, train specialists in instruction and ordinary staff to identify and respond to literacy needs, and provide rewards for improved skills. Because the techniques are still under development and the institutional change entailed is profound, many literacy leaders are understandably wary of this paradigm shift. For the good of the learners, whose interests should be paramount, they must put their scruples behind them. They must seize upon the opportunities provided by the new federal mandates and the emerging corporate and union interest as the occasion to forge a new paradigm.

Governance

Changes in institutional structure alone rarely have much effect on institutional performance. Attitudes must change along with institutions. But as the preceding chapters emphasize, it will be almost impossible to fully achieve the goal of integrating literacy service into other social and economic activities if we rely on the present governance structure of the adult literacy system. Those chapters show that fragmentation of responsibility is very great. At the federal, state, and local levels of government, responsibility is dispersed among education, job-training, and welfare agencies — and agencies of other sorts often play an important role as well. In corporations basic skills instruction is usually the responsibility of personnel or human resource departments, but it is impossible to implement effectively without the cooperation of operations managers up and down the line.

Realistically, close collaboration is unlikely under this governance structure. For example, it is hard to imagine welfare officials making the changes necessary to fully integrate literacy into their service systems, just as it is hard to imagine most educators fully understanding or accepting the complexities and constraints of the welfare system. By the same token, it is hard to imagine personnel managers telling line managers to restructure their operations to accommodate elaborate systems of contextual literacy instruction. And it is hard to imagine that unions can achieve all of their goals unless the system of corporate authority for basic skills instruction is strengthened.

Learners are heavily penalized by this fragmented governance system. Literacy instruction is only one of the needs of a great many people with limited basic skills. In fact, literacy instruction alone is unlikely to do them much good. They very often need a complete package of services that might include, for example, income support, health care, job training, and education. Yet under the present system of governance they are shunted from program to program, and they must contend with separate eligibility criteria, scheduling procedures, and paper-work each time they seek a different service. Many people become discouraged, and many probably do not receive the package of services they need.

These problems are symptomatic of larger shortcomings in the governance of social services in the United States. For the most part, educational, welfare, and job-training services are balkanized. In the public sector, there have been fleeting attempts in the past to integrate them, with little result. But if we believe that education should be linked to real-world out-comes, such as enhanced employability and increased ability to function in everyday life, these reluctant partners must be brought to the altar. This will be a long and complex process. With regard to adult literacy, the first steps toward better coor-dinated efforts are indicated in the preceding chapters. But in the long term, coordination will not be enough. The institu-tional barriers must come down.

At the federal level, this means we must aim at creating a Department of Human Resources, incorporating the present De-partments of Education and Labor as well as all the functions of the Department of Health and Human Services, except Social Se-curity and health. Although the creation of such a department is politically impossible at the present time — and it may be unreal-istic for many years to come — the evolution of federal policy will almost certainly demand it at some point in the future. The recent federal human services legislation discussed in Chapter 10 is only one of many straws in the wind that point in this direction. As a result of that legislation, the Departments of Education, Labor, and Health and Human Services are assuming parallel or closely linked functions. To avoid wasteful duplication and bring about the integration of social services that is both required to meet public needs and called for by recent legislation, a common source of authority will be necessary sooner or later.

For similar reasons, consolidation of authority for human resource programs, including literacy, must also occur at the state and local government levels. We can never have a fully effective human services system in the United States unless both policy and administration are framed in such a way that each individual's needs can be considered as a whole.

In the corporate sector, responsibility for implementing literacy service must be moved up the organizational ladder. The experience of companies that have taken the leadership in this field indicates that effective corporate programs can only be constructed if the chief executive officer demands them and holds subordinates accountable for coordinated action to achieve them (Berger, 1989). Experience also indicates that, in unionized companies, top-level collaboration with organized labor will greatly increase the likelihood of success.

The Challenge to Leadership

Leaders of the adult literacy field have labored in the wilderness for a great many years. Literacy has been the poor relation not only of the educational system but also of virtually every other social and economic cause. In the last few years this situation has changed dramatically. Literacy leaders are now in the national limelight. How well they perform will depend upon the attitudes they bring to this new role.

The nation is demanding a substantial and realistic response to the problem of adult literacy. Literacy leaders are used to doing the best they can with very little. Now they are being asked to accomplish more than may be possible at the present state of the art with far greater resources. The system of service delivery and the goals for performance that have been geared to an environment of limited resources clearly will not be adequate to meet the new demands. Literacy leaders must be prepared to break with past ways of doing business, to pioneer in developing better instructional systems, to join with other social service providers in seeking common goals, to market their wares, and to advocate their cause.

Changes of this sort may be threatening to many leaders of the literacy field. They may fear that they will lose their professional and institutional identities. It is virtually certain that both will be transformed. But this is a risk that must be accepted. Literacy leaders may be able to delay change in their own field, but they cannot stop it. Many fundamental decisions about the directions of the field have already been made by government, industry, organized labor, and other institutions that are in a position to control both the resources and the agenda for adult literacy service.

To emerge as the heroes of the drama that is unfolding in their own backyards, literacy leaders must embrace change. They must use their expertise to seize the initiative in directing the nation toward a solution to the adult literacy problem. If they do, tens of millions of Americans will be deeply in their debt, and the nation will edge away from the social and economic precipice toward which that problem is leading. But if literacy leaders play Hamlet in the drama in which they have been cast, both they and the nation as a whole will meet the future unprepared.

References

Berger, J. "Companies Step in Where Schools Fail." *New York Times,* September 26, 1989.

Brizius, J. A., and Foster, S. E. *Enhancing Adult Literacy: A Policy Guide.* Washington, D.C.: Council of State Policy and Planning Agencies, 1987.

The William T. Grant Foundation Commission on Work, Family and Citizenship. *The Forgotten Half: Non-College Youth in America.* Washington, D.C.: The William T. Grant Foundation Commission, 1988.

Harman, D. *Turning Illiteracy Around: An Agenda for National Action (Working Paper No. 2).* New York: Business Council for Effective Literacy, 1985.

Mikulcky, L. "Second Chance Basic Skills Education." In *Investing in People: A Strategy to Address America's Workforce Crisis,* Background Papers. Washington, D.C.: U.S. Department of Labor, 1989, pp. 216–258.

National Advisory Council on Adult Literacy. *Illiteracy in America: Extent, Causes and Suggested Solutions.* Washington, D.C.: U.S. Government Printing Office, 1986.

Sticht, T. "Adult Literacy Education." In E. Rothkoph (Ed.), *Review of Research in Education.* Washington, D.C.: American Educational Research Association, 1988.

Wirtz, W. *The Boundless Resource: A Prospectus for an Education Work Policy.* Washington, D.C.: New Republic Book Company, 1975.

Index